The English Travels of Sir John Percival and William Byrd II

The English Travels of Sir John Percival and William Byrd II

The Percival Diary of 1701

Edited by Mark R. Wenger

University of Missouri Press
Columbia, 1989

Introduction and scholarly apparatus © 1989 by
The Curators of the University of Missouri
University of Missouri Press, Columbia, Missouri 65211
Printed and bound in the United States of America

Library of Congress Cataloging-in-Publication Data

Percival, John, Sir.
    The English travels of Sir John Percival and William Byrd II :
the Percival diary / edited by Mark R. Wenger.
        p. cm.
    Bibliography: p.
    Includes index.
    ISBN 0–8262–0700–6 (alk. paper)
    1. England—Description and travel—1701–1800. 2. Percival,
John, Sir—Diaries. 3. Percival, John, Sir—Journeys—England.
4. Byrd, William, 1674–1744—Journeys—England. 5. Great
Britain—Nobility—Diaries. 6. Plantation owners—Virginia—
Biography. I. Wenger, Mark R. II. Title.
DA620.P45 1989
914.2'046—dc19   88–27558
                                                              CIP

Dedicated with deepest affection to my family.

Preface

On the fourteenth day of July, 1701, Sir John Percival embarked upon the travels that would ultimately mark the completion of his education. Having concluded three terms of study at Oxford, Percival left the university to begin his "progress round England"—a kind of dress rehearsal for the obligatory Grand Tour of Europe that would follow. Over a period of some fourteen weeks, Sir John visited nearly every major urban center north of London, keeping a diary of his observations on a host of subjects. Trade, manufactures, agriculture, politics, religion, education, art, antiquity, natural philosophy—all find their place in this narrative.

I became interested in Percival's diary through his mentor and traveling companion, William Byrd II of Virginia, one of that colony's leading citizens, and a diarist of some note in his own right. Byrd's secret diary for the years between 1717 and 1721 remains one of the most intimate and revealing accounts of gentry life in Augustan London. Yet, relatively little is known of how Byrd came to be the man we meet in the London diary.[1] Undoubtedly, his journey with Sir John was a significant milestone in that process. This volume presents Percival's account of their experience.

In the introductory chapter, a biographical sketch outlines the major facts of the diarist's life and education, relating the circumstances and events that led up to his English tour. Significant aspects of Percival's narrative are here identified and examined in the larger context of contemporary events and customs. The importance of this document to the study of William Byrd's life has significantly influenced my editorial approach to the diary. Through the annotations, I have attempted to recover, as fully as possible, the meaning and import of Sir John's text. In every case, the intention has been to learn more about the objects, places, people, and ideas Percival and Byrd encountered—to reconstruct, insofar as is possible, their experience. To this end, contempo-

1. For a thoughtful and provocative assessment of Byrd's early years, see Kenneth Lockridge, *The Diary, and Life, of William Byrd II of Virginia, 1674–1744* (Chapel Hill: University of North Carolina Press, 1987).

rary illustrations have also figured prominently in the presentation. Finally, an appendix containing the relevant correspondence of principal characters has been included. These letters, of considerable interest in their own right, have proven to be a helpful and necessary adjunct to the diary throughout the editing process. Taken together, these various elements constitute what is hopefully a useful and reasonably complete record of the journey.

*   *   *

Many people have assisted in the preparation of this manuscript. If there is any merit in what follows, much of the credit belongs to my friend and colleague, George H. Yetter, with whom I began the transcription of this document in my garage, five years ago. Since that time, he has been a constant source of help and encouragement, correcting my mistakes, and, on many occasions, providing information I had despaired of finding.

I also wish to thank Mr. Paul Mellon, whose generosity enabled me to take seven months away from my work at the Colonial Williamsburg Foundation to edit and annotate the diary text. Without such assistance, this volume could not have been completed.

At Colonial Williamsburg I am indebted to Robert C. Birney, Senior Vice President; Cary Carson, Vice President and Director of Research; Nicholas A. Pappas, Foundation Architect; and my immediate supervisor, Edward A. Chappell, for the sympathetic encouragement they have provided throughout the course of my work. As the Foundation's Director of Architectural Research, Ed allowed time for me to write the introductory chapter, contributing helpful suggestions and observations along the way.

I am grateful to still other of my colleagues at Colonial Williamsburg for the many favors they have cheerfully performed. At a critical juncture, Helen Tate created a faultless draft of the annotated diary, and later produced typescripts of three Percival letters. Pam Mendoza provided typescripts of four additional letters written by William Byrd. From John Hemphill came valuable help and advice on a number of matters, especially the papers of His Majesty's Privy Council and the Board of Trade. Margaret Pritchard shared helpful information on early English travel literature and secured a number of the engraved views that appear in this book. Tom Austin, Suzanne Brown, Jim Garrett, Pete Huffman, and particulary Hans Lorenz have also aided me in the procurement of photographic materials. In the Foundation library, Liz Ackert, Susan Berg, John Ingram, Mary Keeling, and Eileen Parris never failed to secure the research materials I needed.

I am especially grateful to the Trustees of the British Library for permission to publish the travel diary of Sir John Percival, along with the relevant portions of his correspondence. I am likewise indebted to the staff of the British Library for the many services they have kindly rendered over the past five years. Dr. D. P. Waley, C. F. Hall, and Kathleen Houghton have been particularly helpful. I also wish to thank the following professionals and their associated institutions: J. D. Culverhouse, Burghley House Collection; A. V. Griffiths, British Museum; Camilla Costello, *Country Life*; Christopher Gatiss, Courtauld Institute; Victor Gray and Janet Smith, Essex Record Office; Jerry Mallick, National Gallery of Art; Pamela J. Wood, Nottingham Castle Museum; Evelyn Newby, Paul Mellon Center for Studies in British Art; J. H. Hopkins, Society of Antiquaries; Virginius Hall and Waverley Winfree, Virginia Historical Society; and Marilyn Hunt, Betty Muirden, and Scott Wilcox, Yale Center for British Art.

For permission to publish privately owned materials, I am indebted to Mr. Paul Mellon, to His Grace the Duke of Grafton, to His Grace the Duke of Roxburghe, to the Right Hon. the Viscount Lambton, and to Mr. John Harris. In addition to lending personal materials, Mr. Harris kindly assisted in the identification of several houses mentioned in the diary.

As I began to work in earnest on Percival's text, Steve and Shirley Devan introduced me to the desktop computer and allowed me to work long hours on their machine—a favor which has made all the difference in my struggle to keep this project on some kind of schedule. To Mrs. Bruce Crane Fisher of Varina, Virginia, is due a special debt of gratitude. Through her kindness I became interested in William Byrd II and, ultimately, in Sir John Percival.

Finally, I wish to express heartfelt thanks to my wife, Becki, and to my children, Jenny and Lauren, who have sacrificed uncounted hours of family life to this project. I will always remain grateful to them for the abiding patience and love which has sustained me.

M. R. W.
Williamsburg, Virginia
May 1988

Contents

Introduction

The Diarist

John Percival, 1st Earl of Egmont, was born in 1683 at Burton, near Cork, Ireland, the second son of Sir John Percival, 3rd Baronet, and his wife, Katherine Dering.[1] The Percivals were Anglo-Irish Protestants—wealthy landowners who had accumulated vast estates in the service of English interests since the time of the early Stuarts. Sir John played a significant role in Irish affairs, having assisted in the suppression of the Tories following the ascension of James II. Trusted by the lords justices and the lord lieutenant, he would surely have been deeply involved in putting down the Irish Rebellion as well had he not died prematurely in April 1686, naming his maternal uncle, Sir Robert Southwell,[2] as guardian of his children and sole executor of his estate in the event of Lady Percival's remarriage.[3] At this time Sir John's title and

1. Anderson, 2:403.

2. Sir Robert Southwell (1635–1702), diplomat and government official; clerk of the Privy Council, 1664; envoy to Portugal, 1665; chief commissioner of excise, 1671; envoy extraordinary to Brussels, 1671; M.P. for Penryn, 1673; vice-admiral of Munster, 1677; envoy extraordinary to the Elector of Brandenburg, 1680; commissioner of customs, 1689; secretary of state for Ireland, 1690; president of the Royal Society, 1690. *Dictionary of National Biography* (hereafter cited as *DNB*), 53:299–303. In 1655, Southwell's only sister, Catherine (1637–1679), married Sir John Percival (1629–1665), 1st Baronet, grandfather of the diarist. See Anderson, 2:361.

3. Anderson, 2:396, 404; Historical Manuscripts Commission, *Report . . . Egmont,* 2:xii. Shortly afterward, Southwell wrote to Sir William Petty: ". . . as I had writt what occurrd on your melancholy queryes, behold a more melancholy subject in the death of my deare Nephew Sir John Percivale . . . What I loose you may easily calculate, when he was the last of 3 Nephewes that I had taken some care to educate to men's estate. I still thought in the course of nature that I should leave young children of my owne to their protection, and soe my care for them was but the patterne of what I proposed for them. But they are all gone before me, and I must renew my care for Sir John's Children; and by the course of nature, when I am gone, those must succeede unto it that I leave." Landsdowne, 198–99.

estates passed to his eldest son, who, at four years of age, became Sir Edward Percival, 4th Baronet.[4]

Fearful of the growing unrest in Ireland occasioned by the papal allegiance of James II, Lady Percival and her minor sons soon embarked for England, taking up residence with their Southwell relatives at King's Weston, in Gloucestershire. Here a third son, Philip, was born.[5] In the fighting that soon swept over Ireland, the family seat at Burton was destroyed by Jacobite forces retreating from their defeat at the Battle of the Boyne.[6]

Within a month of this loss, Lady Percival remarried, effectively placing her children under the sole guardianship of Sir Robert Southwell.[7] For the time being, the family appears to have lived in London, where Southwell owned a house in Lincoln's Inn Fields. It was here, in November 1691, that Sir Edward Percival died "by a Disease occasioned from a Polypus in his Heart."[8] At this time, Sir Edward's title and estates descended to his younger brother, who became Sir John Percival, 5th Baronet. It is with this individual, later created 1st Earl of Egmont, that the present study is concerned.

Education

In August 1692, the Percival family was again visited by tragedy when Sir John's mother died, having suffered a miscarriage.[9] At this time, Sir John and his younger brother, Philip, entered the household of their great-uncle. By all accounts Sir Robert Southwell was an exceedingly affectionate guardian—"a Man of consummate integrity wisdom & piety . . . [who] proved another father to them."[10] Southwell appears to have spared nothing in his efforts to provide for the care and education of his orphaned grandnephews. Percival would later recall that

4. Anderson, 2:401.

5. Ibid., 398, 400. Lady Percival remained in Ireland for about two months to settle her affairs, then left for England.

6. Add. Mss. 47072, f. 5. In addition to the woods and stock destroyed, Burton Hall along with about fifty other buildings on the estate were burned, resulting in losses valued at more than £40,000. Historical Manuscripts Commission, *Report . . . Egmont,* 2:187; Anderson, 2:402.

7. Anderson, 2:404.

8. Ibid., 402; Historical Manuscripts Commission, *Report . . . Egmont,* 2:187–88; London County Council, 59–60.

9. Anderson, 2:399.

10. Add. Mss. 47072, f. 2.

. . . Sir Robert had a peculiar art in directing the education of youth & the care he took of
his Nephews was equall thereto. Besides the instructions they received from Dr Roby . . .
who gave them an early tincture of history Chronology & Geography, he entertaind also in
his house Mr James Pearant a frenchman to teach them that language, arethmetick and
writing . . . St Robert also would examine them himself, oblige them to get bewtifull passages in french & latin Authors by heart to exercise their memories . . . and made them
repeat chosen pieces out of English plays to form their accents and acquire good Action . . .
But above all, a high reverence for God, and a regard to religious duties was what he chiefly
inculcated . . . wherein as in all he led the way by a constant and edifying example.[11]

In 1696 Sir Robert placed Percival and his younger brother in the French
school kept by one Mr. Demeure in Greek Street near what is now Soho
Square, "a Place famous for Education at that Time, where *French, Latin,*
Geography, Musick, Dancing, Fencing, Vaulting, Quarter-Staff, and other
hardy Exercises, were regularly taught . . ."[12] These studies were cut short,
however, when Southwell, hearing of the master's declarations that "the pains
of Hell were not a material fire, but only Sufferings of the mind," withdrew his
nephews from Demeure's establishment. In 1698 they entered Westminster
School, where, to guard against the notorious vices of older boys, the two
brothers were placed in the house of Francis Durant de Breval, a prebendary
of the Abbey church. Here Percival and his younger brother applied themselves to the study of French, Latin, and Greek.[13]

In November 1699, Percival matriculated at Magdalene College, Oxford,
where he studied under Richard Smalbroke, "a Gentleman of great humanity,
Strict principles of religion, and good learning . . ." (Smalbroke was later appointed bishop of St. David's and subsequently translated to the See of Lichfield
and Coventry).[14] After three terms at Oxford, Sir John left the university without a degree to commence the final phase of his education. During the summer
and fall of 1701 he traveled extensively in the northern and eastern portions of
England, making a circuit of the major towns and cities in those regions. From
London, the journey began with a swing through East Anglia, during which
Percival spent several days each in Norwich and Cambridge. Having completed
his inspection of the university, Sir John turned northward, passing through

11. Ibid., f. 6.
12. Anderson, 2:404.
13. Add. Mss. 47072, ff. 6–7.
14. Ibid., f. 7; LeNeve, 1:304, 502, 558.

Sir John Percival. Godfrey Kneller, c. 1702. Courtesy of The Right Hon.
the Viscount Lambton. Photograph: Courtauld Institute.

York en route to Newcastle, thence westward along Hadrian's Wall to Carlisle.
Following a day's excursion into Scotland, he returned to Carlisle and began the
return trip to London, traveling by way of Liverpool, Chester, and Coventry.

Returning to London at the end of October, Percival was shortly thereafter
elected to membership in the Royal Society under the sponsorship of Sir
Robert Southwell. Having bestowed this last favor upon his beloved grand-
nephew, Southwell died the following September at the age of 66.[15] Sir
Robert's death resulted in the postponement of Percival's projected journey
to the Continent, as he later explained:

> S.ʳ John was 19 years old when S.ʳ Robert died, and at his return to London was a consider-
> able time in Suspence whether to comence his travells or Stay at home till he had more

15. *DNB,* 53:302.

Sir Robert Southwell. Copied after Southwell's death from the original of
c. 1695 by Sir Godfrey Kneller. This portrait was among those that hung
in William Byrd's "gallery" at Westover. Virginia Historical Society.

Sir John Percival's Tour of England
July-October 1701

Scotland

North Sea

Irish Sea

Wales

English Channel

Lanwharf
Carlisle
Newcastle
Hexam
Durham
Cockermouth
Penrith
Whitehaven
Keswick
Kendal
Richmond
Ripon
Lancaster
York
Preston
Beverley
Hull
Wigan
Barton
Liverpool
Buxton
Lincoln
Chester
Newark
Derby
Nottingham
Lichfield
Stamford
Norwich
Yarmouth
Peterborough
Beccles
Coventry
Huntingdon
Thetford
Ely
Bury
Cambridge
Newmarket
Northampton
Saffron
Ipswich
Walden
Colchester
Harwich
St. Albans
Chelmsford
London

0   50   100
miles

Sir John Percival's tour of England, 1701.

knowledge of the World, whereby he might be better received abroad, and be more capable of making Such observations as at his return might give him Credit.[16]

Ultimately, Percival elected to defer his European travels and spent the winter in London. Following the death of William III in March 1702, Sir John steered course for Ireland, traveling with the Duke of Ormonde, who as Queen Anne's newly appointed lord lieutenant was to be involved in preparations for the upcoming Parliament. In the general election of 1703, arrangements were made for Percival to be elected without opposition to the Irish House of Commons for the County of Cork. Probably through the influence of Ormonde and that of Percival's near relation Edward Southwell (then secretary of state), Sir John was also appointed to the Privy Council of Ireland the following October.[17]

During this sojourn in Ireland, Percival familiarized himself with the estates that would henceforth provide the bulk of his income—a matter in which he had received admonitions and detailed instructions from his great-uncle.[18] By 1705, Sir John had set his personal affairs in order and was politically established. In August of that year, he embarked for the Continent, accompanied by his "intimate friend Francis Clerke Esq." Spending the winter and part of the spring in Utrecht, Percival sought to perfect his knowledge of fortification, drawing, music, and fencing. In June 1706, he resumed his travels, proceeding to Hanover, Hamburg, Berlin, Dresden, and, by way of Augsburg, to Venice, Rome, and Florence.[19]

Shortly after his return to the British Isles, Percival fell ill and was obliged to remain for several months in London. However, by the spring of 1708 he had recovered, and thereafter withdrew to his estate at Burton.[20] Sir John was soon coaxed out of his rural retirement, though, and returned to London, where in June 1710 he married Catherine Parker, daughter of Sir Philip Parker of Erwarton in Suffolk.[21]

16. Add. Mss. 47072, f. 14.
17. At the time, Southwell was one of the clerks of the Irish Privy Council. By virtue of Sir Robert's death, he was also Percival's guardian, the latter being still underage at the time of his appointment. Anderson, 2:404–5.
18. Ibid.; Historical Manuscripts Commission, *Report . . . Egmont,* 2:208–11.
19. Add. Mss. 47072, f. 21.
20. Anderson, 2:405–6.
21. Ibid., 2:406.

In the general election of 1713, Sir John was again elected without opposition to represent the County of Cork in the Irish House of Commons, and was later sworn a second time to the membership of Ireland's Privy Council. With the ascension of George I the following year, Percival found great favor at court, and in 1715 was created Baron Percival of Burton in the County of Cork, whereby he took a seat in the Irish House of Lords.[22]

In the "unhappy Breach" which soon developed between George I and the Prince of Wales, Lord Percival and his fellow courtiers were obliged to choose whom they would attend, thus declaring their allegiance in the dispute. Fearing the "Imputation of a factious or ungrateful Character," his lordship continued to attend the King while casting his lot with the Prince. Although Sir John later broke with his majesty altogether, he was nevertheless created Viscount Percival of Kanturk in the County of Cork in partial fulfillment of an earlier promise made by the King.[23]

With the ascension of George II in 1727, Percival returned to favor at court and was again sworn to membership on the Irish Privy Council. Wishing to enter the mainstream of English politics, he stood for election in 1727 and was returned to the English House of Commons for the borough of Harwich. In this capacity, he served on the select committee appointed by the House of Commons to inquire into the state of English prisons.[24] Through this channel, Percival became associated with the committee's chairman, James Oglethorpe, in efforts to resettle convicts and debtors in the New World.[25] In 1732, his lordship was appointed first president of the trustees incorporated by royal charter for establishing the colony of Georgia. In this role he functioned for nearly a decade as an energetic and influential advocate of the Georgia enterprise.[26]

Certain of his favored status at court, Percival at length proposed to George II that he be further advanced in the peerage. Accordingly, on 5 August 1733 he was created 1st Earl of Egmont.[27] Suffering in his last years from chronic ill

22. Ibid., 406–9.

23. Ibid., 409–10.

24. Ibid., 431.

25. Tinling, 1:440.

26. Anderson, 2:433. Percival's journal of the trustees' proceedings is now among the collections of the Thomas Gilcrease Institute of American Art, Tulsa, Oklahoma.

27. Ibid., 437; McPherson, xvii.

health, Lord Egmont died in London on 1 May 1748 and was buried at Erwarton, the Suffolk estate of his Parker in-laws.[28]

A Tour of England

As we have seen, Sir John Percival was entrusted to the care of Richard Smalbroke following his arrival at Oxford, where he pursued studies in mathematics, perspective, logic, anatomy, Christian morality, and classical literature. Periodically, Smalbroke reported to Sir Robert on the progress of his pupil. The increasingly apologetic tone of these letters reflected Southwell's growing concern that his nephew was being spoiled by extravagance, scandalous company, and inattention to study. In a letter dated 4 February 1701, Smalbroke sought to allay these fears, explaining,

> . . . I think the greatest occasion of Sr John's Expenses has been his love of Musick, which has engaged him to have more entertainments at his chamber than otherwise he wou'd have had. And at the Same time I must observe to you, that tho this has proved expensive to him, yet I think it has excus'd him himself from drinking more than the greatest part of other Conversation wou'd have done . . . I must do Sr John the justice to Say, that to the best of my knowledge he has not entertain'd any Scandalous Company.[29]

Apparently Southwell took little comfort in this assurance, finding himself by early March in "a mellancolly fit for Sr John."[30] At length he concluded that Percival should leave the university and travel. On 24 April, Smalbroke acknowledged Southwell's instructions to that effect:

> . . . the Diversion you have propos'd to Sr John is very Seasonable, & I Shall take care to improve it by Shewing him Something of fortification before he Sets out for Portsmouth, that he may be able to relish the Entertainments of that place.[31]

The mention of Portsmouth is significant, for it makes clear the fact that Percival was to see his own country before traveling to the Continent—and it

28. *DNB*, 44:369; Anderson, 2:432.
29. Add. Mss. 47025, f. 38v. For Percival's studies, see ff. 36v-40v.
30. Add. Mss. 47025, f. 39r.
31. Ibid., f. 40v.

reveals that his tour was to have begun in the South of England. Smalbroke
was requested to accompany his pupil on this journey, but declined, pleading
a prior engagement of three weeks' duration.[32]

It would appear, then, that Percival was to leave sometime during the
ensuing three weeks—probably around the middle of May. Smalbroke's
refusal made this all but impossible. Resolute in his desire to see Percival leave
Oxford, Southwell turned for assistance to his young protégé, William Byrd of
Virginia, remembered by Percival as "a West Indian Gentleman of good
Fortune & learning, & a Student at the Temple . . . a particular friend of S[r]
Roberts, Fellow of the Royal Society very curious, & of general acquaintance."[33] Indebted to Southwell for many kindnesses (including membership
in the Royal Society), Byrd could scarcely have refused his patron's request.[34]

Preparations

In June 1701, Sir John "quitted the University, with design to travell."[35]
Preparations were soon underway as Southwell secured horses and called
upon various acquaintances for letters of recommendation and for advice
concerning the routes his nephew might follow. In a lengthy epistle, Norfolk
antiquary Peter LeNeve[36] offered detailed suggestions on what and whom
to see in East Anglia. For what was to be the initial leg of the tour, excise
commissioner Francis Parry[37] proposed an itinerary which, beginning in

32. Ibid.

33. Add. Mss. 47072, f. 8.

34. Woodfin, 23–24 and 111–12. Southwell's patronage was acknowledged in the epitaph
that Byrd wrote for his own tomb, now in the garden at Westover:

> Being born to one of the amplest fortunes in this country,
> He was early sent to England for his education,
> Where under the care and direction of Sir Robert Southwell,
> And ever favored with his particular instructions,
> He made a happy proficiency in polite and varied learning.
> By the means of this same noble friend,
> He was introduced to the acquaintance of many of the first
> persons of his age . . . .

Wright and Tinling, 11.

35. Add. Mss. 47072, f. 8.

36. Southwell and LeNeve had probably become acquainted through the Royal Society of
which both were members. See respective entries in the *DNB,* 33:36; 53:301.

37. Ibid., ff. 43r-45r. Southwell and Parry had seen diplomatic service in Portugal and both
were commissioners of the excise. See *DNB,* 53:300; Foster, *Alumni,* 3:1120.

William Byrd II. Attributed to the Studio of Sir Godfrey Kneller, c. 1704.
Colonial Williamsburg Foundation/George Beamish.

Portsmouth, would have followed the coast westward to Penzance, thence up
to Bristol along the northern coasts of Cornwall, Devonshire, and Somerset.
The route envisioned by Parry would have included all of the major ports in
southwest England, as well as the inland towns of Salisbury, Exeter, and
Wells.

Of special interest are Parry's remarks concerning the purpose of Sir John's
undertaking:

. . . give me leave . . . to recomend Some observations to you, relating to your own Country
which in no wise you ought to be a Stranger to, when you launch out into foreign parts. For
as it is very præposterous for a Man to Speak another language better than his own, So it
is for him to be better acquainted with the affairs of another Country than of his own. For
all knowledge of other Countrys that is not usefull to a Man's own is but insignifficant
curiosity. The first Notions therefore of behaviour and business ought to be taken in at
home; for these making the greatest impression, all other Notions will be made to conform
to them . . . In Order therefore to lay a good foundation for the conduct of your whole life,
you are now going to Survey England . . . [38]

Parry's thoughts undoubtedly reflected the convictions of Southwell, who
deemed it proper that Percival

. . . Should first make a progress round England, that after Seeing what was most remarkable at home in arts and natural curiosities, he might be better qualified to make observations abroad, and more welcome to the conversation of foreigners . . . [39]

These remarks, in turn, may have been paraphrased from John Locke's
influential essay *Some Thoughts Concerning Education,* published only a few years
before.[40] According to Locke, one was ill-prepared for travel abroad until

. . . being acquainted with the laws and fashions, the natural and moral advantages and
defects of his own country, he has something to exchange with those abroad, from whose
conversation he hope[s] to reap any knowledge.[41]

In recent years the Englishman's Grand Tour of Europe has enjoyed a good
deal of scholarly attention. Yet students of the Grand Tour have rarely commented on the importance of *English* travel as a prerequisite for one's voyage
to the Continent. In Percival's case it is clear that "the Tour of England" was to
function as a kind of "dry run" for later experiences in Europe. Years earlier
Southwell had prescribed a similar preparatory journey for Sir John's father.
Such a foundation had, perhaps, been laid for Southwell's own journey to the

38. Add. Mss. 47025, ff. 42v-43r.
39. Add. Mss. 47072, f. 8.
40. The catalog of William Byrd's library at Westover mentions an octavo edition of "Locke
on Education." Bassett, 423 (8th Case, 3rd Shelf, octavo).
41. Locke, 256. Henry Peacham offered similar advice in *The Complete Gentleman,* first
published in 1622. See Peacham, 161.

Continent in 1659.[42] This was certainly the case with John and William Blathwayt of Dyrham Park, close neighbors of the Southwells, who in 1703 traveled
for six weeks in the north of England prior to embarking for the Continent.[43]

Unexpectedly, Percival's departure was delayed by some difficulty through
which William Byrd was unable to leave London. Still determined, Southwell
sought to secure a stand-in for Byrd, soliciting the advice of his long-time
friend Sir Hans Sloane:

> . . . Lett me request you to think, where I may find a fitt Companion for My Nephew S.
> John Percivale, who is taking a progresse about England. M. Bird was of the mind to
> partake herein, as well for his owne Recreation, as to obleige me. And I had prepar'd
> Horses and every thing for the purpose. And I was extreamly rejoyc'd in my mind to have
> him. but by an accident that hath happen'd, M. Bird cannot now stirr from the Towne.[44]

The "accident" alluded to by Southwell may have involved Byrd's bid for
the office of secretary of the Virginia colony, a position for which he had
previously petitioned the King.[45] On 13 May, Byrd's petition was read before
the Board of Trade, which, for reasons now unclear, failed to act on the question. Reluctant to leave town with the matter unresolved, Byrd may well have
asked to postpone his departure.[46] For several weeks, it seems, he remained
in London to press forward with his request. In the meantime, Southwell had
been unsuccessful in efforts to find another companion for Sir John.[47] With
summer half over and no resolution of his affairs in sight, Byrd had, at length,
little choice but to oblige his patron and begin the journey. As a result of this

42. Anderson, 2:379; Southwell's notebook, kept while touring Italy, is now in the British
Library, Egerton Mss. 1632.

43. De Blainville, 2, 5–28; Moir, xii-xiv.

44. Sloane Mss., 4061, f. 38.

45. Secretary Ralph Wormeley died sometime before 14 March 1701, when his death was
mentioned in the Executive Journals of the Council of Virginia. Within a short time, Byrd
received intelligence of the resulting vacancy (possibly from his father), whereupon he drafted
and presented his petition to the King. *Executive Journals . . . ,* 134.

46. Within a month of his return to London, Byrd renewed his petition and thereafter
received a favorable recommendation from the Board of Trade. However, on 20 January 1702
Byrd's competitor, Edmund Jennings, was given the appointment. For Byrd's renewed petition
and a summary of his efforts in this matter, see Tinling, 1:215–16.

47. Byrd is the only companion mentioned in Percival's retrospective remarks on his
English tour. See Add. Mss. 47072, f. 8.

delay, perhaps, Percival dispensed with the southern leg of his projected journey, beginning in London rather than Portsmouth.

The Journey

On 14 July 1701, Sir John and his mentor set out on their tour, traveling northward through Brentwood to Colchester. Guided initially by LeNeve's recommendations, the pair frequently presented themselves to knowledgeable clergymen, who furnished "a pretty deal" of information and assistance. At Chelmsford, they encountered the Reverend John Ousley, an eminent authority on the history and antiquities of Essex. Showing the young strangers about Chelmsford, Ousley accompanied them the next day to New Hall, a former royal residence, where the full weight of his knowledge was, no doubt, brought to bear.

Encounters of this sort frequently resulted in recommendations to other men of the cloth. From Norwich Byrd wrote:

> . . . we have by mentioning Mr. Haughtons name, fallen into the acquaintance of Mr. Whitefoot, a clergyman of very great civility & understanding, and he again has made us known to an old acquaintance of yours, Dr. Pridaux, who is subdean here, and master of abundance of learning . . .[48]

In what became typical fashion, Prideaux insisted that his callers come to dine. Treating them with great civility, Prideaux in his turn recommended the two young travelers to still another clergyman, Nicholas Claggett, archdeacon of Sudbury, by whom they were, again, cordially received. But introductions of this sort could not always insure a polite reception. Percival and his mentor "far'd not so well at Ipswich by Mr. Haughtons recommendation, for there his correspondent Mr. Stystead protested he did not know him."[49]

Arriving in Cambridge, however, Percival found John Colbatch, one of the Fellows at Trinity College and an old friend of Sir Robert's. In his account of the university, Byrd remarked:

48. Tinling, 1:211.
49. Ibid.

. . . we owe a great deal of our knowledge of this place to the information and convoy of Mr.
Colebatch. He is a man of distinction for learning and knowledge of the world, and we had
the happiness of haveing abundance of his company.[50]

With Colbatch the two gentlemen travelers paid their respects to Richard
Bentley, then vice-chancellor of the university. Afterward, all were invited to
dine at Bentley's, "where philosophy flew about the table faster then the
wine."[51]

The encounter with Bentley seems to have opened still other doors. In Ely,
Sir John and his mentor called at the bishop's palace, where they dined with
Bishop Simon Patrick. Hours later, they found similar entertainment just
outside of town at Buckden, the country seat of James Gardiner, bishop of
Lincoln. Arriving in Peterborough, Percival and Byrd likewise called on
Bishop Richard Cumberland, who, with characteristic civility, conducted
them on a tour of the Cathedral.

Sir John's frequent resort to these clergymen reflected their special status as
men of learning and, equally, their social accessibility. Having succeeded to
the title of baronet, Percival could expect to be well received by these divines
and their superiors in the clerical hierarchy—prebendaries, deans, arch-
deacons, bishops—even the archbishop of York. Among the secular hierarchy,
Sir John's baronetcy entitled him to the hospitality of merchants, mayors,
gentlemen, knights, and other baronets—but never was he personally received
by the holder of a title more exalted than his own. On the road, as anywhere
else, travelers could expect to find the customary conventions of social distinction rigorously enforced.

Within the compass of one's own social circle, however, hospitality was
given freely—almost compulsively. At Stapleford, the entertainment was "Sin-
gularly good, for the Family pique themselves upon eating and drinking well
and the good old Lady Sherard makes people drink out of charity." In some
cases, hospitality of this sort was to be carefully avoided. Just outside of Ipswich, Percival and Byrd passed by the seat of Thomas Glemham, ignoring an
importunate servant who had been ordered to invite all strangers to the house.
But prospective hosts were not always eluded so easily. In Yarmouth, Percival
and Byrd were unable to examine the local salt works, being forced instead to

50. Ibid., 212.
51. Ibid.

accept the dinner invitation of Richard Ferrier, a local merchant. Returning at day's end to Somerleyton Hall, they found still another formidable host in the person of Sir William Allen, from whom the young travelers "with much adoe broak loose" the next morning, making good their escape to Norwich.

Here they arrived on 23 July, remaining for nearly a week on account of Percival's groom, George, who had fallen ill four days earlier at Saxmundham. In a letter written from Norwich, Byrd offered a fuller description of the illness, possibly appendicitis or a kidney infection:

I am sorry it is our fate to date a second letter to you from Norwich, where we have been arrested by the illness of the groom ever since Wednesday last. The poor fellow began to complain of a pain in his side about a week ago, and was let bloud for it, which we concluded woud cure him. We traveld slowly on his account, imagining his distemper woud wear off, but instead of that it is now turnd to a feaver. The ablest physician in town has been sent for to him, and all other care has been us'd to recover him, and there is some reason to hope that he is passt all danger. But if he do recover, it will be some time before he is fit for travelling, and therefore we have got another groom to supply his place as far as Cambridge, where we shall tarry 3 or 4 days, and if by that time George can get strength, he may follow thither. In the mean time care is taken that he want nothing to finish his recovery.[52]

The delay occasioned by this illness made it necessary to deviate from the itinerary prescribed by LeNeve. Turning south, Percival made his way toward Thetford, eliminating a westward swing through Lynn that would have included visits to Melton Constable, just completed by Sir Jacob Astley, and Raynham Hall, the magnificent seat of Viscount Townsend.[53] News of the groom's recovery caught up with the party at Cambridge, where Percival and his associate waited. This servant, named George, seems to have rejoined the expedition at Stamford.[54]

Traveling on horseback, the party included three persons and at least four horses (assuming that George was mounted). From Harwich Byrd sent favorable reports of the spirited mounts that Southwell had procured, though the journey had not been without incident: "Our horses are not over-rampant, so

52. Ibid., 211.
53. Add. Mss. 47025, ff. 49r-51v.
54. Tinling, 1:213.

that there is like to be no ill consequence from their high-mettle. The sumpter-horse performs very well tho at first he was a little uneasy."[55]

Troublesome as it was, traveling on horseback was preferable to wheeled conveyance, which was exceedingly tedious and fraught with difficulty.[56] This fact may account for the infrequency of Percival's complaints regarding the condition of the roads. At Hockley-in-the-Hole, he noted the existence of an "infamous lane w^{ch} . . . had been allmost impassable for us were it not for a causway wch is thrown up only for horse men."

The journey was not without inconveniences, however. In Northumberland, heavy rains flooded portions of the road, forcing travelers to trespass on adjoining lands as they made their way to Hexam. During a single morning's journey into Scotland, Percival complained of wading rivers as deep as his waist, owing to a complete absence of bridges in that quarter. Arriving, however, in the village of Lanwharf, he was shocked to learn that poor roads and nonexistent bridges were only the beginning. To an Oxford schoolmate he later wrote:

. . . I found the famous Town consisted of 5 mud houses reckoning in the barns. The Kirk indeed was built of Stone, but cover'd like the rest with turf. The best house was a Tavern where I met with very good wine for an English Shilling a quart . . . As Soon as we came to the door, there issued a dirty Female without Shoose or Stockings, who it Seems was our Landlady, & being told it was the custom to kiss our hosts to make them give us the best, we desired her to wipe her mouth, & then fell to our duty . . . So She brought us into another room where there was a table, 2 Stools, & a glass window half a foot Square, a thing rarely Seen in this part of Scotland, Neither was there a house within 16 miles as we were told that had a partition like ours which yet was no other than a curtain which hung down & parted us from the Kitchen, where there was Such a Smoke . . . that we were forc'd to feel where the glass Stood, whereby we unfortunately broak it, and were afterwards obliged to drink our wine out of the Pot . . . I Shall say nothing of the Stink which both the Woman & the House favour'd us with . . . but at first entrance I thought I Shou'd have been Struck down. After all this, we were forc'd to thank our Lady for our good reception with another Kiss, which had certainly brought up my dinner, had not the bread been as heavy as lead in my Stomach.[57]

55. Ibid., 210.
56. Bayne-Powell, 25–26.
57. Add. Mss. 47025, ff. 55r-55v.

Deeply discouraged by the morning's events, Percival and Byrd pondered whether Edinburgh was really worth the trouble. At length they made "resolution to fly the Country" and retraced their steps to Carlisle, where the long journey back to London was to begin.

Books

Comparison of Percival's account with those of contemporary tourists reveals that travel was somewhat more conventionalized by this time than previously supposed.[58] Thomas Baskerville, Celia Fiennes, the Blathwayts, and Daniel Defoe saw many of the places and objects mentioned in Percival's journal. From these and other accounts emerges a series of "attractions" that were rarely missed when travelers were in certain locales. Curious "passengers" frequently called at Littlebury, near Saffron Walden, to view the "odd whimseys and contrivances" of polymath Henry Winstanley. At York, visitors marveled at Ulf's horn or at the "unsupported" ceiling of the cathedral's chapter house. In Northumberland, Hadrian's Wall was a similar object of curiosity and admiration.

Also popular were the so-called "wonders" of Derbyshire's Peak District, celebrated by Charles Cotton in his descriptive poem "The Wonders of the Peak" (1681). Cotton's poem seems to have been required reading for any traveler making his or her way through Derbyshire. Like Celia Fiennes and Daniel Defoe, Percival referred to Cotton's sounding of the "frightful chasm" known as Elden Hole—almost certainly an indication of his familiarity with the poem.[59] Travel had become a kind of literary experience—Defoe cited no less than three authors in his account of Pool's Hole, a cave widely acclaimed for its fantastic limestone formations.[60]

As parallel quotations in the diary annotations will reveal, Percival's observations and perceptions were greatly influenced by these and other works, consulted as part of a planned curriculum of readings. From Harwich Byrd wrote:

> We have begun to read Sir Thomas Smith's republique of England, which we enter upon first, because it contains the most general information. When we have masterd that, twill be time enough to descend to particulars.[61]

58. Moir, xiv.
59. Defoe, 477; Fiennes, 109.
60. Defoe, 470.
61. Tinling, 1:210.

Byrd referred here to Thomas Smith's *De Republica Anglorum* (1583), a suc-
cinct account of the social, judicial, and administrative institutions which
regulated the conduct of English affairs.[62] For guidance in matters more
concrete, Percival consulted James Brome's *Travels through England, Scotland
and Wales . . .* (1700), a general guidebook, focusing primarily on history,
antiquities, and natural phenomena. Though Byrd disapproved of Brome's
"florid" delivery, his companion borrowed freely from this guide. Sir John's
description of poor persons at Pool's Hole, for example, is clearly indebted to
this source.[63]

In Kendall, Percival and Byrd were entertained by the local clergyman,
who, in Sir John's words, "confirm'd to us what we had read" concerning a
nearby waterfall that reputedly signaled the approach of good weather by
growing louder. Brome's description of this waterfall could well have
prompted the remark, though a similar account of the phenomenon was to be
found in William Camden's *Britannia . . . ,* a monumental tome from which
Percival quarried much of his data.[64] Organized by county, this compendium
of Britain's antiquities was an important and nearly ubiquitous guide for early
travelers. Defoe occasionally cited Camden concerning places or objects of
antiquarian interest, and may have carried a copy on his journeys. When
sudden rains interrupted the Blathwayt brothers' visit to Cambridge University, Monsieur De Blainville saw to it that the time was profitably spent in
"Blazoning and reading Cambden." Even Celia Fiennes, who seems to have
cared little for antiquarian pursuits, mentioned this venerable source during
her journey through Northumberland.[65]

Several of Percival's comments were drawn from Bishop Gibson's ampli-
fication of this work, which had first appeared in the folio edition of 1695.
Peter LeNeve undoubtedly referred to this volume in his mention of "a Roman Camp, described in the addition to Camden."[66] This same edition
probably accompanied the anonymous traveler who, in 1697, sneeringly
referred to "our careless enlarger of Camdens *Britannia.*"[67] Although William

62. A different edition of this work appears in the catalog of the Byrd library. See Bassett,
416 (case no. 3, lowest shelf, folio).
63. See diary annotations, note 472.
64. See diary annotations, note 298.
65. Defoe, 481, 519, 538, 553, etc.; De Blainville, 7; Fiennes, 27, 174.
66. Add. Mss. 47025, f. 52v.
67. Historical Manuscripts Commission, *Report . . . Portland,* 2:56.

Byrd's copy of this work is not known to survive, the title does appear as a folio in his library catalog and could have accompanied the expedition.[68]

In addition to Smith, Brome, and Camden, Percival and Byrd appear to have carried some sort of road book. Ogilby's lavish atlas of British roads comes to mind, but would have been exceedingly cumbersome.[69] Percival may have relied instead on an abridged version (an octavo edition appears in the Westover catalog), which included a fold-out map showing the distances between major towns.[70] Byrd, in fact, may have referred to this map when from Lincoln he wrote:

> We had come from Nottingham, which is set down in our books to be but 24 miles from Lincoln, but they prov'd very good measure, and gave us reason to observe that we were travelling in the north.[71]

Percival's heavy reliance on published sources reflected the fact that the journal was to be an educational exercise—a critical essay intended for the perusal of his great-uncle at journey's end. From Norwich, William Byrd assured his mentor, "We are not negligent in our observations, but lay about us for matter to put into our journall."[72] At Cambridge he smugly reported:

> We . . . are so excessively full of questions, that I wish it dont plunge us into a habit of being something impertinent. I fore-see that our journals are like to swell into a volume, and we begin to prefer our performances to those of the florid Mr. Brome already.[73]

Through these journals, Byrd and his charge were made accountable for what was to be an educational experience. The travel diary's function in this regard is especially clear in the case of the Blathwayt brothers' English tour, where the journal entries of Monsieur De Blainville were addressed to the

68. Bassett, 413 (case no. 1, second shelf, folio).

69. John Ogilby, *Britannia; or, The Kingdom of England and Dominion of Wales, Actually Survey'd . . .*, London, 1698, fol. The first edition of this work had appeared in 1675.

70. Bassett, 414 (case no. 1, fourth shelf, octavo). This was probably John Ogilby's *The Traveller's Guide: or a Most Exact Description of the Roads of England . . .*, London, 1699, 8ᵛᵒ.

71. Tinling, 1:214. The distance shown on this map matches that indicated in Byrd's remark.

72. Ibid., 211–12.

73. Ibid., 213.

father of his pupils.[74] Thus, while Byrd found Sir John to be a "jovial" companion with no "tincture of melancholly in his temper,"[75] Percival's narrative nonetheless strikes a sober note, fully in keeping with its serious purpose.

The New Science

The sobriety of this account also reflected the growing influence of experimental science on travel literature of the period. The half-century preceding Sir John's tour had witnessed an astonishing parade of scientific discoveries by such luminaries as Robert Hooke, Robert Boyle, and Isaac Newton. The publication of Newton's *Mathematical Principles of Natural Philosophy* in 1687 had greatly enhanced the prestige of the natural philosopher and the ordered view of nature he professed. Making all the world his laboratory, the virtuoso sought to enlist the aid of travelers in the broadening task of discovery. Increasingly, voyagers were exhorted to keep detailed journals of their observations as a means of providing scientists with a new body of objective, reliable data—an expanding store of "Philosophical stock" upon which to build a truly scientific explanation of the physical universe.[76]

On more than one occasion the Royal Society published detailed instructions concerning what sorts of phenomena travelers were encouraged to observe and how their findings were to be recorded.[77] In all such accounts, the society called for clear, unaffected prose—

> . . . a close, naked, natural way of Speaking; positive Expressions, clear Senses; a native Easiness; bringing all Things as near the mathematical Plainness as they can . . . preferring the Language of Artizanz, Countrymen, and Merchants, before that of Wits, or Scholars.[78]

As a former president of the society, Southwell would certainly have made clear his expectations in this regard. Indeed, a bound folio of "Private Directions for Travels in England," later cataloged among the holdings of the Westover library, may have been drafted by Southwell as he sought to prepare Byrd

74. See, for instance, De Blainville, 24 May 1703, 8–9.
75. Tinling, 1:209.
76. Frantz, 15.
77. Ibid., 15–18.
78. Ibid., 59.

and Percival for their journey.[79] Although this volume has not survived, one cannot help thinking it might have resembled the exhortation that appeared in the introduction to John Churchill's *A Collection of Voyages and Travels . . . ,* published shortly after Percival had completed his journey. Here prospective travelers were admonished that

> . . . they must not pass through a Country as if they carried an Express, but make a reasonable stay at all places where there are Antiquities, or any Rarities to be observ'd; and not think that because others have writ on the Subject, there is no more to be said . . . Let them therefore always have a Table-Book at hand to set down every thing worth remembering, and then at night more methodically transcribe the Notes they have taken in the day. The principal Heads by which to regulate their Observations are these, the Climate, Government, Power, Places of Strength, Cities of note, Religion, Language, Coins, Trade, Manufactures, Wealth, Bishopricks, Universities, Antiquities, Libraries, Collections of Rarities, Arts and Artists, Publick Structures, Roads, Bridges, Woods, Mountains, Customs, Habits, Laws, Privileges, strange Adventures, surprizing Accidents, Rarities both natural and artificial, the Soil, Plants, Animals, and whatsoever may be curious, diverting, or profitable . . .[80]

The ambitious diversity of Sir John's observations reflected the cultivation of this scientific outlook. There can be little doubt that Byrd, a member of the Royal Society's inner council, took pains to insure that some similar set of instructions were assiduously observed by his young colleague. But the whole endeavor was regarded as little more than "insignifficant curiosity" unless one's observations could find some practical application at journey's end. "Useful knowledge" was the traveler's object, and this purpose suffused everything he wrote. Indeed, Byrd himself sounded the appropriate refrain in his account of a visit to Saffron Walden, ". . . where we met with a man very expert at planting & cureing that commodity [saffron]. You will not doubt but we took notes of so usefull a process . . ."[81]

Percival likewise recorded numerous details concerning industrial processes and techniques: the manufacture of saffron near Audley End; the preparation of herring in Yarmouth; the extraction of salt near Newcastle. In Whitehaven he noted what must have been some of the first experiments in

79. Bassett, 438 (case D, second shelf, folio).
80. Awnsham and John Churchill, comps., *A Collection of Voyages and Travels, Some now First Printed from Original Manuscripts . . . ,* (London, 1704), I:lxxv-lxxvi, as cited in Frantz, 23–24.
81. Tinling, I:213.

the use of coke for smelting iron ore—eight years before the first successes recorded at Brosley in Shropshire.

As the owner of considerable estates, Sir John also displayed particular interest in the progress of agricultural methods. In Norfolk he noted the fattening of cattle upon turnips; in Lancashire, the digging of marl for fertilizer; and in Essex, the enrichment of land with crops of saffron and sainfoin. At Warrington he was especially intrigued with the concoction of a local apothecary, which reputedly multiplied the yield of individual corn plants many times over.

Dutifully, Percival examined the plants in question to ascertain the truth of this claim. In his pursuit of the truth, the ideal traveler was expected to bring a skeptical eye to bear upon all he encountered—

> . . . to put a Mark on the Errors, which have been strengthned by long Prescription . . . to separate the Knowledge of *Nature,* from the Colours of *Rhetorick,* the Devices of *Fancy,* or the delightful Deceit of *Fables.*[82]

Influenced by the scientific bent of his mentors, Percival occasionally affected a tone of skepticism in calling attention to the erroneous suppositions of "vulgar Oppinion." At Trinity House, he viewed the "Effigies of a Groenlander who being drove by a Storm So far, and taken, our men would fain have him a Sea monster." On another occasion, he sought to discredit the traditional lore that clung to a rocky Derbyshire hill known as the Mam Tor,

> . . . of wch Hill tis reported that thô it is continually mouldering down yet does it not wast in the least by Reason of some new Supply of matter, but this is fals as any one may plainly discern by Stones wch in Severall places are left bare.

As much as the clarity, objectivity, and wide-ranging diversity of Percival's observations, it is this skeptical, reasoned approach to phenomena which places his account firmly within the scientific tradition of travel literature.

The Poor

Percival was visibly disappointed with Mam Tor, later characterized by Defoe as another of "the wonderless wonders" of Derbyshire's Peak District.[83] But

82. Thomas Sprat, *The History of the Royal Society,* 3rd ed. (London, 1722), 61–62, as cited in Frantz, 31.

83. Defoe, 469.

what Derbyshire lacked in genuine natural wonders was fully recompensed by "observables" of another sort. In this remote, inhospitable place, Sir John, like Defoe, repeatedly experienced face-to-face encounters with the poor. And though he exhibited none of the emotion apparent in Defoe's description of a Derbyshire lead miner's family and home, Sir John's repeated mentions of the poor throughout the diary betray his interest. Emerging from their exploration of Pool's Hole, Percival and Byrd were met by a collection of beggars and poor persons bearing herbs and basins of water in which to wash. They were again assisted at the seemingly bottomless pit called Elden Hole, where "poor people brought up Stones to fling in." Nearby was a second cave known as the "Devil's Arse," where Percival noted a "perfect village" of poor persons' huts standing within the entrance.

In contrast to the humorous tone of his letter describing Scotland, Percival's treatment of poverty in the diary tended toward a kind of analytical detachment, implicitly relating the number of poor in a given community to the state of local commerce and industry. Arriving in Ipswich, he found a poor, half-inhabited town, suffering from the effects of dwindling trade and declining cloth production. Lincoln was similarly forlorn: "The Citty of Lincoln was once in a very flourishing condition having 50 churches now not 15, & a Staple manefacture of wool, but now that is lost 'tis become a very poor town . . ."

In Durham, however, he attributed the appalling condition of the town's inhabitants to the "number and riches" of an unscrupulous clergy, singling out the unconscionable circumstances of one prelate in particular:

The Deanery is worth 1500^{li} a year, besides wch the present enjoyer of it Dr Monntague has the care of an Hospital . . . the charity of wch is very extroardinary, for 30 poor are maintain'd half of whom have but 40p a year, and yet the Governours place is worth 500^{li} per annum.

He was unable to account, on the other hand, for the low circumstances of Northampton, where lived "many gentry who are the Support of the town notwithtanding which the Inhabitants are poor thô they drive a great trade in Shoos & childrens Stockins."

But beyond the causes and extent of poverty, Percival concerned himself with methods of relief and the varying results they produced. In Norwich, he was astonished to learn that "They can not keep themselves from beggars thô there are 5 hospitalls to provide for Impotent & helpless people."

Here, as in many towns, the administrative provisions of poor laws enacted at the beginning of the seventeenth century had proven inadequate. Fixing responsibility for indigent persons at the local level, Parliament had implemented poor relief through the administrative apparatus of the Anglican church. The parish thus became the basic administrative unit in matters of poor relief. In urban areas, individual parishes were only subunits of a larger community, each differing in its ability to provide support. Inevitably, the poor were huddled into distinct localities where there were few resources to be drawn upon by the large number of persons in need. In these areas, moreover, the movement of poor persons, and all it implied for potential charges on the parish, became more difficult to control. These problems had become especially acute in older towns having many small parishes. In Norwich, where Percival had seen many beggars, there were "36 Parish Churches wch Stand very thick, but the Livings are very Small."[84]

The last decade of the seventeenth century saw a new initiative toward the consolidation of relief efforts in such towns. In 1696, Bristol, followed later by other towns, obtained local parliamentary acts that provided for the administration of poor relief through a single organization. Among the first towns to utilize this expedient was Hull, where the visibility of poverty was so far reduced as to pass without mention in the diary. Harwich had taken similar steps, though apparently without the sanction of a local act.[85] Upon his arrival there Percival noted approvingly: "The Government of Harwich is very regular no beggers being suffred, but they who cannot provide for themselves, are distributed among the abler sort who are obliged to maintain them."

Percival and Byrd saw only the beginnings of this change. In most localities poor relief remained a patchwork of statutory and charitable support, delivered in a variety of ways, among which direct payments (in cash or in kind) and maintenance in the homes of parishioners were most common. Institutional options included almshouses and, increasingly, workhouses. The latter alternative reflected a growing trend at century's end toward providing employment for the able-bodied poor. Sir John probably referred to one of these workhouses when, in Warrington, he remarked that "making of pins employs the poorer Sort of people."[86]

While one would hesitate to suggest that Percival's interest in the poor was

84. For administrative problems of poor relief, see Oxley, 34–37.
85. Ibid., 36–37, 81; Jackson, 321.
86. Oxley, 62–87.

solely altruistic, there is evidence that he came away from his travels with some sense of responsibility for the multitude of unfortunate persons he had encountered. As we have seen, Sir John was later instrumental in the introduction of much-needed penal reforms, serving on the committee appointed by the House of Commons to investigate the nation's prisons. At the same time, it is clear that he saw relief programs as a practical solution to the problems indigent people posed to society at large. His work on behalf of the Georgia colony, which entailed the resettlement of "miserable wretches lately relieved from jayl," reflected this outlook. Georgia was to be the instrument through which the "Multitudes, incapable of finding Business at home, might yet be servicable to their Mother Country abroad."[87]

Papists and Dissenters

Besides the poor, the varying circumstances of Catholics and nonconforming Protestants also attracted Sir John's attention. Having suffered indirectly in the turmoil that ravaged Ireland at the end of the seventeenth century, Percival was attentive to the evidences of continuing strife in the mother country. And indeed, it was amidst unhappy circumstances that he surveyed the complex topography of English religion. Since the reign of Henry VIII, scarcely a generation of Englishmen had escaped the yoke of religious persecution and upheaval. And though the worst would soon be over, religious discourse was still conducted in a lingering atmosphere of fear and suspicion, intensified by the inflammatory rhetoric of competing political interests.

In spite of parliamentary declarations, the future of England's Protestant monarchy remained in doubt. Across the English Channel, James, the Pretender, took up his father's claim to the English throne, aided by the Catholic monarch of France. In the meantime, William's embarrassing lack of popularity, together with the ill health of Princess Anne and the death of her only child, the Duke of Gloucester, cast a long shadow over the Protestant succession. Under these circumstances, the Hanoverians, far removed from the scene and notably lacking in charisma, seemed unlikely guarantors of Protestant hopes.[88]

More gripping than these apprehensions, however, were fears of a Puritan resurgence. In his bid for the English throne, William of Orange had pur-

87. McPherson, xviii.
88. Holmes, 188–89.

chased the support of nonconforming Protestants with assurances of greater
religious toleration. Having secured the crown's indulgence, growing numbers
of Dissenters gained access to public office through the practice of "occasional
conformity"—that is, receiving the Anglican sacrament at least once within
the twelve-month period preceding one's election. Thus eluding the provisions
of the Test and Corporation Acts, these Dissenters occasionally gained control
of municipal governments. In some cases this opened the way for high-handed
fixing of parliamentary elections—a development that greatly alarmed Anglicans.[89] Passing through Coventry, Percival remarked that

> . . . the major part of the Inhabitants are quakers Anababtist & Presbiterians wch latter have
> got the Governm^t into their hands, & make themselves very odious by their absolute
> proceedings.

As if to measure the extent of these inroads, Percival sometimes noted the
general distribution of Anglicans and Dissenters in the communities he visited, recording on occasion his own count of meetinghouses and churches. In
Ipswich the predominance of Presbyterian believers was reflected in the construction of a meetinghouse large enough to hold fifteen hundred souls—a
structure which Defoe declared to be as large and as well-appointed as any
such edifice in England.[90]

Elsewhere, the lot of Dissenters was less enviable. In communities like
Newark, besieged by parliamentary forces during the Civil War, the continuing hostility engendered by religious differences was palpable. Here Percival
recorded that the townspeople "Suffer no Dissenters to live among them,"
adding, "totherday a meeting house being attempted to be sett up they pull'd
it down." At Yarmouth, the abiding divisions within the Protestant community were unwittingly memorialized in the parish church, where Sir John
observed that the interior had been partitioned into discreet worship spaces
for Anglicans, Presbyterians, and Independents.[91]

Percival's remarks concerning Catholicism—all recorded in the north—
seem unexpectedly restrained when we remember that he was an Anglo-Irish
Protestant. Although the specter of a Catholic monarch continued to haunt

89. Ibid., 189–96.
90. Defoe, 71.
91. See diary annotations, note 66.

most Englishmen, the old families of recusant Catholics inhabiting the north were viewed with relatively little apprehension. During a visit to Durham, Daniel Defoe observed that the town was

> . . . full of Roman Catholicks, who live peaceably and disturb nobody and nobody them; for we being there on holiday, saw them going as publickly to mass as the Dissenters did on other days to their meeting-house.[92]

Sharing this detachment, Percival was entertained by recusant members of the local gentry on at least four occasions as he traveled from Penrith to Wigan. Having dined at Greystoke Castle, he characterized Charles Howard as "a gentleman of good Sence and learning but a roman Catholick." Accompanied by Howard, the party rode out several miles to call on Sir Henry Fletcher of Hutton-in-the-Forest, whom Sir John esteemed "a very curtius Gentleman, but has chang'd his religion when he was in France." The mention of Fletcher's conversion to Catholicism was incidental. More interesting than Sir Harry's religion were the "vistos" cut through his park and the racing horses bred for his stable.

Architecture and Landscape

Pondering the reconstruction of his own ruined estate in Ireland, Percival regarded the houses, gardens, and parks he visited with particular relish. If Sir John relied on Camden or Brome for certain bits of historical narrative, the remarks he left concerning these houses and gardens were unquestionably rooted in his own observation. From his many descriptions emerges a canonical set of criteria by which he judged each estate he saw. And though the principles implicit in Percival's remarks cannot be said to constitute any coherent theory of architecture, they do reflect an elementary sort of critical capacity.

Was the house located on a rising ground? Was the site well supplied with water? What prospects did it command? (If these comprehended a body of water, the adjacent town, or another gentleman's house, so much the better.) How large was the dwelling? Was it laid out in a "regular" and "convenient" manner? How large was the park—and with what sorts of game was it stocked? Were there warrens, decoys, dovecotes, fishponds, or other sources of provision? What kind of trees did one find in the park? Were there avenues—

92. Cited in Holmes, 188.

woodlands—a grove or wilderness? And what was the disposition of the gardens? Did they have an ornamental body of water?

As these questions suggest, Percival's attention was focused primarily upon the exterior of the dwelling and the larger environment to which it belonged. Like Celia Fiennes, he was unexpectedly facile in the use of certain catchwords and phrases from the gardener's lexicon, commenting on Lord Nottingham's "Severall Visto's" at Burley-on-the-Hill and the "rude prospect" visible from the Duke of Devonshire's garden at Chatsworth. Equally extraordinary is Percival's mention of a canal that functioned like a "ha-ha" in Lord Sandwich's gardens at Hinchingbrook: "They are order'd much after the French fashion being Sorounded on one Side by a Canal w^{ch}: hinders no prospect as generally a wall does." Not until the translation of A. J. Dézallier D'Argenville's *La Théorie et la Practique du Jardinage* in 1712 would such a feature be mentioned in English gardening literature.

Where houses were concerned, only the most sumptuous or otherwise remarkable establishments prompted him to offer anything beyond a basic assessment of interiors or furnishings. Predictably, Burghley and Chatsworth elicited extensive comment. More surprising is his reaction to Lord Orford's house at Chippenham. Being "neither too little nor too big," Chippenham, now gone, was the house he admired above all others. According to Celia Fiennes the hall was wainscoted in walnut, contrasting dramatically with the "lemon" color of the panels and their moldings—all enriched with carved ornament and full-length portraits of the royal family.[93] Ascending the staircase were painted scenes from the battle of La Hogue, conspicuous reminders of Orford's pivotal role in that engagement. These two spaces Percival regarded as "the finest & neatest I ever saw." In the yard, he found a series of "very neat" outbuildings regularly disposed about a court. The stable, which reportedly resembled the Horse Guards at Whitehall Palace, was singled out for special commendation. In domestic building, his praise was consistently reserved for what was modish and classical.

Percival's sympathetic appraisal of certain Gothic buildings therefore comes as a mild surprise. In most cases, his expressions of approval were directed toward work dating from the fifteenth, sixteenth, or even seventeenth centuries.[94] As one might expect, he was especially impressed by King's

93. Fiennes, 140.

94. See Percival's comments on the nave vaulting at Norwich, the west front at Lincoln, that at Beverley, the choir at York, and Bishop Cosin's restoration of the choir at Durham, and

College Chapel, ". . . justly term'd one of the finest buildings in Europe . . . It is built after the Gothick manner & looks on the out Side very bewtyfull & fresh, & the inside is no less fine & neat."

This assessment reflected Percival's liking for the Perpendicular style—a preference made explicit at Beverley Minster, where he characterized the fifteenth-century west front as being "of the finer Sort of Gothick work." Nonetheless, it was Lichfield Cathedral, the product of a thirteenth-century rebuilding, which brought forth his ultimate acclamation as "the neatest of any I ever Saw." Not surprisingly, he found the Norman style less to his taste, censuring the ancient work at Durham Cathedral as "extreemly mean."

Percival's attitude toward the entire range of early ecclesiastical styles finds a striking parallel in the writings of Roger North, produced only a few years earlier. Like Percival, North did not admire Durham Cathedral with its "round upright lumps for columnes." Durham, he asserted, epitomized the shortcomings of the "old way," which "seemed clumsey, and dark, because the supports were great and the apertures small."[95] In spite of his fulminations against the deceitful lightness of later work, North spoke admiringly of its technical virtuosity:

> . . . I must, to doe those good men that built our churches right, profess that in the ordinance of walls and abbutment they have done as much as is possible, to make the stone and lime work its utmost . . . now wee have not any that will venture to set such weight upon so small support . . .[96]

For this reason, he, like Percival, was deeply impressed by the fan-vaulted roof of King's College Chapel, a "broad and massy" span, "wonderfully thought, and executed, the abuttment being small . . ."[97] The intricacy and daring flatness of these vaults spoke to North's aesthetic sense, while the absence of freestanding exterior buttresses removed his greatest objection to the Gothic style. Of this same structural feat Percival would later write:

Peterhouse Chapel at Cambridge. On occasion, Sir John praised earlier work as well. See his remarks on Lichfield and Ely cathedrals, the chapter house at York, and the choir at Carlisle. He was also impressed with classical work of Emmanuel and Pembroke chapels at Cambridge, St. Peter's in Liverpool, and All Hallows in Northampton.

95. Colvin and Newman, 110–11.
96. Ibid., 108.
97. Ibid., 109.

. . . y.ᵉ roof . . . is built of Stone & almost flat without any other Support then the Side walls
of the Chappell, w.ᶜʰ are not thick, and here the art of the builders deserves to be taken
notice of that So flat a roof Should continue So long firm and entire, and evry thing So well
lay'd together as that there falls an equall weight evry where.98

Although Percival shared North's liking for "regular" architecture, his diary
contains none of the classical dogmatizing indulged in by North. Percival's
tolerant—even positive—attitude toward later Gothic architecture may have
resulted from the time he spent at Westminster School—in the shadow of the
Abbey—and at Oxford, where, by the university's very nature, a persistent
ecclesiastical tradition had informed building programs well into the seventeenth century.99

Percival's preoccupation with cathedrals and country houses did not pre-
clude his taking notice of lesser buildings. Sensitive to the distinct regional
characteristics of these structures, he occasionally remarked on the predominance of this or that building material in a particular locality. In Norwich, he
was struck with the extensive use of flint, together with the prevalence of
thatching, of which he disapproved. Crossing the fens around Ely, he implicitly linked the predominance of this covering with the local availability of reeds.
Near Richmond he was more explicit about this sort of connection, remarking
that "The plenty of Stones in the North are the cause of very fair briges &
large houses, of w.ᶜʰ the North is full."

Naturally, Sir John encountered techniques and materials that were unfa-
miliar. At New Hall in Essex, and in Nottingham, he commented on "a Sort
of plaister of Paris" (probably burned alabaster or gypsum) used in making
floors and even walls, "for it may be made into mortar, but it must be
presently us'd otherwise it grows as hard as ever." Near Thetford, walling was
made of chalk quarried in blocks, "which cost but 9 pence a load . . . and may
be cut into the form of brick, or any other Shape, w.ᶜʰ when made in to wall
consolidates, & will last time out of mind." Similarly, among the houses of
Norwich were several which seemed to have been hung or covered with glazed
tiling from Holland, regarded as "proof against time and weather, no rain
being able to moulder or work thrô them."

Less durable were the structures mentioned in Percival's letter written from

98. Add. Mss. 47058, f. 12r.
99. Summerson, 178.

Lanwharf, Scotland, a community of five mud buildings and a stone church, all covered with turf. For a youth who had grown up in Lincoln's Inn Fields, such buildings as Lanwharf's smoke-filled tavern, partitioned with a curtain and illuminated by a window six inches square, must have been a revelation.

In any event, the tour seems to have awakened in Sir John a genuine delight in art, architecture, and landscape—an enjoyment which continued to grow and evolve in the years that followed. During subsequent travels in Europe, Percival assembled a valuable collection of paintings, sculpture, antiquities, books, and music.[100] And though this hoard never reached England, being seized by a French privateer and diverted to St. Malo,[101] Sir John continued to purchase and commission works of art. Among these were several paintings copied after Carracci and a collection of twenty-four "painters heads," possibly intended for thematic adornment of a library or gallery. Percival also acquired several effigies of Roman emperors in ivory, a portrait bust of himself by Vincenzo Felici, and assorted sculptures by Massimiliano Soldani, including at least three unspecified statues.[102]

While in Rome, Percival consorted with painters, antiquarians, sculptors, musicians—and with architect James Gibbs, to whom he extended an offer of patronage.[103] To painter Edward Gouge he likewise offered employment, as a later mezzotint of Lady Percival, copied from Gouge's original, attests.[104]

In Florence Sir John enjoyed great favor with Cosimo III, Grand Duke of Tuscany, an old friend of Sir Robert Southwell's father. In an unusual gesture of friendship, Cosimo presented the young Englishman with a set of gold medals and offered him the choice of any picture in his gallery. Tactfully declining this offer, Percival later presented the Duke with a specially bound collection of English portrait engravings.[105]

100. Add. Mss. 47072, f. 23. Percival's manuscript autobiography contains the intriguing statement that the collection was intended as a gift for "the Accademy of young painters & Sculptors erected by Sr. Godfrey Kneller . . ." Although the academy in which Kneller served as first president was not founded until 1711, Luttrell noted as early as 1698 that "His Majesty is resolved to settle an academy to encourage the art of painting, where are to be 12 masters, and all persons that please may come and practise gratis." Stewart, 58–59.

101. Ibid.; Add. Mss. 47025, f. 70v; Anderson, 2:405.

102. Add. Mss. 47025, ff. 80r, 81r-81v. The portrait bust, dated 1707, is now displayed by the National Portrait Gallery at Beningbrough Hall.

103. Friedman, 7–8, 334, 345.

104. Anderson, 2: plate facing 402.

105. Add. Mss. 47072, ff. 21–22; Add. Mss. 47025, f. 89v.

Shortly after his return to the British Isles, Percival retired to his estate at Burton,[106] finding, at the conclusion of his travels, little pleasure in the enticements of the city,

> . . . a life I am not So fond of as I us'd to be before I fell into Country Improvements which at present fill my hands. I think building, planting gardening & a hundred other amusements I meet at home do infinitely Surpass the busie noise of the town . . .[107]

Years later, Sir John would similarly occupy himself in London, where in the spring of 1719 William Byrd occasionally inspected the progress of his friend's house, then under construction in Pall Mall.[108] In the meantime, Percival had traveled a second time to the Continent, touring for several months in France and the Netherlands. Perhaps it was during this second journey through the Low Countries that he acquired Jacob van Campen's sumptuous volume of engraved views depicting the Amsterdam town hall.[109] In later years, Percival's name would appear among the subscribers to such lavish architectural publications as Colin Campbell's *Vitruvius Britannicus* (1715–1725); William Kent's *Designs of Inigo Jones* (1727); and James Gibbs's *A Book of Architecture* (1728).

In the interim, he was busily assembling a large collection of sixteenth- and seventeenth-century Netherlandish drawings, now preserved at the Yale University Gallery. Some of these, it seems, were obtained through the assistance of his long-time friend George Berkeley, bishop of Cloyne, who traveled in Europe during this period.[110]

No less than painting or sculpture, Percival's delight in gardens found continued expression throughout his life. His enthusiastic and revealing de-

106. Anderson, 2:405–6.

107. Add. Mss. 47025, f. 99r.

108. Wright and Tinling, 244, 258. Following his return to Virginia, Byrd wrote: "When I had the honour to see your Lordship last, I did not forsee that I shou'd tarry long enough here to trouble you with a letter. I thought 3 months wou'd have dispatch'd all my business here, and that before this I shou'd have the pleasure of seeing you compleatly settled in the most elegant house in town." Tinling, 1:328.

109. Jacob van Campen, *Afbeeldin van't Stadt Huis van Amsterdam,* Amsterdam, 1668. Percival's copy of this work, bearing his bookplate, is now owned by the Colonial Williamsburg Foundation.

110. See Wright and Tinling, 133, 170; Haverkamp-Begemann and Logan, xi-xii. Percival's journal of this tour (12 June–30 August 1718) is Add. Mss. 47059, British Library.

scriptions of Hall Barn and Stowe are familiar to students of English garden
history. From these narratives it is clear that Percival was attuned to the asso-
ciative qualities of these early landscape gardens and sensitive to the intentions
underlying their newer elements.[111]

The tour of England was clearly an event of major significance in the forma-
tion of Percival's social, intellectual, and artistic values—a catalytic experience
with consequences for the remainder of Sir John's life and that of his companion.

London and Virginia

Percival and Byrd continued on amicable terms for many years following the
conclusion of their journey, exchanging visits, dining together, or attending an
occasional meeting of the Royal Society. During Byrd's courtship of Mary
Smith, Sir John's name was invoked as one of "most unquestionable honour
and veracity" who would vouch for the suitor's character.[112] During a visit to
Tunbridge Wells in 1719, Byrd spent much of his time with Lady Percival,
upon whom he composed panegyrical verse.

Scattered hints of the 1701 journey appear in the literary exercises produced
by William Byrd during his years in London. Notable among these is the
character of "Melantha," celebrating the virtues of Lady Sherard, to whom
Byrd and Sir John had been introduced during their visit to Stapleford, just a
few months before. In a letter to Lady Mary Caverley, Byrd would later sati-
rize the prodigious drinking of the Sherards and their guests:

> What effect it may have upon the passing of your Waters, to recieve a couple of Billets so
> close upon the heels of one another, I cant determine. If they have the good fortune to please
> you, no doubt but they will make a quart go off as fast as a gallon wou'd do when You think
> of Stapleford . . .[113]

Occasionally, Byrd found an opportunity to mention those Derbyshire
"wonders" examined in Percival's company several years before. On the
occasion of Lady Betty Cromwell's journey to that region, Byrd greeted his
correspondent with the hope she was "safe by a warm fire amongst the

111. Hunt and Willis, 125, 164–65; Martin, 11.

112. Tinling, 1:313. Shortly before Byrd's return to Virginia in 1719, Lord and Lady Percival
provided a quantity of veal broth and an "apothecary shop" to be taken on the voyage. Wright
and Tinling, 337, 344; Tinling, 1:328–29; Woodfin and Tinling, 404.

113. Woodfin and Tinling, 267.

wonders of the Peak." Reflecting on the impending marriage of one of her relatives, he noted that "Prudella has ever since she went down into the country, been in a course of courtship, & is by this time near a worse precipice than any in the Peak, that of matrimony."[114]

In a similar vein, he sought to entertain "Pulcherio" with the news of a mutual friend who had "set out . . . to visit the 8th wonder of y[e] Peak his mistress . . ."[115] Byrd also alluded in this same letter to his experiences with Sir John in Scotland, where unpleasant odors and fear of contracting "the itch" remained salient in his memory: "The many ill-smells we have here wou'd make a man fancy himself at Edinburgh, but that he does not find the same disturbance between his fingers, that he wou'd there."[116] Even in Byrd's now-famous travel narratives, written a quarter-century later, there are faint echoes of the English tour—echoes to which we must now turn.

In 1724, William Byrd was married to Maria Taylor of Kensington, an attractive young woman with a modest inheritance. Together they embarked for Virginia in 1726, and never saw England again. From his plantation seat on the James River, Byrd periodically corresponded with Percival and other London friends, making light of his own exile in "this silent country." Compensating for the chagrin of this banishment, Byrd invited comparison between himself and the patriarchs (each with his flocks and herds—his "bondmen" and "bond-women"), laying stress upon the innocuous, idyllic qualities of his remote existence.[117] Drawing upon the prose imagery of Joseph Addison, he wrote to one friend: "We that are banish't from . . . polite pleasures, are forct to take up with rural entertainments. A library, a garden, a grove and a purling stream are the innocent scenes that divert our leizure."[118]

114. Ibid., 200; Tinling, 1:234.

115. Woodfin and Tinling, 199.

116. Ibid. From Cambridge, Byrd had reported, "If we do not visit Scotland, it will be for want of time, and not for fear of the itch, for we have met with a nostrum for that desease." Tinling, 1:213. While in Scotland, Percival noted: "I eat all the while in my gloves for fear of the itch, w[ch] boldly Shew'd itself on my Landladys fingers & legs, and put me in mind of what an Unkle Dering of mine was wont to Say, that he had been but a fortnight in Scotland, and yet had got their present State at his fingers ends." Add. Mss. 47025, f. 55v.

117. See, for example, his letters to the Earl of Orrey, 5 July 1726 and 2 February 1727, Tinling, 1:354–59.

118. Tinling, 1:413. This passage was probably inspired by the essay on Lenora's library that had appeared earlier in *The Spectator* (no. 37), where Joseph Addison described a widow's love

In 1728, Byrd's service as a commissioner on the expedition to survey the disputed boundary between North Carolina and Virginia provided a yearned-for opportunity to portray his rusticity in a more acceptable light. On his trek through the wilderness, Byrd experienced a kind of literary metamorphosis in which the accustomed roles of courtier and wit were exchanged for more virile characters—adventurer and explorer, the learned man in the wilderness. Amongst members of the Royal Society (and consequently in London society) the young Virginian's provincial ties had always been, to some degree, his entrée. Byrd was fully conscious of the special status his connections with the New World conferred.[119]

Returning from the boundary expedition, he wrote to various friends with news of his adventure, and later produced the parallel narratives that have become the foundation of his literary reputation. The longer of these is a proper "History of the Dividing Line," witty and urbane, replete with descriptions of New World plant and animal life, certain to please those London friends of a scientific bent.[120] A shorter narrative—the so-called "Secret History of the Line"—is a ribald masterpiece of storytelling in which Byrd's penchant for satirical humor was allowed free reign. Here, the sexuality of his fellow commissioners and the uncouth character of local inhabitants were humorously emphasized—subjects which Byrd, no doubt, deemed inappropriate for the politer purposes of the "History."

---

of books and rural retirement. Situated far from the metropolis "in a kind of Wilderness," her estate, like Byrd's, afforded the "rural entertainments" of a library and a "purling stream." *The Spectator,* 1:153–58.

119. At meetings of the society, Byrd's contributions were nearly always based on his familiarity with various aspects of the New World. See Woodfin, 28–34. Significantly, Byrd's portrait, painted for the Earl of Orrery, is a formulaic depiction of a fashionable gentleman—but with the view of a ship in the distance. The significance of this New World imagery is thrown into higher relief by a similar portrait of Sir Wilfred Lawson that once hung at Westover. The pose and attire of the sitter in both of these likenesses is virtually identical, but Lawson stands before a generic, vaguely rendered architectural background. Not only are the background elements of Byrd's portrait different, but they are depicted with greater vigor and detail, a sure indication of their iconographic significance. The Orrery portrait of Byrd, attributed to Hans Hysing, is now owned by the Virginia Historical Society. That of Lawson is exhibited by Colonial Williamsburg at the Wallace Decorative Arts Gallery.

120. It has been suggested that this document was also intended partly as an encouragement to prospective immigrants who might be persuaded to settle on the lands taken up by Byrd along the Roanoke and Dan rivers. Davis, 170. See also Marambaud, 120–29.

The contrasting tone of these parallel "histories" brings to mind Percival's radically differing accounts of the disastrous foray into Scotland. One of these—the diary—is terse and serious in its relation of the event, stated "for the record" and clearly intended to maintain Sir John's pose as the studious traveler. The other—a letter to Oxford classmate Digby Cotes—is humorous and expansive, manifestly intended for the amusement of friends. As in the case of Byrd's "Secret History," the slovenly appearance and uncouth behaviour of persons living on the fringe of civilization were exploited for the entertainment of those in the metropolis. The unsavory topic and sarcastic tone of Percival's letter, acceptable in this context, would have been wholly unsuitable for the diary.

Percival and his mentor amused themselves with the perusal of one another's correspondence,[121] and it is likely that Byrd saw both of these documents. If so, he is certain to have appreciated the distinct purpose and literary possibilities of each. Had Byrd's own journal of the tour survived, we might have observed a similar contrast between the gravity of this document and the lighter tone of his letters to Southwell. As in the case of the Dividing Line expedition, he is likely to have created two very different accounts of this journey, directed toward different literary ends. The tour of England was, quite possibly, Byrd's introduction to the parallel modes of travel narration that later served him so well.

Upon receiving the news of Byrd's expedition, Percival responded with the requisite measures of eulogy and classical allusion, likening his journey to the exploits of Hercules and Caesar.[122] In later years, Percival's involvement in the colonization of Georgia increasingly dominated the correspondence. To Edward Southwell, Byrd would later complain, "I have every year the honour to hear from my Lord Egmont, but Georgia takes up so much of his Lordships thoughts, that he rarely leaves room for private history."[123] Byrd, however, was soon involved in settlement schemes of his own. On his lands at the falls of the James River, he laid off the boundaries of a town to be called Richmond, announcing the sale of lots in the *Virginia Gazette*. Further inland, additional settlements were proposed for his vast holdings along the south side

121. Three days out of London, Byrd reported to Southwell on Sir John's continuing health and good spirits, adding, "I will not say how many good qualitys I discover in him, because he is to see the letter . . ." Tinling, 1:209–10.

122. Ibid., 421–22.

123. Ibid., 2:560.

of what is now the Dan River. Ultimately, he envisioned a network of settlements along the river, all connected by a single road.

The projected layout of these communities, with church and civic structures
fronting a large central square, has been compared with the plan of New
Haven, Connecticut, and with that of an earlier Huguenot settlement at
Manakin, just west of Richmond, in which Byrd's father was evidently involved. It is also possible that Byrd's scheme for the Roanoke settlements
reflected, in a general way, his recollections of Whitehaven, where, some thirty
years earlier, he and Sir John had inspected one of the first postmedieval
planned communities in Britain.

Percival was struck by the regularity of such communities, thinking it worth
remark that the streets of a town should all intersect at right angles.[124] Although Byrd had, by this time, seen Versailles and the rapidly developing
areas on the edges of London, it is unlikely that he had encountered anything
quite like the Whitehaven settlement. Beginning in 1644, the newer portion of
this community had been privately developed by the Lowther family. Laid off
in an elongated grid pattern, the plan of the town provided for straight, broad
thoroughfares and generously sized parcels of land. To encourage settlement,
Sir John Lowther greatly improved the harbor and secured for Whitehaven
the right to hold markets and annual fairs. Prospective settlers were offered
building sites on very favorable terms, sometimes with the addition of capital
advanced at 5 percent interest. As Percival noted, the enterprise was a striking
success. The town's population, about two hundred in 1660, had grown to
nearly three thousand by 1702.[125]

On the scale of a small community, Whitehaven was Byrd's first acquaintance with the orthogonal sort of regularity that later characterized his own civic
planning efforts. But the town was even more important for what it suggested
about the very process of settlement. Given the right conditions (plenty of land,
an advantageous location, and industrious inhabitants), town-building could be
an individual undertaking—a genteel and profitable enterprise. It seems likely
that Byrd's settlements on the James, Appomattox, and Roanoke rivers were
intended to replicate the success of Lowther's paternalistic Whitehaven scheme.

Percival had, in the meantime, been created 1st Earl of Egmont, and on that
happy occasion Byrd seems to have requested a likeness of his old friend to

124. See Sir John's account of Bury St. Edmunds.
125. For an account of Byrd's town-planning activities, see Reps, 195–98, 221–22, 267. For
Lowther's development of Whitehaven, see Hainsworth, xx–xxii; Napper et al., 15–16.

hang in the gallery of worthies he had assembled at Westover. We might regard this collection of portraits as being, in some small degree, a fruit of Byrd's travels with Sir John. Having seen the Duke of Grafton's impressive gallery of images at Euston Hall, the "Little Bedlam" portraits at Burghley, and the royal portraits assembled by Lord Orford in the entry at Chippenham, he understood the role of such collections in making good one's claim to an exalted position in the prevailing social and political order. As if collecting autographs, Byrd solicited the likenesses of powerful and respected friends, which he drew together and displayed to advantage amidst the splendid holdings of the Westover library. Walking to and fro in this long, unobstructed space, visitors contemplated the message these images collectively embodied.[126]

In this and other cases, however, the sentimental impulse underlying such a collection is likewise apparent. Acknowledging the receipt of Lord Egmont's portrait, Byrd wrote:

I had the honour of your Lordships commands of the 9th of September, and since that have the pleasure of conversing a great deal with your picture. It is incomparably well done & the painter has not only hit your ayr, but some of the vertues too which usd to soften and enliven your features. So that every connoisseur that sees it, can see t'was drawn for a generous, benevolent, & worthy person. It is no wonder perhaps that I coud discern so many good things in the portrait, when I knew them so well in the original, just like those who pick out the meaning of the Bible, altho' in a strange language, because they were acquainted with the subject before. But I own I was pleasd to find some strangers able to read your Lordships character on the canvas, as plain as if they had been physiognomists by profession.[127]

Contemplating this token of friendship, Byrd undoubtedly thought himself secure in the Earl's esteem. In a letter written the following year, he ventured to criticize the Georgia colony's monopoly on trade with the Cherokee Indians, thinking it ". . . a little preposterous, for us to send about 500 miles for a licence to trade with Indians that live not half a mile from us, and with whome we have traded time out of mind . . . ."[128]

126. Significantly, it was a short time before Byrd's return to Virginia in 1719 (and the ensuing confrontation with Lieutenant-Governor Alexander Spotswood) that he requested the portrait of his long-time friend (and primary spokesman at court), the Duke of Argyle.

127. Tinling, 2:487; Wenger, 51–54; Meschutt, 19–46.

128. Tinling, 2:521.

John Percival, 1st Earl of Egmont. Attributed to Hans Hysing, c. 1736.
This likeness, a gift from the Earl, hung in William Byrd's gallery of
portraits at Westover. Now tattered and scuffed, it remains a compelling
artifact of their friendship. Courtesy of Mr. Joseph Huger Harrison.
Photograph: Colonial Williamsburg Foundation/Hans Lorenz.

By all appearances, His Lordship was piqued at the liberties Byrd had
taken, for thereafter Egmont's letters ceased. In spite of continued solicitation,
they seem never to have resumed. Thus ended a friendship of nearly forty
years—a bond first established in those fourteen weeks of shared discovery
and travail that were Sir John Percival's "progresse round England."

Editorial Note

Measuring only 6 x 3¾ inches, Percival's English tour diary is a surprisingly small document, suitably proportioned for travel. Shortly after returning from his journey, Percival began to recopy this original narrative, enlarging his earlier sketches and introducing some textual alterations.[1] This transcription (Add. Mss. 47058) was never finished. The original diary thus remains the only complete record of Sir John's tour. As we have seen, Percival was created 1st Earl of Egmont in 1733. Following his death in 1748, the diary descended with the rest of his papers to the 7th Earl of Egmont, and, following his death in 1897, to his widow, Lucy Perceval, Countess of Egmont. In 1950 it was donated by the trustees of her estate to what was then the British Museum. The document is now preserved among the Egmont papers in the British Library, where it bears the designation "Additional Manuscript 47057."

In the texts that follow, the editor has attempted to recover and preserve the original content and meanings of the source documents, recognizing that their significance is more historical than literary. Except as noted below, spelling, punctuation, and capitalization have been retained without alteration. Abbreviations and diacritical markings are likewise rendered as they appear on the manuscript.

Owing to the typographical difficulties inherent in recreating any documentary format, exceptions to this generally literal approach have been necessary. The designation of paragraphs for the diary and accompanying texts is problematic, since the initial sentence of a paragraph is only rarely indented. The beginning of a new paragraph is therefore apparent only where the last line of that preceding ends short of the right margin. Paragraphs have therefore been designated only where the author's intention of such is clear. These designations appear as in the original text, but with the addition of the symbolic notation ¶. No attempt has been made to replicate the erratic spacing observed particularly in the Percival letterbook.

1. A portion of the transcription was made following the death of William III, to whom Percival referred as "our late king." See Add. Mss. 47058, f. 15r.

Likewise, no attempt has been made to preserve the pagination or line-endings of the source documents. As a result, end-of-page and line-end hyphenation, as well as any associated capitalization or spelling changes have been eliminated except where the writer clearly intended to denote a compound word. Similarly, repeated words or parts of words associated with pagination of the source document have also been omitted.

Occasionally, upper-case letters in the middle of such words as "ItSelf" or "DarbyShire" suggest that the writer regarded these terms as compounds. In such instances, the author's original spacing and capitalization have been preserved.

Capitalization of the letters *s* and *k* posed particularly difficult editorial problems. At the beginning of the document, there appeared distinct upper- and lower-case forms of the letter *s,* used more or less in accordance with the dictates of contemporary convention. As the diary progressed, however, Percival's concern with the proprieties of capitalization and other mechanical matters diminished rapidly, resulting in an indiscriminate use of the upper-case form, even in the middle of words. Significantly, this change parallels a marked decline in the quality of Sir John's penmanship. Indeed, by the end of the document the very distinction between upper- and lower-case forms is blurred. In an effort to preserve the evidence of Percival's waning discipline (and flagging spirits?), the editor has reproduced Percival's distracting use of these forms.

Nowhere is this usage more perplexing, however, than with the letter *k.* Here the distinction between upper- and lower-case forms is generally obscure even near the beginning of the document. In all instances where the letter is indisputably upper-case, the upper leg of the *K* is significantly higher than the lower-case letters in the same word. Generally, this *K* is used in marginal notations or where the letter begins a sentence. Otherwise, the general similarity of the upper- and lower-case *k* may have led Percival to use a single generic form with no regard to context. However, the upper leg of the *k* swings decidedly upward on such proper words as *King* and *Kendall* rather than forming a loop. There do appear, then, to be distinct upper- and lower-case forms of the letter. In the edited text, upper-case *K* has been used where the upturned leg appears on a noun or where that leg is significantly higher than lower-case letters in the same word.

Consistent with Percival's ultimate intention, marginal additions have been incorporated into the text of his diary and correspondence. These appear in

Roman text set off with angled brackets ⟨roman⟩ and footnoted, omitting
Percival's referral symbols. Deleted passages from any part of the document,
when substantive and nonredundant, are similarly included and identified.

Inadvertently repeated words, on the other hand, have been silently removed. Interlineations, careted or uncareted, are incorporated, as above,
without comment or notation.

Doubtful readings of text appear in Roman text with a question mark, set
off by square brackets: [roman?]. Where omissions or misspellings seemed
likely to confuse the reader or obscure the meaning of a word or passage, the
missing words or letters have been supplied within square brackets and itali-
cized: roma[*n*]. In cases where the author intentionally left blank spaces to be
filled in at a later time, the appropriate information has been supplied in
italics and set off with square brackets, as above: [*roman*]. If such information
was not available, or could not be inferred from the text, the blank space is
simply noted in accordance with the above convention: [*blank*].

Marginal dates and place-names have been retained, approximating their
original relationship to the text, and are reproduced in the margin.

Finally, some confusion exists with regard to the correct spelling of the
diarist's surname. Some modern reference works have adopted the spelling
used in Anderson's *Genealogical History of the House of Yvery,* that is, *Perceval.*
That work was published in 1742, with the apparent consent and assistance of
the 1st Earl of Egmont, and would therefore seem a reliable source. In Percival's own correspondence, however, and more significantly, in his own
autobiographical sketch, the name is rendered with an *i*: *Percival.* Consequently, the editor has elected to employ this latter spelling in the annotations,
introduction, photocaptions, and other scholarly apparatus.

A Journey thrô Severall
Countys of England 1701

Burntwood
Chelsmford

On monday the 14th of July we set out from London, and came
to Burntwood[1] where we dind, this is a town of no consideration So in the afternoon we proceeded to Chelsford,[2] where
Mr Ously the Parson of Springtree met us. This Gentleman is
a great Antiquary having convers'd much in meddalls and
Genealogys,[3] he told us this town did not begin to flourish till
the reign of Henry the second, when Mauritius Bishop of
London[4] brought the high way thrô it, wch lay before above
half a mile on one side. He also built a bridge over the Chel-
mer wch crosses the town. Here are two large Streets, & a
Church[5] wch by meeting with severall additions has lost its
regularity thô the largeness of it makes amends for it. Here is
a market kept evry Satturday wch supplys London with Corn.
A little without the town are the remains of a Fryary of Bare-
foots founded by Malcome King of Scotland who endow'd it

1. Brentwood, Essex.

2. Chelmsford, Essex.

3. John Ouseley (1645–1708), clergyman and antiquarian. Rector of Panfield near Braintree,
Essex, 1668–1703. Ouseley assembled a considerable collection of manuscripts and notes
relating to the history of Essex. He also supplied information for the chapter on Essex in
Edmund Gibson's 1695 edition of Camden's *Britannia*. Christy, 132–37. William Byrd wrote to
Southwell, describing their encounter with Ouseley, "a great master of the antiquitys of Essex,
but peaks himself chiefly in genealogy. He was very civil, and favour'd us with a pretty deal of
information." Ouseley left the party at Witham. Tinling, 1:209.

4. Maurice (d. 1107), bishop of London 1086–1107; chaplain and chancellor to William the
Conqueror. *DNB*, 37:94.

5. Presently the Cathedral of St. Mary, a fifteenth-century structure heavily reworked in the
nineteenth century. Pevsner, *Buildings . . . Essex*, 102–3.

44

with a yearly revenue of 9[li].[6] But now it is converted into a
Farmhouse and their Chappell into a Barn. In this place king
Henry the 6th founded a free School, w[ch] is not now in a very
thriving condition.[7] ¶

The next morning we left the town to take a vew of New Hall[8]
whither M[r] Ously gave us his company. This Seat Stands 2
mile from Chelsmford & belong'd to the Duke of Albemarl[9]
who bought it of the Duke of Buckingham.[10] It has been a
noble Structure but now is falling to the ground. The walls are
of Brick, and the floors for the most part of plaster of Paris.[11]
Some parts of this was built by Henry y[e] 8th whose arms are
finely cut over the gate, but Queen Elizabeth did afterwards
add much to its bewty & bigness.[12] The Rooms are very Statly
king Charles who resided there making a Pallace of it w[th]
rooms of State, audience,[13] a Guard Chamber,[14] and a Chap-

6. "On the south side of the river stood a house of Black or Dominican Friers; which might
be very antient, but could not be founded by Malcome King of Scotland: for the last of that
name died long before these monks were known in England." Morant, 1:5.

7. The Free Grammar School of King Edward VI, founded c. 1550. *Victoria History . . . Essex,*
2:511.

8. New Hall, Boreham, Essex. A large house purchased by Henry VIII from Sir Thomas
Boleyn. Having laid out considerable sums in its enlargement, Henry dubbed the house
"Beaulieu," a name which, according to Camden, "never obtain'd among the common peo-
ple." Gibson, 346.

9. George Monck (1608–1670), 1st Duke of Albemarle. Cokayne, *Complete Peerage,* 1:87–89.

10. George Villiers (1628–1687), 2nd Duke of Buckingham. Ibid., 2:394–96.

11. "Within their doores also such as are of abilitie doo oft make their floores and parget of
fine alabaster burned, which they call plaster of Paris, whereof in some places we haue great
plentie, and that verie profitable against the rage of fire." Holinshed, 1:315.

12. Henry VIII built a new forecourt and gatehouse with a hall in the east range and a
chapel in the west. The north range was rebuilt by Thomas Radclyff (c. 1525–1583), 3rd Earl of
Sussex, who was granted the house in 1573. (It is this portion that currently survives.) The arms
mentioned by Percival were removed to the present chapel when the gatehouse was demolished c. 1737. Kenworthy-Browne et al., 65–66.

13. The presence or audience chamber, generally the second room in the royal apartment,
immediately preceding the bedchamber. Tudor rulers gave audience in this chamber, to which
"lords, knights, gentlemen, officers of the king's house, and other honest personages" were
allowed access. Colvin et al., *History of the King's Works,* 5:130.

14. The first room in the royal apartment, generally situated at the head of the main stair.

pell. The gardens are quite Spoilt, but there is a grove near the house perhaps the finest in England, at the end of w^{ch}: is a Wilderness; but what adorns it most is a bewtyfull row of Lime and Ash trees w^{ch}: beginning at the high way reaches thrô the Park to it above a mile in length. This is above 60 foot broad, and has a gravell walk on each side, w^{ch}: added to the eveness and Statlyness of the trees makes a noble avenue.[15] We saw nothing els worth observation here, but a prodigious fish Pond w^{ch}: is now choakt up with weeds. ¶

Keldon

From hence we came to keldon[16] a town of no note where we dind, and afterwards went to Felix Hall[17] belonging to Sr Anthony Abney.[18] This is a brick house as are most of this Country and is very irregular, w^{ch}: may well be excus'd thrô its age, for it was in Henry the 8th: time the seat of Sr Robert Southwell.[19] It Stands in the middle of a Park, and commands no other Prospect then that of a Small Grove joining to it. This place lying a mile out of our way we return'd to Keldon, and thence proceeded to Brackstead Lodge, the

BrackStead Lodge.

Quite often these spaces were hung with ornamental displays of arms, as is presently the case with the king's guard chamber at Hampton Court. Ibid.

15. ". . . New-hall . . . in the days of old has been very magnificent, but has nothing now remarquable except a streight shady walk of a mile long, that leads from the entrance of the park to the house, but the view is intercepted by a riseing in the middle; there is besides this a grove of firrs the finest I have seen in England." Tinling, 1:209. According to Thomas Baskerville the avenue was composed, in 1662, of "double rows of lime and hornbeam trees on both sides in exact order." *Victoria History . . . Essex,* 2:626.

16. Kelvedon, Essex.

17. "The house is something irregular but great part of it new; tis finely scituated in the center of a good park." Tinling, 1:209.

18. Sir Anthony Abdy of Felix Hall, Essex (1665–1704), 2nd Baronet. Cokayne, *Baronetage,* 2:99. William Byrd described Abdy as "a gentleman whome the spleen has made very untractable." Tinling, 1:209.

19. According to Byrd, it was another house nearby that was the seat of the Southwells. To Sir Robert, he wrote that Ouseley "gave us to understand that besides this Felix Hall, there was another seat and an extraordinary park about seaven miles distant, belonging to Sir Robert Southwell in king Harry the 8th's time." Tinling, 1:209. LeNeve, on the other hand, referred to "Fælix Hall by Kelvedon formerly the Estates And Seat of Sr Robert Southwell, Kn^t your Ancestor in the time of Hen:8." Add. Mss. 47025, f. 46.

house of Mr Whitcomb a Turky Merchant.[20]¶
This thô it stands on a riseing ground has but little Prospect,
and no conveniencys for water wch is brought half a mile, but
amends is made for this in a Park, warren Fishpond &c.¶
Here we lay one night having met with very kind entertaiment
and the next morning Set out for Colechester. This town is
built upon a hill, and trades greatly in serges,[21] bays,[22] Ois-
ters, & Eringo root[23] w.[ch] being dug above a yard deep out of
the sands near Harwich, is brought hither, & when candid
sent to all parts of the kingdom. It contains within its Libertys
16 Parishes, some of the Churches whereof were ruin'd in the
time of the civil wars. Here are the remains of an Antient
Castle[24] the walls of which in some places are 3 yards thick,
being built of brick and Flint intermix'd. The Proprietors are
evry day pulling it down to sell the materials The bricks again
for building, and the Flints for paving their Streets or mend-
ing their highways.[25] There have latly been found Severall
large Vaults fill'd up with sand, w.[ch] is now Sold for mixing
with Lime. This has formerly been a place of great strength,
but the ditch sorounding it is now fill'd up, and a Stone wall

17.
Colechester

20. Peter Whitcomb of Braxted Lodge, Essex (d. 1703–1707), merchant. Clerk of chancery
1698; was succeeded as sheriff of Suffolk 1702. Whitcomb had purchased the estate in November of the previous year. Essex Record Office, D/DHt T38/9, 25, 27, 29. ". . . we rode to a
pretty seat about 4 [miles] off called [B]rackly Lodge, belonging to a Mr. Whitcomb a freind
of mine, where we quarter'd and met with good entertainment." Tinling, 1:209. In 1708
Braxted Lodge was described as a "large new-built house not above 30 years yet rooms but 12
foot high and but one sash window . . ." Gimson, 21–22.

21. A woolen fabric, often referred to as being worn by the lower classes. More recently the
term refers to a durable twill cloth of worsted or with the warp of worsted and the woof of
wool, used primarily in clothing.

22. Baize. A course woolen stuff with a long nap, used chiefly for coverings, linings, cur-
tains, etc.

23. Eryngo. A root of the sea holly, *Eryngium maritimum,* formerly candied for use as a
sweetmeat and thought to be an aphrodisiac.

24. Built by William the Conqueror, Colchester Castle is an immense eleventh-century
keep, the largest now in existence. King, 1:143.

25. In 1683, the structure had been purchased by a certain John Wheely, who proceeded to
dismantle its upper portions for the salvage of its materials. MacKenzie, 1:260.

wch went quite round the town is now fallen down in many places. On the south side Stood anciently an Abby dedicated to St Peter, wch was afterwards made the seat of Sr Charles Leucas[26] who with Sr George Lisle[27] So valiantly defended the town against the Parliam^t and for wch they were in 1648 in cool bloud Shot to death by Generall Fairfax[28] as is writen on their tomb Stone in St Peters Church.[29] From hence we went to

Harwich

Harwich having from Maningtree thither a view of the river of that name. Harwich in time of peace has but little trade, it depending chiefly upon Passengers who here take Shipping for Holland. The fishing here is very good especially for Lobsters, wch being brought into the market alive, are cary'd fresh

Landguard
Fort

from hence to London. Landguard Fort[30] from hence affords a very aggreable prospect, it is very Strong and Secures the harbour, the Governour is now one Capt Jones.[31] The Government of Harwich is very regular no beggers being suffred, but they who cannot provide for themselves, are distributed among the abler sort who are obliged to maintain them.[32]

26. Sir Charles Lucas (d. 1648), royalist cavalry commander. *DNB,* 34:229.

27. Sir George Lisle (d. 1648) entered the King's service as an infantry commander during the early stages of the Civil War, rising to the rank of colonel. In 1645 he was knighted in recognition of his military exploits and service. *DNB,* 33:340–41.

28. Thomas Fairfax (1612–1671), 3rd Baron Fairfax of Cameron. Commander-in-chief of the parliamentary army during the siege of Colchester. *DNB,* 18:141–49.

29. Following the surrender of Colchester to parliamentary forces in 1648, Lisle and Lucas were shot in the castle yard and buried in the Lucas family vault at St. Giles (not St. Peter's) Church. The tombstone to which Percival referred was erected twelve years after the execution, following the restoration of Charles II to the throne. *DNB,* 24:230. The inscription reads as follows: "Under this Marble ly the Bodies of the two most valiant Captains, Sir Charles Lucas, and Sir George Lisle, Knights, who for their eminent loyalty to their Soverain, were on the 28th day of August 1648, by the command of Sir Thomas Fairfax, the General of the Parliament army, in cold blood barbarously murdered." Cromwell, 1:229.

30. The fortifications on Lungar Point had been completed during the reign of Charles I and probably succeeded an earlier earthwork. Leslie, 3.

31. Lieutenant-colonel Edward Jones (d. 1711), governor of Landguard Fort 1697–1711. Jones had previously served as an officer in the 2nd regiment of Foot Guards (now the Coldstream Guards), having seen active service in Flanders. Ibid., 59, 102–3.

32. In 1673 several almshouses had been built through a bequest of "George Coleman Gent.t." Dale, 56.

⟨good fresh water is here wanting but there is plenty of evry
thing els⟩.³³ We lay at the 3 cupps, where we met w^{th}: particular good Entertaiment. The next morning we Set out for
Ipswich, ferrying over the River Stour to Shotly which is in
Suffolk. We past thrô no considerable town hither, neither did
we see any Gentlemens Seats worth taking notice of. Ipswich
Stands on the Orwall³⁴ about 18 miles before it falls into the
Sea. it has formerly bore a great trade with Holland, but
nothing is now Imported besides Coal, for w^{ch}: Corn is return'd. No Manufactory is he[re] Settled, which makes it that
a town the best Scituated in England for Cõmerce is now
Intirely neglected the Inhabitants being poor, and not filling
above half the town, and of them Quakers & Presbiterians
have a great proportion; the latter have latley built a fine
meeting house large enough to hold 1500 People.³⁵ Here are
twelve Parishes within the town w^{ch}: is govern'd by two Baylifs
who are chosen every year. Here is also a Free Schoole built in
the time of Henry the 8th: and afterwards endow'd by Queen
Elizabeth,³⁶ A town Library,³⁷ an Hospitall,³⁸ and a Shire
house not quite finish'd,³⁹ for want of which the sessions are

Ipswich
18.

33. Marginal note, incorporated.

34. The river Orwell.

35. St. Nicholas Presbyterian (now Unitarian) meetinghouse was erected 1699–1700 by
Joseph Clarke, carpenter. Pevsner, *Buildings . . . Cambridgeshire,* 296. According to Defoe, it was
"as large and as fine a building of that kind as most on this side of England, and inside the best
finished of any I have seen, London not excepted . . ." Defoe, 71.

36. Probably the Ipswich Grammar School, in existence by 1477. It was later dubbed the Ipswich College Grammar School in association with the Cardinal College of St. Mary, founded
through Wolsey's efforts in 1528. Ultimately, it came to be known simply as the Ipswich School.
Victoria History . . . Suffolk, 2:325, 328–29.

37. The library had been formed around a bequest of books made by William Smart in
1598. In 1612 these books were placed in a "spacious room at Christs hospital" where they
remained at the time of Percival's visit. Hepworth, 455–56; *An Account of the Gifts . . . Ipswich,*
140–41.

38. Christ's Hospital, housed in buildings previously occupied by a community of Domin-
icans or Blackfriars. Hepworth, 456.

39. Following the decay of an earlier sessions hall in the fourteenth century, justices found
Bury a more convenient stop on their circuit between Cambridge and Thetford. In 1698 an
attempt was made to attract the assizes back to Ipswich by erecting a new sessions house. The

held in the town Hall,[40] but the sises are held in Bury, thô this
is the County town, and might justly chalenge the right of
having them held here.¶
The two houses of note in this town are ChristChurch[41] w^{ch}
belong'd to the late Ld Hereford,[42] and Sr John Barkers
house.[43] Both are large brick buildings, but the first is Situated the pleasantest for Standing on a rising ground, it co-
m̄ands at once a view both of the town and river wch co-
m̄ands plenty of fish. This Seat was first erected by Cardinall
Woolsey a native of this place who designed it for a Colledge:
But Since it has been turn'd into a noblemans Seat it has been
sorounded with a Park in wch are severall Fishponds. Sr John
Barkers house is much loftyer, but Stands not so advantagiously as ChristChurch But the Gardins are much better.[44]
This is a burrow town and is a mile broad, & of the same
length. Upon leaving it we past thrô Woodbrige, and Wick-
ham to Saxmundum. Within 3 miles of this town Stands
Glenham house[45] belonging to a Gentleman of that name.[46]

---

citizens of Bury retaliated, however, subscribing "towards especially respectful and generous
entertainment of the judges." In the end, Bury prevailed. Redstone, 102–3.

40. Formerly the Church of St. Mildred. Cross, 3–4.

41. Christchurch Mansion, built 1548–1550 by Edmund Withipoll on the site of a twelfth-
century Augustinian priory. (Percival's association of Cardinal Wolsey with the construction of
Christchurch was erroneous.) The house was later rebuilt by Leicester Devereaux (1617–1677),
6th Viscount Hereford, following a fire that nearly gutted it in 1674. Much of what now
constitutes the mansion's distinctive appearance (the interiors, the transom windows of the
upper story, and the Dutch gables with their surmounting pediments) dates from this rebuilding. Pevsner, *Buildings . . . Suffolk,* 298.

42. Edward Devereux (c. 1675–1700), 8th Viscount Hereford. Lord Hereford was succeeded
by his cousin Price Devereux (1664–1740), 9th Viscount. Cokayne, *Peerage,* 6:480–81.

43. Sir John Barker of Grimston Hall, Suffolk (c. 1680–1731), 5th Baronet. M.P. for Ipswich
1708–1710 and 1710–1713; for Thetford 1713–1715; for Suffolk 1722–1727 and 1727–1731. Cokayne, *Baronetage,* 1:192.

44. ". . . there are 3 gardens on the one side with grass and gravell walks all kept neate and
good fruite; on the other side is one large garden with a sum̄er house in which stands a large
statue, black of a gigantick form and proportion, this answeres the fine green house on the
other side . . ." Fiennes, 135.

45. Glemham Hall, erected during the latter part of the sixteenth century, probably by Sir
Henry Glemham. Around the beginning of the eighteenth century the estate passed into the

Christchurch Mansion, Ipswich. Detail from John Ogilby's map of Ipswich, 1674. British Museum.

we call'd not here to see him as his man Importund us who had without doubt order to invite all Strangers who accidentaly come out of their way to see his house. This thô old has not met wth much alteration as is easy to be gues'd from its regularity. It Stands in the middle of a Park 3 mile round and well Stock'd wth Deer, and has great conveniency for water. ¶ Saxmundum is a very Small market town, & contains nothing

Saxmundum 20.

possession of Dudley North (c. 1686–1730), under whose ownership the house assumed its present appearance. Begun no earlier than 1705, North's alterations were completed by 1722. Tipping, 406–7, 410; Venn and Venn, 3:265.

46. Thomas Glemham of Glemham Hall, Suffolk (c. 1648–1704), "a Gentleman endow'd with great civility as inheritor of the Vertue & Estate of Sr Sackville, Sr Thomas & Sr John Glemham his Ancestors." Add. Mss. 47025, f.46v; Foster, *Alumni*, 2:571.

worth observation, So we easily prevail'd upon our Selves the next day when Dinner was done to leave it and go to Beccles. Had not my Groom fell Sick here we had made more hast and layn at Yarmouth, w^{ch}: was our first design, but this mischance forc'd us to lodge here. In our way we past thrô Bliburrow,[47] in w^{ch}: is a very lofty Church[48] (where one of our Kings before the Conquest is bury'd)[49] and the ruines of An Abby.[50] The Church is not only very large, but as regular & bewtyfull on the out Side. We went to the top of it, and took a view of Severall fine Prospects, perticularily of Sould,[51] w^{ch}: Standing upon a riseing Ground is seen at the best advantage. The Church and Abby could not have been better Situated it being on the top of a Small hill, at the foot of which there runs a very fine Stream thrô a meddow w^{ch}: reaches some miles. Having Sattisfy'd our curiosity we went on, and in our way Saw S^r: John Rouse[52] and M^r: Garnishes[53] house both which are old

47. Blytheburgh, Suffolk.

48. Holy Trinity Church, a fifteenth-century structure of knapped flint. Pevsner, *Buildings . . . Suffolk,* 102.

49. Anna (d. 652), king of the East Angles. Slain by Penda, king of the Mercians. Holinshed, 1:619–20.

50. Blytheburgh Priory, a community of Augustinian canons founded during the reign of Edward I. According to one commentator, remains of the priory were "Yet to be seen about a hundred and fifty yards N.E. of the parochial church." Dugdale, *Monasticon Anglicanum,* vol. 6, pt. 3, 587–88.

51. Southwould, Suffolk.

52. Sir John Rous of Henham Hall, Suffolk (c. 1656–1730), 2nd Baronet. Sheriff of Suffolk 1678–1679; M.P. for Eye 1685–1687; for Suffolk 1689–1690. Cokayne, *Baronetage,* 5:114.

53. Possibly Edward Garneys of Redisham, then deceased. His daughter Francis Garneys (then Francis Jacobs, widow) and his son-in-law George Pretyman (whose late wife was Elizabeth Garneys) sold off respective portions of the estate in 1700 and 1706. Although there existed several other Garneys estates in the vicinity of Beccles, only Redisham lay directly along Percival and Byrd's route of travel. In 1847 Redisham Hall was described as being an Elizabethan structure, having "some good and lofty apartments," and being "rich in the clustered ornamented chimneys which so especially marked the domestic architecture of the era in which it was erected." Suckling, 1:62–66. It is possible that Percival, following the recommendation of Peter LeNeve, visited Roos Hall rather than Redisham, which "by purchasse, came to the family of Garnish . . . but this was long Since Sold, acknowledging Sr Robt Rich Bar^t lately deceas'd as Lord thereof." Add. Mss. 47025, f. 47r.

brick buildings and very large. ⟨Beccles is a market town,   Beccles
Standing on the river waveney, in it is a gramar School with an
endowm[t] of 10 Schollarships for Emanuell Colledge in Cambrige.⟩[54] [At?] Beccles we met wth Sr John Plater[55] a very odd
old fashion'd Gentleman who thô he makes a Concience of
rideing a horsback on a Sonday will set to drinking from
Satturday evening to 4 a clock next morning. M[r] Le Neve of
Norfolk recomended us to him,[56] and who brought us
acquainted with Sr Edmund Bacon, a Parliatn: Man that has a
Seat within a mile of this town.[57] He invited us next day being
Sunday to dinner w[ch] being over we went to Somerly the house   Somerly
of S[r] Richard Allen[58] within 4 mile of Yarmouth, while my
man who remain'd still out of order went on to that Place.¶
This Gentleman is mary'd to the Daughter of Sr Henry Ashurst of Oxford Shire,[59] and both have very good Accomplish-
ments and live happily together. His Seat wch is built of Brick
thô as old as Queen Elizabeths time looks extreamly well with

54. Marginal text, incorporated.

55. Sir John Playter of Sotterley, Suffolk (d. 1721), 2nd Baronet. Cokayne, *Baronetage*, 1:220–21.

56. Peter LeNeve (1661–1729). Norfolk antiquary and genealogist; elected president of the Society of Antiquaries 1687; fellow of the Royal Society; made Norroy king-at-arms 1704. Though LeNeve appears to have published nothing, his extensive collection of genealogical notes later became the basis of Blomefield's history of Norfolk. *DNB*, 33:36–37. LeNeve had directed Percival to Playter's house "where, if S[r] John will be pleas'd to call, he will find a piece of mutton and other honest Country fare, S[r] John having married a relation of mine." Add. Mss. 47025, f. 47r.

57. Sir Edmund Bacon of Gillingham, Norfolk (d. 1721), 4th Baronet. M.P. for Orford 1700–1708. Cokayne, *Baronetage*, 2:32.

58. Sir Richard Allen (previously Richard Anguish) of Somerleyton, Suffolk (d. 1725), 1st Baronet. Having in 1696 inherited the estate of Somerleyton by the death of his maternal uncle Sir Thomas Allen, Richard Anguish assumed the name and arms of Allen and was in 1699 created a baronet. He was M.P. for Dunwich 1703–1710. Cokayne, *Baronetage*, 4:181. Concerning the unusual circumstances of Allen's identity, Peter LeNeve wrote to Percival, ". . . he has lately assum'd his name without any warrant from the King preceding, or other Authority than that of his being call'd by y[e] name of Allen . . ." Add. Mss. 47025, f.47v.

59. Sir Henry Ashurst of Waterstock, Oxfordshire (1645–1711), 1st Baronet. M.P. for Truro 1681–1695 and for Wilton, Wiltshire, 1698–1702. Cokayne, *Baronetage*, 4:151. His only daughter, Frances, married Sir William Allen, though not in 1710 as is supposed. Ibid., 181.

the additions he has made to it. Round it he has a large Park
in which are Deer, Sheep, & Oxen for he kills his own meat.
Besides this he has a Warren, Dove house, Fish Ponds, Decoys,[60] & all manner of game within half a mile of it, w^{ch}.
house is so situated, that from a Lanthorn on the top of it he
can see Norwich Spire wch. is 18 miles distant, on the other
Side he can see the Sea, and what Ships sail in it, So that S^{r}.
Richard has all conveniencys either for the Eye or mouth.[61]
The Land his house Stands upon is call'd the Island, because it
is sorounded on one side by the Sea, and on the other by a Salt
water & Fresh water Stream,[62] wch. are hindred from meeting
by a Damn call'd S^{t}. Ouls Bridge wch. also divides the Countyes
of Norfolk & Suffolk. In this Country Oxen are generally fed
With Turnups wch. fatten them very much and soon, but they
must not be kill'd, till after they have been taken up & fed
with hay for a fortnight, otherwise they eat rank and have the
perfect tast of the turnup.[63] towards October great Number
of these are drove to London Markets ¶

Yarmouth
22.

While we were here we took a trip to Yarmouth, our cheif
design being to Se the manner of the Herring trade wch. is
drove there but we came in a rong Season, it beginning 3

60. Defoe referred in the Fen country to "duckoys; that is to say, places so adapted for the
harbour and shelter of wild-fowl, and then furnished with a breed of those they call decoy-
ducks, who are taught to allure and entice their kind to the places they belong to, that it is
incredible what quantities of wild-fowl of all sorts, duck, mallard, teal, widgeon, &c. they take
in those duckoys every week, during the season." Defoe, 101.

61. "Here the Spectator may view a noble Royalty (He being Lord Paramount of this whole
Hundred or Island call'd Lothing land) a fair Park, formerly celebrated Gardens when in the
possession of S^{r} J^{n}. Wentworth, Several large Broads, (a word used here & in Norfolk for a
poole, or where a River Spreads itself over the adjacent ground) Several Decoys, & a Warren.
For these reasons this Gentleman is reckon'd to have a great advantage over his Neighbours in
Speedy & cheap providing for his Sudden Guests . . ." Add. Mss. 47025, f.47v.

62. Oulton Broad and the river Waveney.

63. "This part of England is remarkable for being the first where the feeding and fattening
of cattle . . . with turnips, was first practised in England . . . And though some have objected
against the goodness of the flesh thus fed with turnips, and have fancied it would taste of the
root; yet upon experience 'tis found, that at market there is no difference nor can they that
buy, single out one joint of mutton from another by the taste." Defoe, 82–83.

weeks before Micklemas,[64] & lasting ten weeks. We were
forc'd hereupon to Sattisfy our curiosity with what was only
told us, and as far as we could learn their way of ketching
them is to go out into the sea near a mile or two and then
Spred their long nets wch go over near 15 acres in length these
sink on one side to the bottom by leads fastned to them, and
the other side is kept up wth Corks. In these Nets the Herrings
wch Swim in Shoals are cought by the Gills and so brought in
Boats on Shoar. After this they are cured wch is the term for
drying them in great rooms wth billets of beach lay'd a cross,
and So contriv'd as that the Smoke only reach the Fish, for the
fire it Self dos more hurt then good. These are thus a curing a
Shorter or longer time, according as the Place is distant to w^{ch}
they must be sent, wch is to Holland, but cheifly to Leghorn,
wch makes the Inhabitants dread a War. The key of this town
whence goods are Ship'd off is Said to be the finest in England, being near a mile long. The town is well fortify'd, having
a Strong wall built in King Johns time, wch encompases it
toward the Sea,[65] and two mounts on wch Stood many Guns
before King James dismounted them. These defended the
town on that Side, thô there is no great danger of an Enemys
invading it by Sea, because the harbour is So choakt up with
Sand, that tis very dangerous for any Ship to venture in that
has not an expert Pilot to conduct it. The whole town is but
one Parish, So it requires a large Church wch it indeed has, &
the Chancell to it is the largest of any belonging to a Parish
Church in England; In the late Civil Wars The Presbiterians
did service in one part & the Church of England in another,

64. Michaelmas. The feast of St. Michael, occurring on 29 September, one of the quarter-
days of the English business year.

65. The walls of Yarmouth were begun after 1260 and completed in the fourteenth century.
Encompassing the medieval town (excepting that side toward the river Yar), these walls are
approximately 2,280 yards in length, punctuated at intervals with sixteen towers and ten gates.
Pevsner, *Buildings . . . North-East Norfolk,* 224. ". . . it is likewise inclosed with a very strong
Wall, upon which, besides Towers, is cast up a Mount towards the East, and are planted
several Pieces of Ordnance to defend the Town and command the Sea." Brome, 134.

for w^ch: reason there ran a partition which divided the Chancell from the body of the Church, and this has taken much from the bewty of the Inside,[66] w^ch: is built Cathedrall wise, & kept very neat. There is now a jetty or Fence making to hinder the Sea from breaking in upon the banks, and by act of Parliam^t: a Shiling is lay'd on evry chadron[67] of Coals w^ch: Shall be us'd in the County. by this 2000^li is propos'd to be rais'd, but The design is like to come to nothing, Severall Gentlemen of the Country being as much against it as others are for it as forseing how little twill answer the Expense.[68] Neer this Place Stand the ruines of an Antient Castle call'd Burrow,[69] whose antiquity is evry day confirm'd by the great quantity of meddalls w^ch: are found there. Not far also from this town are brine Pits for making Salt, the gain accruing from them baring So little proportion to the cost of them that the Undertaker M^r: Bendish is ruin'd by them. These we had not the time thô curiosity to see, by reason of a kind Invitation from M^r: Ferier a Merchant living in the town,[70] w^ch: we were forc'd to accept. ⟨The Streets in this town are generally So narrow that carts cannot pass, So instead of them there is a certain conveniency call'd a Curry or Yarmouth Coach made use of, the figure of which is this:⟩[71] We return'd in the Afternoon to S^r: Richard

66. St. Nicholas Church. In 1650 dissenting sects had taken over portions of the church. The north aisle was used by Presbyterians, who separated it from the rest of the church by filling in the arches on the north side of the nave. Independents were accommodated in the chancel, separated from the nave and aisles by a wall that filled in the chancel arch and the great arches in the east walls of the transepts. Lupson, 9.

67. Chaldron. A dry measure amounting to thirty-six bushels when used in regard to coal.

68. "An Act for the Clearing, Repairing, Preserving and Maintaining the Haven and Piers of Great Yarmouth in the County of Norfolk." Among other things this act provided for a duty on "every Chaldron of Coals, Winchester Measure . . . such Sum or Sums of Money not exceeding the Sum of Twelve Pence." *Public Acts, 1698–99, 10–11 William 3.* c.5, 49.

69. Burgh Castle. A Roman fort overlooking the harbor of Caister-by-Yarmouth, ostensibly erected to protect a Roman naval dockyard formerly in that location. Built of brick and flint, it is roughly quadrangular, covering an area of approximately six acres. Pevsner, *Buildings . . . Suffolk,* 129.

70. Richard Ferrier (1670–1728). M.P. for Yarmouth, 1708, 1710, 1713–1715; mayor of Yarmouth 1706. Venn and Venn, 2:134; Blomefield, 5:1644.

71. Marginal text, incorporated. See facing page for Percival's drawing of the cart.

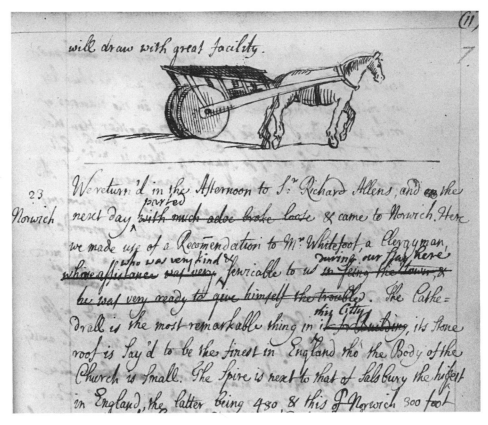

will draw with great facility.

23
Norwich

We return'd in the Afternoon to S.r Richard Allens, and on the
next day parted came to Norwich. Here
we made use of a Recomendation to M.r Whitefoot, a Clergyman,
who was very kind & during our stay here
he was very ready to give himself the trouble. The Cathe=
dral is the most remarkable thing in this City, its stone
roof is say'd to be the finest in England tho' the Body of the
Church is small. The Spire is next to that of Salsbury the highest
in England, the latter being 480 & this of Norwich 300 foot

Yarmouth Cart. Sir John Percival, c. 1701–1702. From Percival's unfinished copy of the diary.
British Library.

Allens and on the 23 with much adoe broak loose from him to   23.
come to Norwich. Here we made use of a recomendation   Norwich.
from M.r Haley[72] to M.r Whitefoot a Clergyman[73] who being a

72. Probably Edmund Hallcy (1656–1742), the noted astronomer, whom Sir Robert Southwell would have known through the Royal Society. *DNB*, 24:104. According to Byrd, however,
it was "by mentioning Mr. Haughton's name" that the two travelers were introduced to
Whitefoot. Tinling, 1:211.
    73. John Whitefoot (1646–1731). Fellow of Caius College, Cambridge University, 1671–1677;
rector of Hellesdon, Norfolk, 1682–1731; minister of St. Gregory's, Norwich, 1682–1731, and of
St. Peter Mancroft, 1720–1731; commissary of Norwich and clerk of the Convocation. Venn,
4:391. Byrd characterized Whitefoot as "a clergyman of very great civility & understanding."
Tinling, 1:211.

24.   Gentleman of good Sence & knowledge, we were glad of his
assistance in Seing the Citty. We first went to the Cathedrall to
Prayers, where neither the Singing, nor Quire is much to be
comended.[74] The Cathedrall is Say'd to have the finest Stone
roof of any in England,[75] but the body of it is Small. The Spire
is next to that of Salsbury the highest in England, being above
300 foot high, and that of Salsbury more then 480. Here is a
Dean & 6 Prebends w[ch] Chapter in many cases is independent
of the Bishop. The 6 Prebends are allways put in by the L[d]
Chancelor. We went afterwards to the top of Muscle hill,
where are the ruines of a Chappell, w[ch] Kett the rebell[76] in
Edward the 6th days turn'd into a Fort to batter the town, and
since his time it has been call'd Ketts Castle.[77] No citty in
England except London Stands upon more ground then this,
and the Citty walls are larger in Circumference then those of
London.[78] The Streets are pav'd exceeding bad wth a rugged
Flint of w[ch] allmost all the Churches are built, but being first
broke Square in the manner of bricks, no building can be
Smoother, or Stronger then those of this Sort. the Art of so
Squaring them is no[w?] entirely lost.[79] Here are 36 Parish
Churches w[ch] Stand very thick, and the Livings are very Small,

74. The choir stalls survive, though not in their original locations. A portion of these date
from 1420, the remainder from 1480. Pevsner, *Buildings . . . North-East Norfolk,* 224.

75. Begun during the last quarter of the fifteenth century, the vault is enriched with a
complex network of tierceron and lierne ribs, punctuated at their intersections with richly
carved bosses, several hundred in all. Ibid., 216–20.

76. Robert Kett of Wyndomham (d. 1549), tanner and leader of a rebellion aimed at
diminishing the powers of manorial lords. Following a riot in Attleborough, Kett and his
brother led a mob to Norwich, where a fight for the city ensued. Both were captured following
the defeat of the rebels and executed on 7 December 1549, after which Robert Kett's body was
hung in chains from the top of the castle. *DNB,* 31:76–77.

77. ". . . the Mount on the East-side of the City, called *Ket's-Castle,* must not be passed by in
silence, for it was the Harbour and Nest of *Ket,* a Tanner of *Windham,* that notorious Ring-
leader of Rebellion in King *Edward* the Sixth's Days . . ." Brome, 138–39.

78. First erected in the twelfth century and subsequently rebuilt 1294–1320, the walls of
Norwich are approximately two and a quarter miles in length. Pevsner, *Buildings . . . North-East
Norfolk,* 258.

79. ". . . there are 12 gates in all and 36 Churches . . . they are built all of flints well headed
or cut which makes them look blackish and shineing . . ." Fiennes, 136.

but the Inhabitants are very numerous and these are here of
every Sect, which have each their meeting houses. They can
not Keep themselves from beggars thô there are 5 hospitalls to
provide for Impotent & helpless people. The town has been
fortify'd by a wall which Sorounded it on every Side except the
East wch the River Yare protects, and afterwards runs thrô the
middle of it. Over this are 5 briges and Severall houses built
upon Piles. The Castle[80] which Stands in the heart of the town
upon a mount wth a dry ditch round it, has probably been very
antient, but it was never finish'd nor never will, for it now is
gone to decay, and Serves only for a Prison for Debtors &
Mallefactors. The Duke of Norfolk[81] has a house in this town
which Stands very ill and is now tumbling down. The rooms
in it are very lofty but it has no Gardens nor conveniencys to
it.[82] The houses here are many of them thatch'd, wch takes
much from the bewty of the town. Among those which are
otherwise I took notice of the Street call'd St Andrews the tiles
of wch are glas'd over, being Sent So from Holland, these are
proof against time and weather, no rain being able to moulder
or work thrô them. Here is a good Exchange wch was formerly
a Church, and Severall other good Structures as the town Hall,
and Sr John Hubbards house,[83] wch latter is rather most co-
mendable for its good Situation. Here is also a large Free

80. Norwich Castle, a Norman keep, erected on an enormous motte c. 1160. Nearly as large
as the White Tower in London, the castle is remarkable for the unity and consistency of its
exterior ornament. Pevsner, *Buildings . . . North-East Norfolk,* 256.

81. Thomas Howard (1683–1732), 8th Duke of Norfolk, had only recently succeeded his
uncle, Henry Howard (1655–1701), 7th Duke, who died in April 1701. Cokayne, *Peerage,*
9:628–31.

82. In 1681 Thomas Baskerville was likewise unimpressed with the Duke's house: ". . . we
rowed under 5 or 6 bridges, and then landed at the Duke of Norfolk's Palace, a sumptuous
new-built house not yet finish'd within, but seated in a dung hole place . . . for it hath but little
room for gardens and is pent up on both sides on this and the other side of the river, with
tradesmen's and dyer's houses, who foul the water by thier constant washing and cleaning their
cloth . . ." By 1711, the building had fallen into such disrepair that the Duke ordered its demoli-
tion. Kent, 84–85.

83. Possibly Sir John Hobart of Blickling Hall, Norfolk (1693–1756), Knight. Created Baron
Hobart of Blickling, Norfolk, 1728 and Earl of Buckinghamshire 1746. Cokayne, *Baronetage,*
1:13, and *Peerage,* 2:401.

School, & on Satturday a market counted the finest next to
Leadenhall in England. The River is not navigable for Ships of
great burthen near the town, but barges may come into the
town. The cheif trade drove here is weaving Callimanios,[84]
Druggets,[85] Says[86] but cheifly the famous Norwich Stuffs, w^ch:
imploys a great number of the people in preparing Wool for
the Weavers use. Here we got acquainted w^th: D^r: Prideaux[87]
one of the Prebends, a Gentleman of Sound Learning,
especially in the Eastern Languages & history. He Shew's us a
bundence of civility and made us dine with him before we left
this place.[88] ⟨This Citty is perticularly famous for large
Gilliflowrs,[89] w^th: w^ch: it keeps a Flora's Feast[90] once a year,
and because Earwigs[91] are great destroyers of this flowr, They
hang on the top of the Stick w^ch: bares it up Sheep hoofs, into

84. A woolen stuff, having a glossy surface, woven with a satin twill and checkered in the
warp, so that the checks are visible on one side only.

85. Drugget. A woolen textile, sometimes with linen or silk, used primarily in clothing.

86. Say. A fine-textured cloth resembling serge; in the sixteenth century sometimes partly of
silk, later entirely of wool.

87. Humphrey Prideaux (1648–1724), clergyman. Prebendary of Norwich 1681–1702; archdeacon of Suffolk 1688–1702; dean of Norwich 1702–1724. Prideaux was best known for his
Life of Mahomet, a copy of which was listed among the books in William Byrd's library at
Westover. Prideaux was also author of *Marmora Oxoniensia . . .* (1676), a catalog of the Arundel
marbles. *DNB*, 46:352–53; LeNeve, 2:490, 499; Bassett, 439. In Norwich, LeNeve had recommended that the two travelers seek out "Dr. Prideaux . . . a Searcher into the Antiquities of the
Cathedrall Church & City." Add. Mss. 47025, f. 49r.

88. In his account of Norwich, Byrd wrote: ". . . Mr. Whitefoot . . . has made us known to
an old acquantaince of yours, Dr. Pridaux, who is sub-dean here, and master of abundance of
learning; he values himself particularly upon his skil in Arabique, by virtue of which he has
convers'd more with the Alcoran and the comments upon it, than some other doctors have
with the Bible." Tinling, 1:211.

89. Gillyflower. The clove-scented pink *Dianthus caryophyllus* and other similar flowers. "One
remarque I have made here, is, that their clove-gilliflowers are exceeding large, and they use
some art to make them so. They shelter the top of the flower with a thin board from the dew
(which they call capping of it) and by this precaution it thrives much better." Ibid., 212.

90. "On Tuesday next at the duke of Norfolks pallace will be a solemnity they call the Feast
of Flora, where will be a collection of the finest of these flowers that the country affords, but we
shant be tempted to stay to see it, not tho all the old divertisments of Flora's Feast were to be
seen there." Ibid.

91. An insect, *Forficula auricularia,* called such in the belief that it entered one's head
through the ear.

which these insects [creep?][92] to defend themselves from the
Sun and So are taken & destroy'd.)[93] having remain'd here 5
days upon account of my Grooms Feaver, and finding it
continued upon him, I was forc'd to take another, in hopes
during my Stay at Cambrige to be over taken by him. ⟨In the
mean time I took Sufficient care that nothing Should be wanting wch. might contribute towards his health during his
absence, and so⟩[94] I set forward on the 28 for Thetford. At
Attleburge wch. is a market town we din'd where we got
acquainted with M^r. Bickly Parson of the Parish.[95] We took
notice here of a very large Church[96] which he told us was
anciently a Sort of Cathedrall, when Mortimer Earle of
March[97] in the Reign of Edward the third Founded an Abby
near to it.[98] The best house here abouts is that of S^r. Francis
Bickly's who has newly rais'd it out of the ruins of an ancient
Seat of the Suffolks which by mariage[99] fell into his hands. It

Attleburge
28.

92. Illegible on Percival's manuscript, this word has been rendered *creep* based on the text of
Byrd's very similar version. See Tinling, 1:212.

93. Marginal text, incorporated.

94. Text struck through. Byrd's correspondence gives us a more detailed account concerning the groom's illness: ". . . we have been arrested by the illness of the groom ever since
Wednesday last. The poor fellow began to complain of a pain in his side about a week ago, and
was let bloud for it, which we concluded woud cure him. We traveld slowly on his account,
imagining his distemper woud wear off, but instead of that it is now turnd to a feaver. The
ablest physician in town has been sent for to him, and all other care has been us'd to recover
him, and there is some reason to hope that he is passt all danger. But if he do recover, it will be
some time before he is fit for travelling, and therefore we have got another groom to supply his
place as far as Cambridge, where we shall tarry 3 or 4 days, and if by that time George can get
his strength, he may follow thither. In the mean time care is taken that he want nothing to
finish his recovery." Tinling, 1:211.

95. Richard Bickley (1639–1706), vicar of Attleborough 1683–1708. Venn and Venn, 1:148.
He was a first cousin of Sir Francis Bickley (see note 99). Burke, *Extinct and Dormant Baronetcies,*
61.

96. St. Mary, a fourteenth-century structure in the Decorated style, incorporating an earlier
Norman crossing tower. Pevsner, *Buildings . . . North-East Norfolk,* 78.

97. See note 244.

98. Actually it was the executors of Sir Robert Mortimer, Knt., who, about 1406, founded a
chantry or college dedicated to the "Exaltation of the Holy Cross." Dugdale, *Monasticon Anglicanum,* vol. 6, pt. 3, 1400.

99. Sir Francis Bickley of Attleborough Hall, Norfolk (d. 1746), 4th Baronet. Cokayne,
Baronetage, 3:230. Bickley had previously been a captain in the Duke of Norfolk's regiment

Thetford.

Stands upon an easy ascent, by which it has a Small prospect of the town; it moated round according to the old manner, and when finish'd will prove a plesant Country house. After Dinner we went on to Thetford a Market & burrow town, where there are now but 3 Parishes, but formerly were many more it being a Bishoprick till about 1100 Herbert translated the See to Norwich.[100] The only Gentleman of note living in this town is S.[r] John Woodhouse.[101] This place is remarkable for nothing but a high mount thrown up on one side of it, but for what design I cannot guess.[102] It Seems much too big to have been the burying place of any Generall, & is to far out of the town, either to attaque or defend it. The most probable conjecture is that this was the burying place of all the Soldiers Slain in a battle that was fought neer this place, the tradition of which is Still handed down.[103] On the other end of the town are the remains of the Cathedrall when this was a bishops See in 1500,[104] which Shows it to have been much biger then that at Norwich. ⟨The walls here abouts are often built of chalk w.[ch] cost but 9 pence a load ready dug. and may be cut into the form of brick, or any other Shape, w.[ch]

during the wars in Ireland. Cokayne, *Baronetage,* 3:230; Burke, *Extinct and Dormant Baronetcies,* 62. The circumstances under which Bickley might have obtained "an antient Seat of the Suffolks" are unclear. According to Blomefield, it was by purchase, about 1657, that Bickley's great-grandfather obtained the estate from John Radcliff, Esq., son of Sir Alexander Ratcliff, adopted heir of the Earl of Sussex. Cokayne, *Baronetage,* 3:230, and *Peerage,* vol. 12, pt. 1, 471; Blomefield, 1:352.

100. Herbert De Losinga (1054–1119), 1st bishop of Norwich and founder of the cathedral church. Herbert moved the see from Thetford to Norwich 1094–1096. *DNB,* 34:143; Powicke and Fryde, 242.

101. Sir John Wodehouse of Kimberly, Norfolk (1669–1754), 4th Baronet. M.P. for Thetford, 1695–1698, 1701–1702, and 1705–1708; M.P. for Norfolk, 1710–1713; and recorder of Thetford. Cokayne, *Baronetage,* 1:52.

102. Probably the same earthwork later described as "an huge Mote thrown up to a great Height, and fortify'd with a double Rampire, and (as tradition has it) with Walls at first, tho' now little or no Signs appear of them." Cox, 3:337. One authority believes the complex to be an eleventh-century motte built within the confines of an earlier Iron Age fort. Wilson and Hurst, 257.

103. "King *Edmund* . . . engag'd the Danes hard by {Thetford] for seven hours together, not without vast loss on both sides . . ." Gibson, 384.

104. Possibly the suffragan bishopric of Thetford, instituted in 1534. John Salisbury was suffragan bishop of Thetford 1536–1570. *Victoria History . . . Norfolk,* 2:254; Powicke and Fryde, 272.

Euston Hall, Suffolk, view from the southeast. English school, c. 1676. Courtesy of His Grace the Duke of Grafton, KG. Photograph: National Gallery.

when made in to wall consolidates, & will last time out of mind.⟩[105] This town thô it is very poor, Yet the Inhabitants are very industrius, and cheifly drive the Linnen weaving trade, but their greatest Support is a Small navigable River running by their town, wch brings them from Cambrige, Lyn and Norwich what they cant be furnish'd with at home as wood, Cole &c in exchange of wch they return Corn, whereof this Country Sows great quantitys every year. From Thetford we Set out next morning for St Edmunds Bury,[106] and Euston Hall[107] Standing but two miles from whence we set out, we

29.

105. Marginal text, incorporated.

106. Bury St. Edmunds, Suffolk.

107. A palatial house much enlarged by the Earl of Arlington (see note 109) following his acquisition of the Euston estate in 1666, after which further enlargements were made by Matthew Brettingham in the 1750s. Much of the interior was destroyed when the house burned in 1902. Two ranges of the house (those rebuilt following the fire) were pulled down about 1950. Kenworthy-Browne et al., 230–31. "It is seated on a flat, and in a fair pleasant Champian Country; which induc'd the Earl of *Arlington* to raise a noble Structure there call'd by the name of *Euston-hall;* adorn'd with a large *Nursery* containing great quantities of Fruit-trees of several sorts, with artificial fountains, a Canal, a pleasant Grove, a large Warren, &c . . ." Gibson, 380.

took it in our way. This was once the Seat of the Ld Desmond,[108] of whom my Ld Arlington[109] bought it, The
Dutchess of Grafton has it now for life, at the end of which it
falls to the present Duke.[110] This is a large brick building,
and has a fine Canal running on one side of it.[111] It has a Park
10 miles round adjoining, and Severall Gardins w^{ch}: are not
extraordinary good, but it com̃ands two or three good Prospects, and has a noble Avenue to it.[112] The inside is not very
extroardinary Save a very handsome Staircase and severall
Cælingrooms[113] painted by Vario being the first of his doing
upon his coming over to England;[114] there are also Severall
fine pictures of other mens work, especialy in a Gallery that
runs the whole length of the house.[115] This work being over

108. George Fielding (c. 1614–1666), 1st Earl of Desmond. Cokayne, *Peerage*, 4:257–58. The
Earl had acquired the estate from the Rookwood family in 1655. Oswald, 58.

109. Sir Henry Bennet (1620–1685), 1st Earl of Arlington. Cokayne, *Peerage*, 1:216–18. According to Evelyn, the Earl was "given to no expensive vise but building and to have all things
rich, and polite, and Princely." Evelyn, 264.

110. Isabella (c. 1667–1723), Duchess of Grafton, was the only daughter and heir of the 1st
Earl of Arlington. She was married first to Henry Fitzroy (1663–1690), 1st Duke of Grafton.
Upon her death in 1723, the estate passed to her son, Charles Fitzroy (1683–1757), 2nd Duke of
Grafton. Cokayne, *Peerage*, 1:216–18; 5:493.

111. "The Canale running under my Ladys dressing chamber window, is full of Carps, and
fowle, which come and are fed there with great diversion: The Cascade at the end of the Canale
turnes a Corne-mill . . ." Evelyn, 263.

112. ". . . 4 rows of Ashes . . . reaches to the Parke Pale which is 9 miles in Compas . . ."
Ibid., 263.

113. The royal apartment, criticized by North for its "lowness . . . smallness of the windoes
and consequently darkness of the ceilings . . ." North, 143.

114. Antonio Verrio (1639–1707), decorative painter, born and trained in Italy. After working for a time in France, Verrio came to England, probably in 1672 at the invitation of Ralph
Montague (later 1st Duke of Montague), who was then ambassador extraordinary to the French
court. It was probably through Montague as well that Verrio was commissioned by Lord
Arlington to work at Euston Hall. Subsequently he worked for both royal and private patrons,
most notably at Windsor Castle for Charles II and at Burghley for Lord Exeter. Croft-Murray,
50–58. "In my Lords house, and especialy above the Stayre Case, the greate hall and some of
the Chambers and roomes of State, is painted in fresca, by the hand of Signor Virrio the same
who has painted all Winsor being the first worke which he did in England." Evelyn, 239.

115. From Celia Fiennes we learn that the gallery was "hung with pictures at length—on the
one side the Royal family from K. Henry the 7th by the Scottish race his eldest daughter down
to the present King William and his Queen Mary, the other side are forreign princes from the

we proceeded to Bury, a burrow town & place where more
Gentry meet, then in any other Country town in England, &
for that reason call'd little London. It has every thing that can
be desir'd for the necessarys of Life, and Stands in a noted
good Air. There are only two Parishes in this town, whose
Churches are very neat, and large and are join'd by one
Churchyard.[116] Before the Dissolution of Abbys this town was
very famous & mightily resorted to upon account of the Mar-
tirdom of K: Edmund who was Shot to death by the Danes for
not forsaking the Christian faith & here bury'd.[117] And here
are the remains of an Abby Said to have been the Second or
third in England.[118] The ruins are also yet to be seen of many
religious house wth which this heathfull town abounded w^{ch}
clearly Show how well the Clergy of those times understood
what was both for their health & Pleasure. This place is famous for three things Bewtyfull women, bad wives; Good
malt, bad beer; and fine Streets wth very bad houses; for the

---

Emperour of Moroccoe the Northern and Southern princes and Emperour of Germany; there
is a square in the middle where stands a billiard table hung with outlandish pictures of Heroes
. . . at the end of the roome is the Duke and Dutchess of Graftons pictures at length also . . ."
Fiennes, 139.

116. St. James (now the cathedral) and St. Mary, both medieval churches. Pevsner, *Buildings
. . . Suffolk*, 133, 141–43. "To this adjoins two large Churches of curious Architecture, dedicated
the one to St. *James*, and the other to St. *Mary*, and in that spacious Church Yard . . . they both
stand . . . being only parted by a decorous shady Walk of Trees . . ." Brome, 123.

117. In 869, "the most Christian King, because he would not renounce Christ, was by the
most inhuman Danes . . . bound to a tree, and had his body all over mangl'd with arrows. And
they to increase the pain and torture with showers of arrows, made wound upon wound, till
the darts gave place to one another." Gibson, 375.

118. The Abbey of St. Edmundsbury, one of the wealthiest and most powerful Benedictine
monasteries in England. Although there seems to have been a monastic establishment on this
site as early as 633, it was not until the eleventh century that it began to assume great importance. Two gates (the twelfth-century Norman Gate and the fourteenth-century Great Gate)
plus fragments of several buildings within the precinct are the only remains. Pevsner, *Buildings
. . . Suffolk*, 132, 138. "The Town it self hath been very famous for a large and stately Monastery
. . . it appeared rather like a City than a Monastery, so many Gates it had for entrance, and
many of them Brass, so many Towers, and above all a most glorious Church . . . there remains
nothing now, but the Carcas of that ancient Structure; and yet even still by its Ruins it is easie
to conjecture what a majestick Fabrick it once was." Brome, 122–23.

Streets cut one another at right angles,[119] w[ch]: makes the town very regular. Here is a very large Free School,[120] and a good market, & Market Cross. We were recom̄ended by D[r.] Prideaux to Arch Deacon Claggett,[121] who Show'd us much civility and is a cheerfull affable man. While we were here we visited M[r.] Harvy[122] who is building a fine house within three or 4 mile of this Place. Not far from hence lives S[r.] John Bigs,[123] a Gentleman who tis hop'd will Shortly oblige the world with the History of NorfolkShire. There is now an act of Parliam[t.] for making a river Navigable from [*Long-Common*] to it w[ch]: will very much raise the trade of the town.[124] Our time pressing us we Set out next morning for Newmarket, 3 miles from w[ch]: Stands Chipnam[125] the Seat of the Earle of Or-

30.
Chipnam

119. The town was laid out on a rectilinear plan by Abbot Baldwin of St. Edmundsbury. The grid pattern, with its elongated blocks, resembles the contemporary plan of Ludlow nearby. Pevsner, *Buildings . . . Suffolk,* 140.

120. The Free Grammar School of King Edward VII, founded by that monarch in 1550. Elliott, 13; *Victoria History . . . Suffolk,* 2:313. In 1730 it was described as "a flourishing Free-school of a Royal Foundation, having King Edward VI's Busto, who was the founder, on the Front." Cox, 5:335.

121. Nicholas Claggett (1654–1727). Preacher of St. Mary's, Bury St. Edmunds, 1680–1726; rector of Thurlow Parva 1683; archdeacon of Sudbury 1698–1727; rector of Hincham, Suffolk, 1707–1726. Venn and Venn, 2:338.

122. John Hervey of Ickworth (1666–1751), later created Baron Hervey of Kidbrooke, Kent, in 1703 and 1st Earl of Bristol in 1714. Deputy-lieutenant of Suffolk 1692; M.P. for Bury 1694–1703. Venn and Venn, 2:324; Cokayne, *Peerage,* 6:576. Following his inheritance of Ickworth in 1700, Hervey adapted one of the farmhouses on the estate for use as a residence. Hussey, "Ickworth, Suffolk," 678–79.

123. Possibly Sir John Bigs of Petersfield, Hampshire, recorder of Portsmouth, who was knighted in 1675. Shaw, 2:230.

124. "An Act for making the River Lark, alias Burn, Navigable." This act provided for clearing the channel "from a place called Long-Common, a little below Mildenhall-Mill on the said River . . . to East-gate Bridge, in East-gate Street, in Bury St. Edmunds." *Public Acts 1698–99, 11–12 William 3.,* c.22, 348.

125. Chippenham Park, a late seventeenth-century house of brick, demolished during the eighteenth century. Kenworthy-Browne et al., 11. ". . . here are severall good gardens well kept; a coach yard and stables in the middle of which is a large gate into the ground and built over with a high lanthorn where hangs the clock and bell, this stands higher than the house like a tower, the house being a flat roofe leaded and railed round full of chimneys, but this tower I saw 10 mile off; all the out offices built round a court very handsome . . ." Fiennes, 140.

ford,[126] which we thought worth our while to se, thô we went
3 mile out of our way. This house is neither too little nor too
big, and has latly receiv'd the addition of two wings Since this
Earle came to it w^{ch}: is neer 15 years. The Hall & Staircase that
are here are the finest & neatest I ever saw the Hall being
wenscoted with wallnut tree and addorn'd w^{th}: severall peices
of Carv'd work and pictures.[127] The Stair Case is finely finish'd, and is set of[f] w^{th}: representations of Sea fights, Particularly the feats of this L^{d}: when Admirall before La Hogue.[128]
The Offices about the House are very neat, especially the
Stables, w^{ch}: are built after the manner of Whithall.[129] The
Gardins are about being made very fine, and cheifly two walks
meeting in a right angle, on one Side of which there runs a
long Canall. Besides this there is an Aviary, wilderness, and
Greenhouse w^{ch}: is extroardinary pleasant, and well finish'd
within. My L^{d}: has very latly taken in above three mile for a
Park, and encompas'd it w^{th}: a handsome brick wall. We Staid
here no longer then was necessary for vewing the place, and So
Set forward for Newmarket, a poor town if it were not for the   Newmarket
horse racing w^{ch}: is there kept twice a Year.[130] In the Evening

126. Edward Russell (1652–1727), 1st Earl of Orford. Cokayne, *Peerage*, 10:77.

127. ". . . the hall is very noble paved with freestone a squaire of black marble at each
corner of the freestone; there are two fine white marble tables veined with blew, its wanscoated
with Wallnut tree the pannells and rims round with Mulbery tree that is a lemon coullour and
the moldings beyond it round are of a sweete outlandish wood not much differing from Cedar
but of a finer graine, the chaires are all the same: its hung with pictures att full proportion of
the Royal family . . ." Fiennes, 140.

128. The battle of La Hogue, fought between the French and Anglo-Dutch fleets near
Cherbourg in May 1692. Admiral Russell's victory foiled an intended invasion of England by
forces under the exiled James II. For his service in this and other naval engagements, Russell
was elevated to the peerage in 1697. *DNB*, 49:430–31. ". . . the staircase is wanscoated, very
noble fine pictures, there is the battle at La Hogue a large sea peice with an inscription of the
Admiralls valour when the great ship the Gunn was burnt, mightily valued by the French
King." Fiennes, 141.

129. The Horse Guards, Whitehall Palace, erected 1663-1664 to house both mounted and
unmounted units of the Life Guards. Colvin et al., *History of the King's Works*, 5:433.

130. Newmarket had prospered "chiefly from the frequent Resort of the Court thither for
Horse-Races, and other Diversions, sometimes twice a Year, which brings multitude of Spec-
tators thither; for it stands on a Plain very commodious for those Sports; and on the Cam-

Cambrige   we parted from hence and got over the Downs to Cambrige
                wch is distant from it 10 miles.¶
                Some miles on this Side of Newmarket we past over a deep
                trench call'd the Devils ditch wch was probably a boundary
31.   between the kingdom of Mercia and that of the east An-
                gles.[131] The next day Mr Colebatch Fellow of Trinity Col-
                ledge[132] came to see us, and after dinner gave himself the
                trouble to Show us the town. This Gentleman was Chaplain to
                Mr Methwin[133] when he went envoy to Portugall and has his
                Share of curtesy & learning. The first thing we went to See was
                St Mary's Church[134] where the whole University meet on
                Sunday to hear a Sermon, having Prayers at each Colledge
                first. This Church is not So large as that of Oxford[135] nor So
                well contriv'd, there being no gallerys wch are both convenient

bridge side there is an House built on purpose for the reception of our Kings. The Plain . . . is
call'd from the Town, New-Market-Heath, and the soil thereof is indeed Sandy and Barren; but
the surface is green and dry, fit for such Exercises." Cox, 5:218.

131. The Devil's Dyke. A vast earthwork seven and a half miles long, possibly raised in the
sixth or seventh centuries by the East Angles or the Mercians. Pevsner, Buildings . . . Cambridgeshire, 264.

132. John Colbatch (1665–1748), clergyman. Fellow of Trinity College 1689; for some years
chaplain to the English "factory" or mercantile establishment at Lisbon; prebendary of Salisbury 1702–1720; rector of Orwell, Cambridgeshire, 1720–1748; professor of moral philosophy
and casuistical divinity, Cambridge University, 1707–1744. Venn and Venn, 1:365. ". . . we owe
a great deal of our knowledge of this place to the information and convoy of Mr. Colebatch. He
is a man of distinction for learning and knowledge of the world, and we had the happiness of
haveing abundance of his company. He desird me to let you know, that he is under great
concern, that he cant dispatch the affair you were pleas'd to commit to him, with so much
expedition as he promis'd." Tinling, 1:212. It may have been at Sir Robert Southwell's request
that Colbatch showed Percival and Byrd about. Southwell had previously corresponded with
Colbatch regarding the identity of various persons, including a "Richardus Southwell," one of
Sir Robert's ancestors. Add. Mss. 22905, f. 5.

133. John Methune (1650–1706), diplomat. M.P. for Devizes 1690; envoy to Portugal 1691;
lord chancellor of Ireland and speaker of the Irish House of Lords 1697; again sent to Portugal
1702; ambassador extraordinary to Portugal 1703, where he concluded the commercial treaty
that bears his name. DNB, 37:310.

134. St. Mary the Great. Built during the late fifteenth and early sixteenth centuries, it
follows in the pattern of East Anglia's larger, late Perpendicular churches. Pevsner, Buildings . . . Cambridgeshire, 217.

135. St. Mary, the parish church for Oxford, used for university ceremonies until completion of Wren's Sheldonian Theater. Pevsner, Buildings . . . Oxfordshire, 238.

and add bewty to one. From hence we went to See the Publick
Library w:^ch comes not any thing neer the Bodlayan at Oxford,[136] tis full indeed of Books, but that is owing to the Smal-
ness of it (there being only two narrow rooms) & an obligation
upon evry bookseller to present it w:^th a Copy of what ever
book he prints.[137] The most valuable book we Saw here was a
Great testam:^t w:^th the Latine on the Sides Say'd to have been S:^t
Ironeus's[138] own, of w:^ch oppinion Bera[139] himself was, who gave
it to the Library, & that S:^t liv'd w:^th [in] 200 years of Christ.¶
After this we went to See the Publick Schools w:^ch are nothing
to compare to those at Oxford, nor So many in number. From
hence we went to kings Colledge Chappell,[140] w:^ch is justly
term'd one of the finest builings in Europe. In length it is 304
feet, in breadth 73, & in height 91. It is built after the Gothick
manner & looks on the out Side very bewtyfull & fresh, & the
inside is no less fine & neat. On the windows w:^ch are counted
of the largest Size is painted the history of the bible, entirely
preserv'd.[141] About the Quire is a great deal of very curious

136. The Bodleian Library, Oxford University.

137. The Licensing Acts of 1662–1679 and 1685–1695 had stipulated that all publications be licensed and registered at Stationers' Hall. Three copies of each publication were to be delivered to the master of the Stationers' Company, who would forward one each to the Royal Library, to Oxford, and to Cambridge. These acts were enforced with only partial success. Following their expiration in 1695, delivery of books ceased altogether, only to resume with passage of the Copyright Act in 1709. Oates, 290; Partridge, 31–34.

138. St. Irenaeus (c. 130–200), bishop of Lyon c. 178–200. One of the great early Western ecclesiastical writers. Farmer, 204.

139. Richard Bere (d. 1524), abbot of Glastonbury 1493–1524. *DNB*, 4:323–24.

140. One of England's great medieval buildings, erected in three phases between 1446 and 1515. It followed in the typical form of royal chapels as first seen in the fourteenth century at St. Stephen's, Westminster Palace. Details of the chapel's plan and appearance were spelled out by Henry VI in his so-called "will" of 1448. His instructions read like an epitome of the English Perpendicular style, calling for a building "in large fourme clene and substantial, setting a parte superfluite of too great curious workes of *enteille* and besy moulding." The "curious" heraldic carving in the western portion of the interior dates from the time of Henry VIII. Pevsner, *Buildings . . . Cambridgeshire,* 94, 102–6.

141. The most complete series of church windows to have survived from the time of Henry VIII. Beginning with the story of Joachim and Anna at the west end, the scenes move in a clockwise direction toward the Crucifixion in the east window, culminating with the Last Judgment in the west window. Ibid., 109–11.

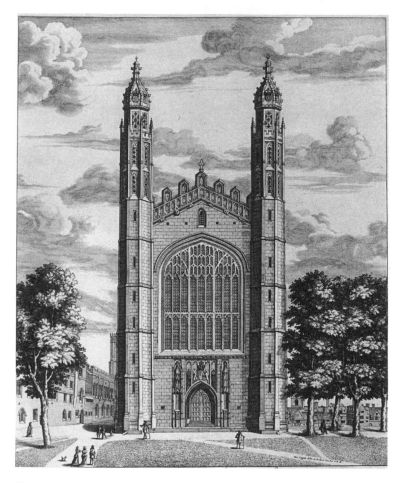

King's College Chapel, Cambridge University, west front, David Loggan,
c. 1678–1690. Colonial Williamsburg Foundation/Hans Lorenz.

carving,[142] but the noblest part of the Chappell is the roof,
w^{ch}: is built of Stone, & allmost flatt wth: out any Pillar to Support it.[143] Within this Place is a very handsome Library and a

142. In Pevsner's words, "the purest work in the early Renaissance style in England." The
sumptuously carved choir screen was probably created c. 1530–1536 by Italian or French
artisans. The stalls are believed to represent contemporary English work. The finely carved
coats-of-arms above these stalls, along with the cornice and its supporting balusters, were
added in 1633. Ibid., 108–9.

143. The fan-vaulted ceiling, designed and executed c. 1480–1515, during the tenure of
master mason Simon Clerk. Ibid., 105–6.

King's College Chapel, Cambridge University, interior view looking east, David Loggan, c. 1678–1690. Colonial Williamsburg Foundation/Hans Lorenz.

Skeleton of M.^{r} keel[144] of Oxfords Setting together, w^{ch}: is the
cleanest and most exact of any I ever Saw. Kings Colledge its
Self is nothing answerable to its Chappell the building in w^{ch}:
the Society live being only the out houses of a much nobler
Colledge desin'd by Henry ye 6, who had he liv'd & got cleer
of the troubles w^{ch}: brought him to his end, would have gone
on wth: the foundations w^{ch}: are yet to be seen.¶
From hence we went to Peter house which is the antientest of
all the Colledges or Halls in Cambrige, & was founded in
1256.[145] Here we met wth: nothing worth our curiosity no more
then at Bennet Colledge remarkable only for a Library consisting mostly of Manuscripts relating to the Reformation. After
these we Saw Clare Hall w^{ch}: is now building & will Shortly be
very neat.[146] We past by Severall other Small Colledges &
Halls & afterwards came to Trinity Colledge, the cheifest in
the University. This has two very large Quadrangles thô neither of Such extent as that at Christ Church in Oxford. The
cheif thing here to be seen is the Library[147] w^{ch}: is indeed a
very noble Structure, it is built Plain, Strong, & very large
being a very long room one Story high, pav'd wth: black &
white Marble. The Staircase going up to it is of Stone & is
wainscoted wth: Cedar, & has a well wrought iron rail to it. It
Stands upon three rows of Pillars w^{ch}: make two handsome
cloisters. On the inside is Some very fine carv'd work by M.^{r}
Gibbons,[148] and a Statue w^{ch}: cost 200[li] done by the Same

144. James Keil, M.D. (1673–1719), lecturer on anatomy at Oxford and Cambridge; author
of *The Anatomy of the Human Body abridged; or A Short and Full View of All the Parts of the Human
Body,* London, 1698; F.R.S., 1712. Venn and Venn, 3:3; K. F. Russell, *British Anatomy 1525–1800*
(Wincester, Hampshire: St. Paul's Bibliographies, 1987), 120.

145. Peterhouse, founded 1284. Pevsner, *Buildings . . . Cambridgeshire,* 129.

146. Clare College. Construction on the west range of the quadrangle had been suspended in
1676. Work resumed in 1705 but was not completed until 1715. Ibid., 56–59.

147. Trinity College Library, built 1676–1690 to the design of Sir Christopher Wren. Ibid.,
172.

148. Grinling Gibbons (1648–1720), woodcarver and statuary. Discovered by John Evelyn

Trinity College Library, Cambridge University, David Loggan, 1678–1690. Colonial Williamsburg Foundation/Hans Lorenz.

hand, of the present Duke of Somerset[149] who gave 500^li towards the building. On the further end is a large bellcony w^ch: requires a better Prospect then is now to be seen. This Library is not over well Stock'd w^th: books, but evry day it receivs Some additionall presents. It has a Stone rail on the top upon which Stand 4 Statues viz: of Divinity, Mathematiks Phisick & law w^ch: are bigger then the life, and Show very well from below. We paid our respects to Dr Bently[150] who is master of

August
1.

---

in 1671, he was introduced to the king and other future patrons including Sir Christopher Wren, who employed him at St. Paul's and several other London churches, as well as at Trinity College Library. From the time of Charles II to that of George I he was master-carver in wood to the crown, working at Windsor, Whitehall, and Kensington. Examples of his work are also found in many private houses of the period. *DNB,* 21:259–61.

149. Charles Seymour (1662–1748), 6th Duke of Somerset, often referred to as "the Proud Duke"; chancellor of Cambridge University 1689–1748. Cokayne, *Peerage,* vol. 12, pt. 1, 77–82.

150. Richard Bently (1662–1742), noted scholar and critic. Vice-chancellor of Cambridge

3.   this Colledge & now Vicechancelor and din'd wth him on
            Sunday. The Colledge was built entirely by the Fellows, w^ch
            they were abler to do then any other Colledge, their revenue
            being so large, for in the falling of a Shilling in a bushell of
            corn they loose 1000^li.¶
            As for the town of Cambrige it is Scituated in a wholsome air,
            thô Some think otherwise by reason of the Fens wch are neer
            it. but they are 7 mile distant, & dont affect it. The river Cam
            runs thrô it wch is navigable to Thetford, & Lyn, by wch the
            University is Supply'd wth Coles and other necessarys. The
            Sizes are kept here, and the Same High Sherif is chosen for
            Cambrige and Huntington Sheirs. On one end of the town is a
            mount thrown up, and Severall ditches about it. probably
            Some Saxon work,[151] from the top of this we had a Prospect
            of the whole University, & town wch is very Small & has but 13
            poor Parishes, poor because the tradesmen had rather live
            from hand to mouth upon the Schollars, then grow rich by any
            labour of their own, for were a Manefacture settled here it
            might turn to very good account. Our time lying on our
            hands, we thought we could not Spend it better, then in Seing
            Some of the Country about this place So we went on Satturday
Littleburrow   to Littleburrow wch is 10 mile from Cambrige, & there Saw the
            odd whimseys & contrivances of Mr Winstanley[152] a great
            Projector, who has built a very handsome house neer the road,

---

University 1700; master of Trinity College 1700–1742. *DNB*, 4:306; LeNeve, 3:608. "We din'd
yesterday at Mr. Vice-Chancellour's, where philosophy flew about the table faster than wine."
Tinling, 1:212.

   151. The motte of a castle erected by William the Conqueror in 1068. By 1606, the
gatehouse was the only intact building remaining. Pevsner, *Buildings . . . Cambridgeshire*, 232.

   152. Henry Winstanley of Littlebury, Essex (1644–1703), architect and engraver. Best
known as designer of the Eddystone lighthouse near Plymouth, Winstanley is also credited
with the design of his own house at Littlebury and was employed by the crown as clerk of the
works at Audley End from 1679–1702. His engraved suite of plans and views of Audley End,
completed sometime after 1676, was one of the earliest such productions to depict a single
English country house. Winstanley produced views of other country houses as well, apparently
with the intention of assembling a volume similar to that produced by Leonard Knyff and
Johannes Kip some years later. Harris, 88–89.

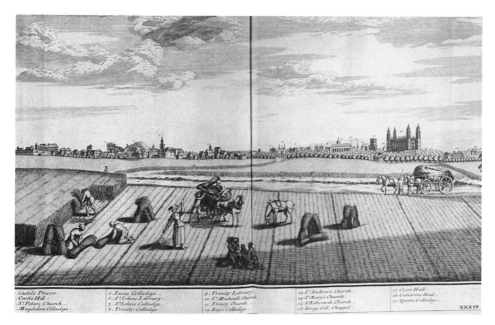

Cambridge, view from the west. An engraving of c. 1713, based on David Loggan's earlier view of c. 1678–1690. Yale Center for British Art, Paul Mellon Collection.

w^ch: Passengers never fail to see.[153] We were first Shown into a room where there is a perpetuall motion. There are two balls or one w^ch: run[s] up and down a Spirall Engine, & when got to the bottom fall into a Sort of Scale w^ch: raises it again to the top & Setts it going. We were not admitted into the Secret of it, & it was So plac'd that we could not examine it much.[154] In the Same room we Saw a picture done by M^r: Winstanly

153. "Here are several . . . contrivances, which like the greatest part of modern philosophy, relish more of whimsy than advantage to mankind." Tinling, 1:213.

154. "Amongst other things there's a perpetual motion, performd by a brass ball, that runs by a gentle declension down several spiral ledges, till comeing to the bottom tis instantly drawn up by a pully, and so repeats its tour again." Tinling, 1:213. In 1703 De Blainville described this same mechanism: ". . . a perpetual motion contrivance which comes about by means of a copper ball which is placed above a cabinet which ball finding the slope drops down to the bottom after it reaches 18 circuits in the space of two minutes, at the end of which the ball falls into a funnel where a spring sends it up to the very top of the cabinet from where it rolls down as before, and always in that manner without stopping." De Blainville, 6.

Littlebury, Essex. Henry Winstanley, c. 1680.

himself wth a pen, on wch if you look'd full you might See king Williams Head & underneath Gulielmus 3 Rex dei gratia &c. if you look'd Slanting towards the right it was King James picture wth Jacobus 2:Rex:&c., and if Slanting to the left Carolus Secundus &c. The thing is very ingenius but Ime told that in France there is a picture wch Shows all the princes of the bloud after the Same manner.[155] We went afterwards into another room where there is a chair in wch whoever Sits, will sink 20 yards into the Earth whence being let out & lead into a chamber where there rises up a Ghost out of the floor wch vanishes again before the consternation the party is in be over.[156]¶

155. De Blainville also mentioned this picture, ". . . an engraving of a half length portrait in which can be seen a head with 3 noses, 3 chins, 3 mouths, 6 eyes &c. and drawn with such artistry and so skillfully engraved, and artfully contrived that looking from three different places it perfectly represent[s] three different Kings, namely Charles II, James II, and William III, with their special inscriptions . . ." Ibid., 6. Winstanley's drawing and the French picture mentioned by Percival may have been inspired by Jean François Niçeron's *La Perspective Curieuse ou Magie Artificiele des Effets Merveilleux . . .* (1638), a treatise on perspective and geometrical optics that included a similar portrait of Francis I.

156. The chair was "placed in the most respected position in the room where those who

This being over we went into another room where Sitting
down the chair runs away w:th one above a hundred & fifty
yards into a Garden,[157] at the end of w:ch is a prospect of a
Summar house w:ch changes to a room w:th a table in it where
we went & Set down no sooner were we out but it turn'd into a
bed chamber w:th a chimney & every thing Seutable.[158] In a
corner of the garden Stands a Moddle of the Light house near
Plymouth that is 6 Score foot from the foundation a Small
rock Standing 3 leagues from Shoar.[159] In Stormy weather the
waves will beat quite over it but it is So contriv'd as to keep
dry, & break their force. In it is a bed room for the watch
man, & a room of State for any Prince to go into,[160] over
these is the turret in w:ch the fire is made to guide Ships into

---

enter the room are invited to sit; this chair poised in some sort of balance remains stable, but
as soon as someone sits on it all of a sudden one descends from the upper room into the
cellar." De Blainville, 6.

157. This chair was "suspended upon 4 pulleys that one hardly notices . . . a door opens
behind the chair and one is carried with speed about 800 feet; because of the slope of a little
hill upon which the house is situated." Ibid., 6.

158. According to De Blainville this "garden closet" was "made of wood concerning which
one notices the position of the door, windows, chairs &c. hardly had we left than we were led
back to it; and we found a chimneypiece, a large bed, and quite another positioning of the
windows, of the door, of the chairs; this change results from a wheel upon which this closet is
placed, by means of which one turns it to whichever side one wishes." Ibid., 7.

159. "The eighth [curiosity], is the model of the lighthouse that one sees out at sea a few
miles from Plymouth, which is built of bricks in the garden, with all the measurements
reduced to a small scale in height and circumference. One sees yet another model of this same
lighthouse in one of the rooms of the house wrought in silver; we were assured that this work
had cost more than ninety pieces." Ibid., 7. One of the models had previously been on display
at Winstanley's "Water Theater" near the "lower end of Piccadilly," as evidenced by the
following description from his 1699 engraving of the lighthouse: "This Draught was made &
Engraven by Henry Winstanly of Littlebury, Gen.t and is Sold at his Waterworks where is also
to be seen at any time ye Modle of ye said Building & principal Roomes for six pence a Peice."

160. On Winstanley's engraving of the lighthouse, the state room was described as "being
10 Square 19 foot wide, & 12 foot high, very well Carved & Painted, with a Chimney, & 2
Closets, & 2 Sash Windows, wth Strong shutters to Bar and Bolt." Also shown are a kitchen
and bedchamber with "2 Cabbin Beds, & all Conveniencies for a Dining Room." Winstanley
was killed in 1703 in the great storm that destroyed this lighthouse. As late as 1712, his widow
had continued to exhibit Littlebury and the Water Theater at a charge of 12 pence per head.
DNB, 62:208–9; "Notes and Queries," 63.

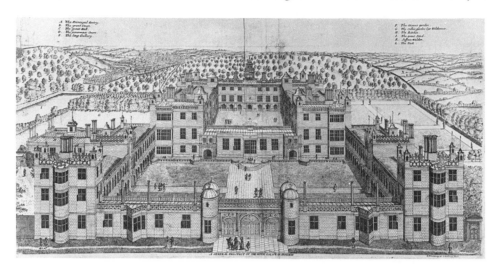

Audley End, Essex. Henry Winstanley, c. 1676. Essex Record Office.

Audley End
               Harbour. Having Seen evry thing here, we went to Audly
End[161] the Seat of the Earle of Suffolk.[162] This is the largest
Subjects house in England, is built of Stone, but for want of
repair would fall to the ground of it Self, were there not a design to pull it down it being So large that it would cost 15000^{li}
to just keep it Standing & 5 or 600^{li} a year only to look after
it.[163] It Stands in a moist low ground by the river Cam w^{ch}
runs thrô a very large Court and has 3 handsom briges over it.
In these Fenny Grounds the owners only mow as much hay as
is for present use, and burn what the[y] leave, wch brings a
very Great Crop next year. There is a Gallery in Audly end
the largest in England, tis So long that two persons can not

    161. Audley End was the largest newly built house of the Jacobean era. Begun in 1604 for
Thomas Howard (1561–1626), 1st Earl of Suffolk, it was originally built around two courtyards,
according to the designs of Bernard Janssen. Pevsner, *Buildings . . . Essex,* 57–61.
    162. Henry Howard (1626–1709), 5th Earl of Suffolk. Cokayne, *Peerage,* vol. 12, pt. 1, 471–73.
    163. Some demolition must have been carried out soon after Percival's visit. In 1697 Celia
Fiennes placed the number of Audley End's rooms at 750, whereas by 1703, that number had
shrunk to 365. Fiennes, 77; De Blainville, 5. According to Pevsner, however, the entire west or
outer quadrangle was pulled down by Sir John Vanbrugh, probably in conjunction with his
alteration of the stair c. 1718. Still other portions were demolished in 1749. Pevsner, *Buildings
. . . Suffolk,* 59.

know one another Standing one at each end it is propor-
tionally broad & high.[164] it was built in Queen Elizabeth, time
and since king Charles the 2^{ds}: time met wth: no repairing. He
bought it of the Earle, but paid only half the money aggreed
for, So this king rather then pay the remainder return'd it
to the first owner.[165] From hence we went to Waldon[166] to   Waldon
dinner, this is a very good Market town, & has a fine Church,
wth: the largest and neatest alterpeice of any Parish Church in
England.[167] Formerly this town Sent Burgesses to Parliam^t:
but voluntarily parted wth: that right, petitioning Henry the 8
to ease them of it upon account of the Charge. ⟨Since that
time their right of chusing Parliam^t: men is restored.⟩[168] This   growth of
waldon is in Essex, and is famous for the growth of Saffron,[169]   Safron
being from thence call'd Safron Waldon.[170] This is a Sort
of flour like a crokus out of w^{ch}: grows 3 or 4 little Streaks
w^{ch}: is the Safron.[171] The heads of this flour are Set in a light
rosom[172] ground, the nearer chalk the better, w^{ch}: must be
well clear'd of Stones & filth. The time of Planting is in mid-
sumar, when they are put 3 inches deep & as many wide into

164. ". . . they showed us there amongst other things a very beautiful gallery, 240 feet long,
and 32 wide: its plaster ceiling depicts realistically the labours of Hercules, and the meta-
morphoses of Ovid . . ." De Blainville, 5.

165. In 1669 the 3rd Earl of Suffolk sold Audley End to Charles II for the sum of £50,000.
This sum was never paid in full, however, and in 1701 the house was returned to the Earl in lieu
of an outstanding balance of £20,000. Colvin, 131.

166. Saffron Walden, Essex.

167. St. Mary the Virgin, one of the largest parish churhes in Essex. The structure was
largely rebuilt c. 1450–1525 along lines typical of the East Anglian churches of Suffolk and
Cambridge. Apparently the grand altarpiece alluded to by Percival does not survive intact,
though fragments of a fifteenth-century alabaster altar are now to be seen in the south porch of
the church. Pevsner, *Buildings . . . Essex,* 304–5.

168. Marginal text, incorporated.

169. The autumnal crocus, *Crocus sativus.*

170. ". . . we proceeded to Saffron Walden, where we met with a man very expert at
planting & cureing that commodity. You will not doubt but we took notes of so usefull a
process . . ." Tinling, 1:213.

171. An orange-red substance produced from the dried stigmas of the *Crocus sativus,* formerly used in medicine as a cordial and sudorific.

172. Perhaps rosin—i.e., resembling or having the color of rosin.

the ground & then covred about half a foot thick with Earth.
In Octobre tis gathred, & the first year yeilds but a little crop,
the Second more but the third is very advantagious, for the
flour Spreads greatly. At the end of 3 years this must in August
be again transplanted when the third crop is over, into fresh
ground. There s an old verse belonging to the managment of
this Plant w^ch: runs

> If any one would know
> When Saffron does grow
> Let him ask when he's Sober
> He'l be told in October..

The way of drying it is to lay it in a kiln a foot Square, in the
middle of w^ch: is a haircloth Strain'd very hard. upon this are
laid Severall Sheets of cap paper, and upon those the Safron is
laid about a foot thick, & just pick'd from the flour. The
Safron is covred again w^th: Safron paper, and over those Sheets
a peice of woolen cloth, Upon all this is afterwards lai'd a
Pellock[173] or Pilaber[174] of Straw, and a board w^ch: presses all
close by the help of a hundred weight or less, and is made to
fit the inside of the kiln. The Cake made of the Safron thus
Squeez'd together must be turn'd often, especially the edges
w^th: a knife, and let to dry gradually over a deliberate charcole
fire under the kiln, and now and then moistend w^th: Some of
the wet Safron viz: w^ch: is just gather'd and Steept in Small
beer.[175] Care must be taken that the cake is not dry'd too
much, for it often Seems wet when it is very well cured.¶
The ground where this is Sow'd is afterwards very fertile for
corn, but if first Sow'd with Sanfoild,[176] will hold 14 years
without other manuring then Sinder dust Scatter'd about the

---

173. A wooden vessel, generally used to carry bait for fishing lines. Wright, *English Dialect Dictionary*, 4:462. Also a ball or projectile thrown from a crossbow, hackbut, or cannon. Thus, Percival may have used this term in the sense of "ball" or compacted mass of material.

174. Pilliver. A pillow case or, in this instance, a bag.

175. Weak or poor quality beer.

176. Sainfoin, a low-growing perennial herb, *Onobrychis sativa*, frequently grown as a forage plant.

lands after the manner that corn is Sow'd. No vermin will touch this plant, hairs only mischeive it by eating the grass wch grows on the top of the root out of wch Springs the flour. The town is very well Scituated, and had a castle thrown up neer it wch is now tumbled down.[177] Before I left I learn't a certain cure for the itch, wch is to Take as much Stone brimstone[178] beat to very fine powder as will Lye upon a Sixpence. Take it in the middle of your hand, & drop into it 3 drops of olive oil, rub your hands together very hard till it be dry'd in wch will not be long a doing, & then go to bed, repeat this 3 or 4 times and twill prove an infallible cure.[179]¶

From Waldon I return'd over Gogmagog hills to Cambrige, these are So call'd from being an ancient fortification of the danes, among other works there is a Castrum Sorounded with a threefold trench, where now the Stables for race horses Stand.[180]¶

On munday we went to See St Johns Colledge wch is three very   4. large courts of Brick.[181] The Library[182] was what we cheifly went to see, wch is a very large one, well fill'd. We were Shew'd there, a cheese petrify'd, a chinese book, and Some other

177. A twelfth-century keep of flint-rubble, dismantled in 1158 by Henry II. King, 1:147; Pevsner, *Buildings . . . Essex,* 306.

178. Sulphur.

179. Percival may have copied this prescription from a written source, as Byrd's version is quite similar. See Tinling, 1:213.

180. Wandlebury hill-fort, Stapleford, Cambridgeshire. A roughly circular earthen fortification built during the 3rd century B.C. and later strengthened in the 1st century A.D. The stables mentioned by Percival were either part of, or perhaps succeeded by, the present Gogmagog House, which, according to Pevsner, is an eighteenth-century complex. The horses were, no doubt, to run at Newmarket. Pevsner, *Buildings . . . Cambridgeshire,* 459–60; *Victoria History . . . Cambridgeshire,* 3:227–28. "Not far from this place appears aloft a certain ridge of *Hills* called *Hog-magog-Hills,* fortified of old by the *Danes,* when they infested these Parts, with a threefold Trench, some part whereof is still to be seen." Brome, 67.

181. These three courts lay along a single axis terminating at the river Cam. The first court was completed by 1520; the second by 1602; the third, on the river, by 1671. Pevsner, *Buildings . . . Cambridgeshire,* 145–49.

182. Built of brick in 1624, the library is an early example of self-conscious Gothic Revival work. It formed the north range of the college's westernmost court, extending down to the river Cam. Ibid., 148–49.

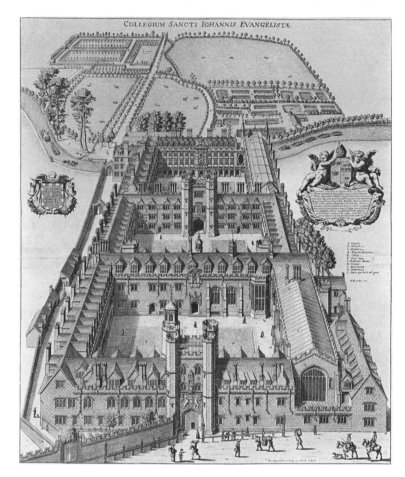

COLLEGIUM SANCTI IOHANNIS EVANGELISTÆ.

St. John's College, Cambridge University, view from the east, David
Loggan, c. 1678–1690. Colonial Williamsburg Foundation/Hans Lorenz.

things w^ch: are not uncomon in Collections of that kind, & there
are Severall pictures of inlaid Marble done very fine. I went
afterwards to Se the Chappells of Peter house,[183] Emanuell
Colledge,[184] & Pembrok Hall,[185] w^ch: are all very neat & fresh.¶

183. An extraordinary mix of Gothic and Classical elements, Peterhouse Chapel was completed in 1632 under the mastership of Matthew Wren. Ibid., 132.

184. Emmanuel College Chapel and its adjoining colonnades were designed by Christopher
Wren and built between 1668 and 1674. Ibid., 72.

185. Pembroke College Chapel was one of Christopher Wren's earliest designs, and the first
purely classical building at Cambridge. It was completed in 1665. Ibid., 125.

Emmanuel College Chapel, Cambridge University, David Loggan, c. 1678–1690. Colonial
Williamsburg Foundation/Hans Lorenz.

Within a mile of Cambrige is a Small village call'd Sturbrige
where once a year in September there is a great resort of
gentry there being a Fair wch lasts a fortnight together.[186]
Having receiv'd news of my grooms recovry,[187] I Set out on
teusday for Ely, wch is counted 8 miles distant from it but
when measur'd prov'd to be 15. We travell'd over a Fen[188]
most part of the Way, into the Island of Ely wch is allmost all
Such containing 28 Parishes. In winter time tis generally quite
under water, but when that is gone off it proves very rich in

5.

186. ". . . nothing is more remarkable . . . than the great Fair annually kept . . . in *September,*
called by the name of *Sturbridge* Fair . . . 'tis supposed the largest, and best stored with all kind
of Wares and Commodities, which the *Londoners* take special care to import hither. When you
are within the Limits, you would rather be ready to imagine your self in some great Town, by
the variety of Shops and multiplicity of Booths . . . Now those Booths are always built for the
time in which it lasts, which is about a Fortnight . . . here is always a great concourse of People
from all parts of the Nation." Brome, 66–67.

187. ". . . we shall proceed to Stanford, where I hope we shall meet the groom, who we
understand is recoverd." Tinling, 1:213.

188. Low-lying land covered with shallow water or subject to frequent inundations.

Ely

grass and affords much willow for baskets, & reeds for thatching.[189] The Citty is very Small & poor, there being neither a
good Street nor Gentlemans house worth notice except the
Bishops Pallace.[190] And there being no manefacture to Employ the poorer Sort of People, have a many beggars. The only
remarkable thing in the town is the minster a very bewtyfull &
Spacious Structure.[191] The first Foundations of it are very
Ancient. but in Henry the first's time Hervy the first Bishop
of this Place[192] rebuilt it. The Isle is very long and was once
adorn'd wth Severall Noblemen & Bishops Seats till the fury of
the troubles in 48 defac'd them, and evry thing that was fine
in it.[193] The Bishoprick is a royall Franchise, and the Bishop
is evry thing in civile matters. For there is no Major nor Bay-
liffs, but a judge whom the Bishop appoints, & no cause under
5 pound can be carry'd up to Westminster to be try'd. The
town consists but of two Parishes w[ch] are well inhabited and
the Air is counted very good for consumptive People. Round
about it have been found in the Fens Severall Smiths Forges,
Ankors, Sickles, & layers of grass, w[ch] is an argument that the
country was once a dry Land, & free from these inundations,
but when the Danes infested these parts, the mounds &
Sluices w[ch] kept out the water were neglected, & the land

189. The Fens of Huntingdonshire and the Isle of Ely provided ample quantities of the reed
Phragmites communis, the best material for thatching. Elsewhere, straw and heather were extensively used. Clifton-Taylor, 338.

190. Built before 1501 for Bishop Alcock, the palace stood just west of the cathedral's
southwest transept. Only two towers now remain. According to Celia Fiennes it was unfur-
nished. Pevsner, *Buildings . . . Cambridgeshire,* 378; Fiennes, 142.

191. Ely Cathedral. Built during the twelfth century, the structure still retains its Norman
nave, crowned by an early timber ceiling. The crossing and chancel date primarily from the
fourteenth and fifteenth centuries. Pevsner, *Buildings . . . Cambridgeshire,* 339–41.

192. Hervey (d. 1131), bishop of Bangor and in 1109 the first bishop of Ely. *DNB,* 26:276–77.

193. "There are very good monuments there is one of white marble laying at length and so
exactly cut that the hand lookes extreamely natural the sinewes and veines and very turn of the
fingers so finely done as to appear very proper; there is another that was a Bishop made by
Queen Elizabeth, whose garments and all are marble and so finely embroydered carv'd and
painted and gilt, and a verge all down before and round the neck with the figures of the
apostles done in embroydery as it were, all marble very fine . . ." Fiennes, 142.

became overflow'd So that it could never thrôly recover it Self.
The Bishop being at his Pallace,[194] he invited us to Dinner   6.
after which we went to Huntington. In our way I took no
notice of any Gentlemans Seat, & the weather was So excessivly hot, that we Sat not out till the cool of the evening &
travell'd by moonshine to Huntington. This is the county town   Huntington
finely Scituated on the river Ouze.[195] Formerly it was very
large but now there only 3 Parishes in it. On one Side is Port-
sholm a meadow famous for horseraces. Three miles from it
Stands Bugden,[196] the Pallace of the Bishop of Lincoln,[197]
who being there, we went & din'd wth him the next day. The   7.
house is large, thô not much to be comended either for bewty
or convenience, but his gardins are well Stock't wth fishponds,
& his orchards wth fruit, wch yeild him very good Sider. In our
return to Huntington we went into the gardins of my Ld Sand-
wiches house[198] wch was the birth place of Oliver Cromwell.
They are order'd much after the French fashion being Sorounded on one Side by a Canal[199] wch hinders no prospect as

194. Simon Patrick (1626–1707), bishop of Chichester 1689–1691 and of Ely 1691–1707. *DNB*,
44:45–46.

195. The river Ouse.

196. Buckden, a tower house of diapered brickwork, set within a quadrangular enclosure
and entered through an outer court. The great tower and both gatehouses survive, all dating
from 1472–1494. Buckden had been an episcopal residence as early as the mid thirteenth
century. Pevsner, *Buildings . . . Bedfordshire*, 215.

197. James Gardiner (1637–1705), bishop of Lincoln 1694–1705. *DNB*, 20:413–14.

198. Edward Montague (1670–1730), 3rd Earl of Sandwich. Cokayne, *Peerage*, 11:434. The Earl's
house, Hinchingbrooke, was originally an Augustinian nunnery, taken over by the Cromwells in 1538
and enlarged during the sixteenth and seventeenth centuries. Most of the surviving work dates from
this period, though altered somewhat in the nineteenth century. In 1627 the estate was sold to Sir
Sidney Montagu, whose son became the 1st Earl of Sandwich. Pevsner, *Buildings . . . Bedfordshire*, 26.
". . . we enter a good lofty hall, in it hangs the Ship in which he [Lord Sandwich] was lost that is the
representation of it cut out in little and all things exactly made to it; there is a large dineing roome
above with good tapistry hangings and its ceil'd with Irish oake carv'd with points hanging down
like fine fret worke . . . there are good bed chambers with good furniture and fine Pictures, over
one of the Chimneys is a fine picture of Venus were it not too much uncloth'd . . ." Fiennes, 82.

199. ". . . we went to see the gardens of My Lord Sandwich's which are assuredly very fine. If
one considers their grandeur, their walks, their terraces, their neatness, and their vistas; that
which one finds the most curious is a canal which runs along one side which is 800 feet long."
De Blainville, 10.

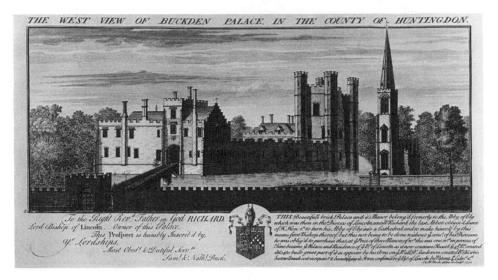

THE WEST VIEW OF BUCKDEN PALACE, IN THE COUNTY OF HUNTINGDON.

Buckden, Huntingdonshire. Samuel and Nathaniel Buck, 1730. Yale Center for British Art, Paul Mellon Collection.

generally a wall does.[200] They run down by a gentle declension near a quarter of a mile, and on one Side is a Park & a wilderness design'd. They are not very regular, nor well Supply'd wth water.[201] The house Stands upon a rising ground, & comãnds Severall good Prospects but it is not regular, nor handsom, but large & convenient.[202] When this was over we return'd to Huntington, & the next day Set out for Peterborrow, whither we got, passing thrô Stilton & Yaxley; this being 13 miles we din'd here. In the Afternoon we waited on the Bishop[203] who gave himself the trouble to Show us the Cathe-

8.
Peterburrow.

200. An early instance of the "ha-ha" concept employed in an English garden. Not until the translation of A.J. Dézallier D' Argenville's *La Théorie et la Practique du Jardinage* by John James in 1712 was this device mentioned in English gardening literature. Hunt and Willis, 11, 25.

201. ". . . the Gardens and Wilderness and Greenhouse will be very fine when quite finish'd, with the dwarfe trees and gravell-walks, there is a large fountaine or bason which is to resemble that in the privy garden at White hall which will front the house . . ." Fiennes, 82.

202. According to Walpole, it was "old, spacious, irregular, yet not vast or forlorn." Pevsner, *Buildings . . . Bedfordshire,* 264.

203. Richard Cumberland (1631–1718), bishop of Peterborough 1690–1718. *DNB,* 13:289–90.

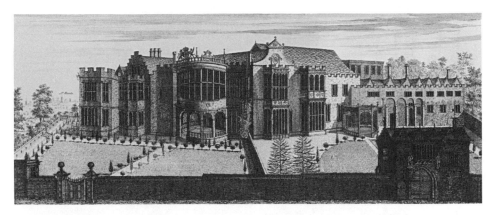

Hinchingbrooke, Huntingdonshire. Samuel and Nathaniel Buck, 1730. Society of
Antiquaries.

drall[204] w.ch was first erected a monastery to S.t Peter by Wolpher king of the Mercians.[205] Afterwards the Danes about
800 years after Christ destroy'd, & killd the Abbot[206] &
Monks who ly all buried in the Church yard. But King Alfred[207] who restored learning in England, rebuilt it. It
receiv'd additions in King Stephens raign, & So lasted a Monastery till Henry the 8.th erected it into a Bishoprick, assining
Northamptom Sheir and Rutland for its Dyocess. The Pile in
respect of its antiquity is very fine, & the Quire is very large,
in w.ch were buried Katherine Queen of Spain,[208] & Mary
Queen of Scotts whose Coffin was remov'd to Westminster.
There is nothing but a Plain Stone on w.ch is writ Queen
Catherine to Show where She lyes, for Henry the 8.th being
prest to build Some fine tomb over her, he reply'd all the

204. Peterborough Cathedral. Having begun life as a monastic church, it only later became
a cathedral when, in 1541, Henry VIII made Peterborough a bishopric. The existing building is
Norman, dating from the twelfth century, with significant thirteenth-century additions to the
west front. Also dating from this period is the timber ceiling, a rare survival. Pevsner, *Buildings
. . . Bedfordshire,* 305–6.

205. Wulphere (d. 675), king of the Mercians, the first such to be baptised. *DNB,* 43:170.

206. Hedda was abbot at the time of the monastery's destruction in 870. Dugdale, *Monasticon Anglicanum,* 1:346.

207. Aelfred (849–901), king of the West Saxons, son of Ethelwulf. *DNB,* 1:153–62.

208. Catherine of Aragon (1485–1536).

Peterborough Cathedral, interior view. Thomas Eayre, c. 1721. British
Museum.

Church Should be her Monum.ᵗ & thereupon repair'd it.²⁰⁹
On the windows were printed the History of Wolpher the
Founder, & the Succession of Abbots till the troubles of 41
when the Rebbells broke them down as they did a famous
alter peice w.ᶜʰ went by Steps to almost the top of the Church.
The town is not large having but one Parish Church,²¹⁰ nor is
it counted very healthy, by reason of the Marshes w.ᶜʰ in Some
places come within a mile of it. The great trade here is wool-
coming & Malting being a great corn country, for w.ᶜʰ there is
a very good market on Satturday. Here is much fish taken
hereabouts, but tis deer because the higlers,²¹¹ by it to carry

209. According to one source, an earlier, more elaborate tomb was destroyed during de-
predations by the parliamentary army in 1643. *A Concise History . . . ,* 34. Purported fragments
of this monument are presently displayed next to the plain black stone described by Percival.
210. St. John Baptist, built 1402–1407 in the Perpendicular style. Pevsner, *Buildings . . .
Bedfordshire . . . Peterborough,* 325.
211. Higgler. An itinerant dealer who exchanges petty commodities for poultry, dairy
products, or, in this case, fish.

up to London. The next day we Set out for Stanford[212] This is
a large town (in wch are 6 Churches) wall'd about, it chuses
Parliam^t men, having an Alderman & 24 Burgesses, and
enjoys divers priviledges. In Edward the 3^ds reign it was an
University, and had two Colledges in it, till that king Sur-
press'd them.[213] The Houses are many of them very large &
new being built all of Stone & for the most part til'd. The
Stone is brought from kettle a Small town 3 miles off, whence
great quantitys are carry'd to Pauls, & Greenwich.[214] Not far
from hence runs the river Welland well Stor'd wth fish, but for
the conveniencys of the town there was cut a river near 7 mile
long wch runs thrô it, & afterwards falls again into the old
Stream. The Inhabitans are great Maltsers, but otherwise are
very idle. Within a mile Stands Burleigh[215] the famous Seat of   Burleigh
the Earl of Exeter.[216] It Stands in the middle of a large Park
upon a rising ground, by which it comands a Prospect not
only of Stanford but many vilages & Gentlemens houses. The
Park is very thick Set with Ash & Oak, and has many Avenues
thrô it leading to the House, before wch is a large Court raild
in wth a Semicircle of Iron bars finly work'd. In the Court is a

212. Stamford, Lincolnshire.

213. Founded during the reign of Edward II, the "university" was later suppressed, owing to
the large number of faculty and scholars who had retired there following a major dispute at
Oxford. Marrat, 2:223–31.

214. St. Paul's Cathedral and Greenwich Hospital, both being built at the time under the
surveyorship of Wren. Colvin, *Biographical Dictionary,* 919–20.

215. Burghley House. Basically, the house assumed its present form (encompassing two
courtyards) during enlargements carried out by William Cecil c. 1556–1587. Most of the interiors,
however, date from a subsequent remodeling by the 5th Earl of Exeter (see note 217) during the
1680s and 1690s. Pevsner, *Buildings . . . Bedfordshire,* 218, 223. "This house, built all of free-stone,
looks more like a town than a house, at which avenue soever you come to it; the towers and the
pinnacles so high, and placed at such a distance from one another, look like so many distant
parish-churches in a great town, and a large spire covered with lead, over the great clock in the
centre, looks like a cathedral, or chief church of the town . . . .The late Earl of Excester . . .
contrived the house itself in a most magnificent manner; the rooms spacious, well directed, the
ceilings lofty, and the decorations just, yet the late Earl found room for alterations, infinitely to
the advantage of the whole; as particularly, a noble stair case, a whole set of fine apartments, with
rooms of state, fitting for the entertainment of a prince . . ." Defoe, 421–22.

216. John Cecil (1674–1721), 6th Earl of Exeter. Cokayne, *Peerage,* 5:220.

Burghley, Northamptonshire, view of the inner court. John Haynes, 1755. *Country Life.*

very large bason. The House is all of Stone & looks majgestic-
ly, being built after the old manner wth two great Courts on
the inside. Without it is finly addorn'd wth towers & Statues,
but within it is much finer, being furnish'd wth multitudes of
pictures & Statues done by the finest hands in Italy, & brought
over at Severall times by the Late Ld Exeter,[217] who was ex-
tream curious this way, & at a great charge in procuring them.
The Rooms are all large, & lofty, being either hung wth pictures, or wth the finest tappestry made at the Goblins in Par-

217. John Cecil (1648–1700), 5th Earl of Exeter. Ibid., 5:219–20. "My Lord Excetter in his
travells was for all sorts of Curious things if it cost him never so much . . ." Fiennes, 83–84.
The Earl had made no less than three trips to Italy, where he acquired numerous works of art
to be brought back to Burghley. Lees-Milne, *English Country Houses*, 60.

is.[218] The chimney peices are mostly marble, Set off wth fine
chany, or Statues in Minature of wood, carv'd by Mr Gibons,
& other ornaments wch are plac'd over all the doors & Chimneys & are the neatest workmanship I ever Saw. The Cælings
are either of Fretwork or finly painted, Especially the Appartment where Vario was Employ'd[219] wch if furnish'd suitably
will prove the finest rooms in England. The Floors are many
of them inlay'd like the finest tables, of wch there is one of
Stone very remarkable, in wch cards, counters, & Such like is
So admirably inlay'd that one would really think company had
been playing upon it.[220] In Short the furniture of all Sorts is
the finest that could be bought for mony, The beds are of
needle work, & the hangings wch are not of tappestry is of the
finest Brocade. It would take up a week to See evry thing, &
our time Streigtening us we were forc'd to conclude wth Seing
the Chappell and Library wch is for a private one, maybe one
of the finest in England, for the number of Books, the choice
of them, & the ornamentary part being all curiusly guilt &
plac'd in exact order.[221] I had allmost forgot to mention the
two Rooms call'd live & dead Bedlam wch we were in, in one
of these hange the pictures of all the Gentlemen who dy'd out
of the Socyety wch was a meeting of the neighbouring country
Gentlemen at this place to drink hard,[222] & they who dy'd

218. Percival's attribution of these tapestries may have been incorrect. Christopher Hussey
discusses three sets of tapestries at Burghley, all attributed with varying degrees of certainty to
John Vanderbank or his shop. Hussey, "Burghley House," 2106, 2166.

219. The state apartment or so-called "George Rooms," painted by Verrio c. 1690–1696.
This apartment included the Saloon or "Heaven Room," generally regarded as Verrio's masterpiece. In spite of the painter's scandalous conduct, the Earl maintained Verrio in considerable
luxury during his extended employment at Burghley. Croft-Murray, 57–58, 236.

220. For a similar tabletop in needlework, see Roque, 320–21.

221. This library was moved to its present location in the hall during the nineteenth
century. Pevsner, *Buildings . . . Bedfordshire,* 55n.

222. The Honourable Order of Little Bedlam, an aristocratic drinking club founded in 1684
by the 5th Earl. According to a circular later issued by the 6th Earl in 1706, there were
originally twenty-seven members, among whom were Sir Godfrey Kneller, Antonio Verrio,
and the Duke of Devonshire. Stewart, 33–34, 34n.

Sir Godfrey Kneller, self-portrait, c. 1688. It was to this painting that
Percival referred in his description of the "Little Bedlam" portraits. Courtesy of the Burghley House Collection. Photograph: National Gallery.

Martyrs to good FellowShip had their pictures decently put
into black frams & hung in order about dead Bedlam, but
those who Still Survive have their pictures hung up in live
Bedlam, among wch is Sr Godfrey Nellers who painted them
all.[223] The Gardins we had not time to See, (but they are very

223. Sir Godfrey Kneller (1646–1723), noted portrait painter. Each member was represented by a portrait, bearing his likeness along with that of an emblematic animal—in Sir
Godfrey's case a unicorn. Not all of these were painted by Kneller, however. In addition to his
own self-portrait and his likeness of Verrio, Bedlam portraits of Dean Hascard (by Dahl) and

Burley-on-the-Hill, Rutland, view from the south. Peter Tillemans, c. 1729. Courtesy of His
Grace the Duke of Roxburghe. Photograph: National Galleries of Scotland.

fine tis Said) So we return'd to our Inn, & Stay'd the day   10.
following being Sunday & heard the Bishop of Peterbur-   11.
row²²⁴ make a very good discourse. On munday we Set out   Burleigh on
for Burleigh on the Hills²²⁵ wch is in Rutland & 7 miles from   the hills.

the 3rd Earl of Gainsborough (by Closterman) hang in the present billiard room at Burghley.
Still other portraits from among the Bedlam group survive elsewhere, including Sir James
Robinson (by Dahl), and James, 2nd Lord Griffin, Henry Nevil, and the 1st Duke of
Devonshire, all by Kneller. According to Stewart, these likenesses were "in intention and
general effect, if not in format, forerunners of the Kit-cat portraits." Ibid., 33–34, 34n. It was
undoubtedly to these portraits that George Vertue referred when remarking on the "many
heads of Gent. & some Noblemen" that hung "in the drinking Room." Walpole Society, 34.
    224. See note 203.
    225. Burley-on-the-Hill, a large stone house flanked by symmetrically arranged subsidiary
buildings. "One of the most sweeping compositions of its date in England," it was erected
1696–1708 by the 2nd Earl of Nottingham (see note 226) at an estimated cost of more than
£30,000. Pevsner, *Buildings . . . Leicestershire,* 289; Habakkuk, 141, 153. "This house would

Stanford. This is a new build Seat of the Earle of Nottinghams[226] the body being but just erected, & the yards and Gardins not finish'd.[227] it is built of Stone[228] design'd to last Some
ages as well as to be bewtyfull. It is very regular & long being
197 feet in Front and it is as convenient on the inside as bewtyfull on the out, & has a great deal of Room. All the out houses
as brewhouse, bakehouse, kitchen, & Stables are So plac'd as
not to be an Eysore to it and the latter are very large, for there is
room for 40 horses, & another Stable is on the other Side design'd to answer it of an equall bigness.[229] The house Stands in
a Park about 4 miles round, well Stock'd w.th Deer & extroardinary well wooded in w.ch are cut out Severall Visto's, &
Severall Avenues leading to the house of above a mile long, w.ch
look very noble. The Gardins when finish'd will be very fine,
being all upon a Declension, and at the foot of them, there is a
Pond as broad as the Thames at Putney, & proportionably
long. The House Stands on a rising ground, & from the topp of
it w.ch is leaded, may be Seen Severall Prospects, as to Lincoln
w.ch is 30 mile from it. While we were here we went to See
Exton[230] a Seat of my L.d Gainsburrows,[231] the house is old,
inconvenient, & irregular, but there is a fine Park 7 mile

---

indeed require a volume of itself, to describe the pleasant situation, and magnificent structure,
the fine gardens, the perfectly well-finished apartments, the curious paintings, and well-stored
library . . . at present, all I can say of it is, there may be some extraordinary palaces in England,
but I do not know of a house in Britain, which excells all the rest in so many particulars, or that
goes so near to excelling them all in everything." Defoe, 419–20.

226. Daniel Finch (1647–1730), 2nd Earl of Nottingham, later 7th Earl of Winchelsea.
Cokayne, *Peerage*, 12:782–85.

227. The Earl and his family had moved into the house in 1699. By 1700 it was structurally
complete, though much remained to be done toward decoration of the interior and toward
completion of the grounds, where George London and Henry Wise were busy laying out the
gardens. Habakkuk, 152; Lees-Milne, *English Country Houses*, 117–18.

228. The stone was quarried nearby at Clipsam. Habakkuk, 149.

229. These stables, the last remnant of the Duke of Buckingham's earlier house, burned in
1705 and were subsequently rebuilt and enlarged. Ibid., 152.

230. Exton Park, a stone house of the Jacobean era, destroyed by fire in 1810. Portions of the
gutted shell still stand. Pevsner, *Buildings . . . Leicestershire*, 298; Harris, 168.

231. Baptist Noel (1684–1714), 3rd Earl of Gainsborough. Cokayne, *Peerage*, 5:395.

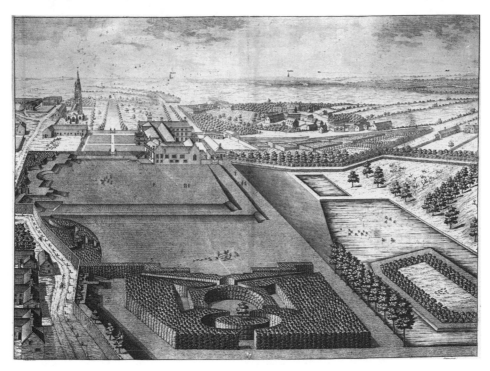

Exton Park, Rutland, view of the house and park. Thomas Badeslade, c. 1739. Courtesy of Mr. John Harris.

round neer it, in wch are Deer, & a very large fishPond. About my Ld Nottinghams house is a variety of game, Especially good hunting. It is So contriv'd that Should one Side of it be on fire it could go no farther then the middle of the house for every partition wall is 3 foot thick, So that the Family have time to Secure themselves in the other part of the house. The Library wch joins to it is well Stock'd & will be very fine, and there is a Green house design'd on the other Side to answer it, that all may be regular. From hence we had much ado to part, & gain my Ld Sherards house²³² wch is 5 miles from it. ¶

232. Bennet Sherard (1621–1700), 2nd Baron Sherard of Leitrim, Ireland. Ibid., 11:674. Lord Sherard's seat was Stapleford, in Leicestershire. The house consisted of a remarkable fifteenth-century range, repaired in 1633, to which three additional wings were added by the 2nd Lord Sherard in 1670, forming an H-shaped plan. Lees-Milne, *English Country Houses*, 130.

Stapleford.   This is a very old house built at Severall times, wch makes it
                  neither regular nor convenient, formerly it was according to
                  the old fashion moated round, The out Offices are not ex-
                  troardinary good, & there is a very indiferent Gardin, wch is
                  Shortly to be improv'd at the expence of a thousand Pound.
                  The Entertaim^t we met wth here was Singularly good, for the
                  Family pique themselves upon eating and drinking well and
                  the good old Lady Sherard[233] makes people drink out of
                  charity. The old Ld Sherard has been dead about a Year, & has
                  left a Son[234] who is very much a Gentleman, who has [to
                  wife?] Lady of no less bewty then wit.[235] The Scituation of the
                  house is very bad being low & consequently without Prospect,
                  but this is made amends for by the good Neighbourhood
                  about it, and the conveniency of Racing, of wch this Lord is a
                  great Lover and promoter. What between importunity to
18.   Stay, & the good usage we met wth we parted not from hence
Nottingham   till monday when we left this place and came to Nottingham.
                  This is counted one of the finest towns in England both for its
                  healthy Scituation, fine houses, & good manefacture. It Stands
                  on a hill in wch are cut Severall houses wth chimneys and Sel-
                  lers and is Sorounded by Severall fine Seats as the Earle of
                  Rutlands,[236] Holm Pierpoint, Earle of Kingstons,[237] Sr Thom-

233. Lady Elizabeth Sherard (d. 1713), daughter of Sir Robert Christopher of Alford, Lincolnshire. Cokayne, *Peerage*, 11:674.

234. Bennet Sherard (1677–1732), 3rd Baron Sherard of Leitrim, Ireland, later 1st Earl of
Harborough. In 1696 he married Mary the daughter of Sir Henry Caverley of Eryholme,
Durham. Ibid., 6:295–96. William Byrd did not share Percival's esteem for the younger Lord
Sherard. In a character of Lady Sherard, written some time after her death in 1702, he praised
her "delicacy of Person which pleas'd every body, but an awkward tactless Husband." Her
virtue, he continued, was "a Guard invincible, both against the addresses of the most accom-
plisht Lover, and the provocations of the most ridiculous Husband." Woodfin and Tinling,
228.

235. "There was a certain Dolce piquante in her Conversation that pleas'd all but Wounded
none." Woodfin and Tinling, 228.

236. John Manners (1676–1711), 9th Earl of Rutland, later 1st Duke of Rutland. Cokayne,
Peerage, 11:264–66. Belvoir Castle, in Leicestershire, was the Earl's seat. Having been demolished during the Civil War, it was rebuilt c. 1662–1668 by the 8th Earl in a form resembling
nearby Nottingham Castle, as rebuilt by the Duke of Newcastle.

237. Evelyn Pierrepont (c. 1665–1726), 5th Earl of Kingston-upon-Hull, later 1st Duke of

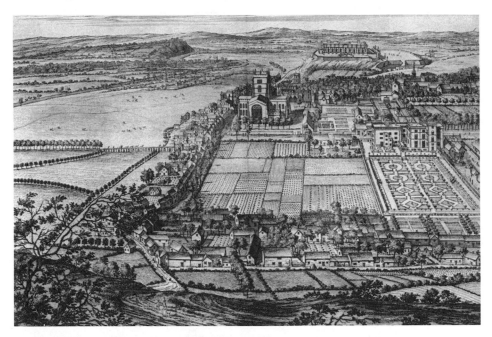

Nottingham, view from the east. Johannes Kip after Leonard Knyff, c. 1710. Paul Mellon
Center for Studies in British Art.

as Willowbys,[238] the Ld Fairfaxs,[239] Ld Hows,[240] and others,
besides Clare Hall[241] & Severall wch. are in the town, and a
Noble Pallace of the Duke of Newcastles[242] built from the

Kingston-upon-Hull. Ibid., 306–7. Standing adjacent to the town of Nottingham, Holme
Pierrepont had been the seat of the Pierrepont family until the 1680s, when Thoresby superceded it as the Earl of Kingston's primary residence. The oldest portions of the house appear
to date from the early sixteenth century, with early seventeenth century additions and alterations. Binney, 842, 845.

238. Sir Thomas Willoughby of Wollaton Hall, Nottinghamshire (c. 1670–1729), 2nd Bar-
onet. Created Baron Middleton, Warwickshire, 1712. Sheriff of Nottinghamshire 1695–1696;
M.P. for Nottinghamshire 1698–1710 and for Newark 1710–1712. Cokayne, *Baronetage,* 4:85–86;
Cokayne, *Peerage,* 8:697–98. Willoughby's seat was Wollaton Hall, one of England's most
noted Elizabethan houses, built 1580–1588 for Sir Francis Willoughby by Robert Smythson.
Pevsner, *Buildings . . . Nottinghamshire,* 208.

239. Thomas Fairfax (1657–1710), 5th Lord Fairfax of Cameron. Cokayne, *Peerage,* 5:231–32.

240. Scrope Howe (1648–1713), 1st Viscount Howe. Lord Howe's estate was Langar, Nottinghamshire. Ibid., 6:596.

241. Unidentified.

242. John Holles (c. 1662–1711), 1st Duke of Newcastle-upon-Tyne. Cokayne, *Peerage,* 9:529.

ruins of an antient Castle, wch William the Conquerer erected, and was afterwards ruin'd in King Stephens reign. This Castle Stood on the west Side of the town upon a very Steep rock, and was formerly very Strong being Sorounded by a deep trench and a wall Some remains of wch yet appear, but king Charles the :1. making it a Garison for here it was he first pitch'd his Standard, when he forsook it the Parliam^{ta}ians destroy'd it, after wch in his Sons reign the late Duke of New-castle built a very fine house after the new mode.[243] This house is not furnish'd but there is one appartment wainscoted wth Cedar & one room (whos floor is of the Same finly inlaid) is hung wth rich Tapestry being the 4 Evangelists, bought by the Duke when he fled wth Prince Rupert to Antwerp, & cost 2000^{li}. We went underneath the castle thrô Mortimers Vault wch is high enough for a man to walk upright, and wide enough for 5 a brest to go, being cut out of the solid rock. The Passage from this into Queen Isabellas chamber by wch Ed-ward the 3 Secretly made himself master of the Castle & kill'd Mortimer,[244] is now wall'd up, as is the Prison where David king of Scots was detain'd. The town is on one Side invirond wth hills, & on the other wth fruitfull meadows and the river Lean wch runs about a mile off into the trent. The Manefacture here is Malt, Silk Stockins, Earthen ware, & Glass. Here is a very good Market for Corn, butchers meat, Sheep, beasts &c. the Market place is very large & famous having a distinct quarter for all those comoditys. The Inhabitants are numer-ous, there are 3 Parish Churches & Severall Sectary Meetings.

243. Nottingham Castle, erected by the Duke of Newcastle (see note 242) after he had acquired the site of the old castle in 1674. Based on the Capitoline Palace in Rome and on plates from Rubens's *Pallazi di Genova,* the Italianate design, with its balustraded flat roof, anticipated the silhouettes later created by Talman at Thoresby and Chatsworth. Hill and Cornforth, 237.

244. Roger de Mortimer (1287–1330), 1st Earl of March. On the night of 18 October 1330, conspirators acting on behalf of Edward III made their way to the Earl's lodgings by way of a secret passage revealed to them by the governor of Nottingham Castle. Mortimer was seized and tried before Parliament. Pronounced guilty, he was hanged at Tyburn on 29 November. Cokayne, *Peerage,* 8:441.

The houses are most modern & built of brick, & the floors are
many of them lay'd w.th a Sort of plaister of Paris. It is compos'd of a Stone as hard as Marble wch like it will bare Pollish-
ing. This Stone being burnt like lime and Sifted fine is Strued
on the floor, and when water is afterwards thrown on it, it
grows in an howers time So hard that one may walk on it, and
continues very hard, lasting very long. Some times the walls of
houses are built of it, for it may be made into mortar, but
must presently be us'd, otherwise it grows as hard as ever. The   19.
next morning we left this place, and came to Newark a pretty   Newark
considerable burgess town, having a good Market on frydays
and a Market place where Ld Bellasis[245] drew up 10000 men
when he defended the town against the whole Scotch army in
the troubles of 41.[246] Here are the Ruines of a very large
Castle,[247] & there is a Church very large, built Cathedrall
wise.[248] The Inhabitants will Suffer no Dissenters to live
among them, & totherday a meeting house being attempted to
be sett up they pull'd it down. King John here ended his life. 3
miles from hence is Beckingham a Small town where on
Wednesday the 6.th of this month happen'd Such a Storm of
hail as Spoilt 600 pounds worth of corn thrashing the grain
out as w.th a flail. Many of the hail Stones when taken up were
found to be 5 or 6 inches about. A thunderbolt at the Same
time fell & past thrô a gentlemans house in Newark, it broke
thrô the tiles & one floor turning up at last & carrying a piece

245. John Belasyse (1614–1689), 1st Baron Belasyse of Worlaby, Lincolnshire. Lieutenant-
general of the king's forces in York and Nottingham. Ibid., 2:89–90.

246. Acting on orders from Charles I, Lord Belasyse, against his will and that of the
garrison, surrendered Newark to parliamentary forces on 6 May 1646. *Victoria History . . .
Nottinghamshire*, 1:353.

247. Newark Castle, a single ward, erected c. 1130 by Alexander, bishop of London, with
additions in the thirteenth century. Only a twelfth-century gatehouse and the thirteenth-
century west or riverfront wall and towers now remain. Pevsner, *Buildings . . . Nottinghamshire*,
110–11; King, 2:380.

248. St. Mary Magdalene, one of the grander parish churches in England, completed during
the fifteenth century. The west tower and the crossing are earlier, dating from the thirteenth
century. It is the later, Perpendicular work of the fifteenth century, however, that visually
predominates. Pevsner, *Buildings . . . Nottinghamshire*, 106–7.

Lincoln

of a window away wth it, & doing no other damage then Scortching a picture. From Newark we got to Lincoln, & now we found we approach'd the north by the length of the miles.[249] The Citty of Lincoln was once in a very flourishing condition having 50 churches now not 15, & a Staple manefacture of wool, but now that is lost 'tis become a very poor town, the Minster[250] & Gail being the only considerable things in it. This first is very large & has been very fine on the west End especially, till the [*troubles of*] 41 destroy'd all that was magnificent about it.[251] To the Cathedrall there are 44 Prebends a Chancellor a Chaunter, & other heads wch have Such good Preferment that this Church is counted one of the finest in England, & certainly it was So before Peterburrow, Ely & Oxford were taken out of it. Within the Minster are the tombs of Severall Noblemen, & one very remarkable one of Dr Honeywood viz:¶

Here lyeth the body of Michael Honywood D^{D} who was Grandchild, & one of the 367 persons that Mary the wife of Robert Honywood Esq: did see before she dyed, lawfully decended from her that is 16 of her own body 114 grandchildren 228 of the 3^{d} Generation, & 9 of the 4th [252]¶

249. In the northern counties the statute mile of 1,760 yards had not yet superceded the old British mile of 2,428 yards. Moir, 8–9. "We had come from Nottingham, which is set down in our books to be but 24 miles from Lincoln, but they prov'd very good measure, and gave us reason to observe that we were travelling in the north." Tinling, 1:214.

250. Lincoln Cathedral, built in three major phases during the eleventh to fifteenth centuries. Predominant among these phases is the Early English work, carried on during most of the thirteenth century. This construction incorporated earlier Norman work at the west end and was later augmented with fourteenth- and fifteenth-century additions, most notably the towers. Pevsner, *Buildings . . . Lincolnshire*, 82.

251. ". . . the Workmanship of the whole Fabrick is very curious and admirable, and the carved Images on the Front of the West-end were such unimitable pieces of Art, (till some of them in our late unhappy broils were sacrificed to the fury of the Insolent Soldiery, who committed a new Martyrdom upon the Saints in Effigie) that they did even allure and ravish the Eyes . . ." Brome, 147.

252. Michael Honeywood (1597–1681) was dean of Lincoln 1660–1681. He was the son of Robert Honeywood, Esq., of Charing, Kent. His grandmother, Mary Honeywood, died in 1620 at the age of ninety-three. Noted for her piety, she reportedly became despondent in her later years. *DNB*, 27:249–51.

The Prison is the ruins of the Castle[253] w^{ch}: was very large
having a great court wall'd round which the Debtors walk
in[254] & a bowling Green & town hall within it. The Castle is
on the higher part of the town has a very deep ditch round it,
& the town was wall'd about formerly. The town is famous for
wildfowl and is very well Supply'd wth: fish thô theres a very
Small rivulet that runs up to it w^{ch}: Small boats only at certain
times can pass. We were very well entertaind by M^r: Paul-
ing,[255] & M^r: Kentril[256] while we Staid here, & the next place
we design'd for was Hull. The first days journey was to Brigds,   22.
but we din'd first at Spittle a Small village where there is an   Spittle
Hospitall built 300 years ago for 6 poor people,[257] & a Sheer
house.[258] The road was very fine from Lincoln to Brigds w^{ch}: is   Brigds
20 mile from it. Here is a pretty Chappell new built at the
charge of the town. The Dissenters here are Superior both in

253. Lincoln Castle. Built in 1068 by William the Conqueror within the southeast corner of
the old Roman *castrum* overlooking the town. The walls form a circuit of 650 yards, encompassing an area of 6 ¼ acres. Standing on a mound at the southeast corner of the enclosure is a
Norman tower with a fourteenth-century addition on its east side. In the center of the south
wall is a polygonal Norman shell-keep, dating from the late twelfth century. Pevsner, *Buildings
. . . Lincolnshire*, 149–51.

254. The marking out of prison bounds in which debtors were allowed to walk was
customary in England and the colonies. The following passage from the Virginia statutes
undoubtedly reflects contemporary practice in England: ". . . the justices of every county shall
be . . . impowered and required, to mark and lay out the bounds and rules of their respective
county prisons, not exceeding ten acres of land, adjoining to such prison . . . every prisoner,
not committed for treason, or felony, giving good security to keep within the said rules, shall
have liberty to walk therein, out of the prison, for the preservation of his or her health . . ."
Hening, 5:508.

255. Probably Edward Pollen (1672–1731), son of John Pollen of Andover, Hampshire.
Foster, 3:1177. "At Lincoln we fell into the hands of Mr. Pollen a friend of mine, that made
much of us for 2 days." Tinling, 1:214. It was undoubtedly during his studies at the Inns of
Court that Byrd had become acquainted with Pollen. Both were admitted in April 1692—
Pollen to Lincoln's Inn and Byrd to the Middle Temple. *The Records . . . of Lincoln's Inn*, 1:345;
Marambaud, 17.

256. Probably Richard Cantrell (1671–1712), clergyman. Prebendary of Lincoln 1694–1712;
rector of Thorpe-on-the-Hill 1700. The latter lay along the road traveled by Percival and Byrd
from Newark to Lincoln. Foster, *Alumni Oxonienses*, 1:234; LeNeve, 2:143.

257. The hospital called "Spittal on the Street," built in 1396 and administered by the dean
and chapter of Lincoln. *Victoria History . . . Lincolnshire*, 2:235.

258. A cloth manufactory.

Number and wealth to those of the church of England, and
both Quakers & Presbiterians have their meeting houses. This
is a market town [*and*] is well Supply'd wth fish, fowl, & flesh
on thursdays & drives a great trade for wood, iron & cole w.^ch

23.
Barton

are brought up to it by a pretty deep river. From Brigds we
came to Barton a market town containing two Parishes & is
famous for Dottrells[259], & Pints.[260] It lys on the Extremity of
LincolnShire having a fine Prospect over the river Humber
(wch divides this County from YorkShire) to Hull whether we
Crost in an howers time being 4 mile & the tide being With

Hull

us.[261] Hull is a round compact town, being half a mile long
evry way, tis govern'd by a Major Sherif & aldermen is a
Market town contains two Parishes & chuses Parliam.^t men.
The Houses are cheifly built of Brick being large, new fashion'd & very neat. Sectarys are here very numerous, Quakers
having one & the Presbiterians two meeting houses. The trade
of this town was formerly very great yet Still it deals very much
wth Holland whether it transports Cheese, Cloth, Butter &
Corn. ⟨Here was once 250 Ships belonging to the Port but
now not above 150.⟩[262] This is a Garison town & is counted
the Second for Strength in England. It can lay all the country
round it for 3 or 4 miles underwater, but the works towards
the Sea are very much out of repair. King Edward the 1:st
made this a town & Burrow, & it grew So rich that in a little
time it built a wall at its own charge round the town & a
double ditch to deffend it.[263] Thrô the town there runs a little

259. Dotterel. A species of plover, *Eudromias morinellus,* so called from the ease with which it
allows itself to be approached and taken. In his *Worthies of England,* William Fuller described
this "mirth-making bird, so ridiculously mimical, that he is easily caught (or rather catcheth
himself) by his over-active imitation . . . As the fowler stretcheth forth his arms and legs going
towards the bird, the bird extendeth his legs and wings approaching the fowler, till surprised in
the net." Fuller, 325.

260. Pink. The chaffinch, *Fringillia coelebs,* called "pinks" in the Midlands from their constant repetition of that sound. Wright, *English Dialect Dictionary,* 4:512–13.

261. ". . . we embarqu'd our selves and horses to cross the mouth of the Humber which is 5
miles over, to Hull. It blew fresh, and was rough-water, but for all that we coud not be sick, tho
we thought of all the nasty images in the world to provoke us to it." Tinling, 1:214.

262. Marginal text, incorporated.

263. In 1326 the town petitioned and was granted royal license to construct fortifications,

Kingston-upon-Hull, view from the southeast. Samuel and Nathaniel Buck, 1745. Yale Center for British Art, Paul Mellon Collection.

river out of the Humber, w^{ch}: goes about 6 miles up & is So deep that Ship of great Burthen can Sail up. One of the Parish Churches here is so large that once two Seperate congregations met at a time & tis built after the manner of a Collegiat Church.[264] In the town are Severall Almshouses an Endowment for Blewcote boys,[265] & an Hospitall call'd Trinity house[266] where is show'd the Effigies of a Mairman who wth: his boat was found & taken in 1613 Some legues from the Shoar. This is the vulgar oppinion but when we Saw it we found he was a Groenlander who being drove by a Storm So far, & taken, our men would fain have to be a Sea monster.[267]¶

the cost of which was defrayed by a toll on all goods entering or leaving Hull. Tickell, 17–19.

264. Holy Trinity Church, the largest parish church in England, built on a cruciform plan at various stages from the fourteenth to the sixteenth centuries. Pevsner, *Buildings . . . Yorkshire . . . The East Riding,* 268.

265. Charity Hall, the town's poorhouse, had been enlarged in 1699 to allow for the training of pauper children in various trades. These children were outfitted with a blue-coat uniform, the boys having stockings and caps like those of Christ's Hospital in London—hence the term *Blewcote boys. Victoria History . . . Yorkshire . . . East Riding,* 348–49.

266. Having begun as a religious establishment in the fourteenth century, Trinity House ultimately became a sort of mariners' guild. During the seventeenth and eighteenth centuries it exercised considerable control over maritime affairs and maintained a hospital for indigent seamen and their dependents. Pevsner, *Buildings . . . Yorkshire . . . The East Riding,* 272.

267. "In Trinity House which is an hospital for 28 poor seamen, or their widdows, there hangs up the effigies of a poor Laplander, that almost 100 years ago was taken up with his little boat by a Greenland ship and in those dark times was taken for a mereman & by most people is stil believd as such." Tinling, 1:215. A description of this effigy by "the curious and ingenious

24.
Beverly:

From hence we Set out to Beverly, this is a large Market town being above a mile long, contains two Parishes and chuses Parliam.ͭ men. Here is a great resort of Gentry upon account of its pleasant Scituation for game, nearness to York, and goodness of the town, the Streets are broad, & well pav'd, the houses, new, large, & handsome & the Churches very bewty-full. At one end of the town Stands a Minster w.ͨͪ thô tumbling down, Shows how noble large & bewtyfull a work it has been.[268] It is of the finer Sort of Gothick work,[269] & in a Nich on the west Side Stands a Statue of Some person the work of w.ͨͪ is So fine that few of our moderns can pretend to better,[270] the rest are fallen thrô age. Within the quire is the tomb of the famous Earl Perrcy of chivy chase who lys here bury'd as dos his Lady[271] in 2 different tombs the Stonework

Mr. *Ray*" is quoted by Bishop Gibson in his additions to Camden: "In the midst of this room hangs the effigies of a native of *Groenland,* with a loose skin-coat upon him, sitting in a small boat or *Canoe* cover'd with skins; and having his lower part under deck. For the boat is deck'd or cover'd above with the same whereof it is made, having only a round hole fitted to his body, through which he puts down his legs and lower parts into the boat. He had in his right-hand (as I *then* thought) a pair of wooden oars, whereby he rowed and managed his boat; and in his left, a dart, with which he strikes fishes. But it appearing by the Supplement to the *North-East Voyages* lately publish'd, that they have but *one* oar about six foot long, with a paddle six inches broad at either end, I am inclin'd to think, that the boat hanging so high, I might be mistaken . . . This on his forehead had a bonnet like a trencher to fence his eyes from sun or water. Behind him lay a bladder or bag of skins, in which I supposed he bestowed the fish he caught. Some told us it was a bladder full of oyl, wherewith he allured the fish to him. This is the same individual *Canoe* that was taken in the year 1613 by *Andrew Barkar,* with all its furniture and boat-man. The Groenlander that was taken refused to eat, and died within three days after." Gibson, 745.

    268. Beverley Minster, originally a collegiate church. Built primarily in the thirteenth and fourteenth centuries, with the addition of the Perpendicular west front during the first half of the fifteenth century. Pevsner, *Buildings . . . Yorkshire . . . The East Riding,* 170–72. By 1716 the minster had become so delapidated that "its restoration was despaired of," the north transept being virtually a ruin. Cobb, 52.

    269. Percival probably referred here to the Perpendicular-style work of the west front.

    270. Possibly the effigy of Henry Percy on one side of the north tower. This is the only original figure now surviving in association with the west front. Pevsner, *Buildings . . . Yorkshire . . . The East Riding,* 171.

    271. Owing, no doubt, to Brome's account (p. 153), Percival confused Henry Percy (1394–1455), commonly regarded as the 2nd Earl of Northumberland, with his father, Sir

over that of the Earls is counted Some of the finest work being
a Canopy wth: our Savior & Angels.[272] Neer them is St Johns
free Stool into w^{ch}: if any debtor or Criminall could escape, he
was Secure from the hands of Justice.[273] Without the Quire
on the left hand is painted on the wall the picture of king
Athelstane[274] and St John[275] who was bury'd here between
whom are these these words written

> Alls free make I thee
> As hert can wish
> Or Eyh may See.[276]

Henry Percy (1364–1403), the famous "Hotspur" of the Battle of Otterburn (Chevy Chase).
DNB, 44:405–8. Lady Percy was Eleanor, daughter of Ralph Neville (1364–1420), 1st Earl of
Westmoreland. Cokayne, *Peerage*, 9:715–16; and vol. 12, pt. 2, 544–49.

272. According to one authority this monument was "probably not a tomb at all and almost
certainly had nothing to do with Lady Eleanor Percy . . . It is far more likely to have been an
Easter Sepulcher erected at the expense of Lady Idoine Percy." Stone, 171. ". . . that which one
finds the most remarkable is a stone Mausoleum in which are buried the Counts of Northumberland. I can truly say that of all the stone figures that I have seen in Italy, there was not
one in my opinion which deserves comparison with the 12 or 15 of those that one sees on this
Mausoleum; and if I may be permitted to use a hyperbole to express my thoughts, I shall say
that in considering the delicacy, one would take them rather for copper-plate miniatures than
works of sculpture . . ." De Blainville, 16.

273. "Nor were there only Privileges granted to the Town, but even Foreigners did reap
great Benefit hereby . . . for here formerly stood an old Chair of *Stone*, which by its description
did declare as much:

> *Hæc sedes lapidea Freed-Stool, i.e. Pacis*
> *Cathedra, ad quam Reus fugiendo perveniens*
> *omnimodam habet Securitatum.*
> *That is,*
> *This Chair of Stone is called Freed-Stool, that is,*
> *Chair of Peace, unto which whatsoever Offender*
> *fleeth or cometh, hath all manner of Security."*

Brome, 153.

274. Athelstan (895–940), king of the West Saxons and Mercians. *DNB*, 2:215.

275. St. John of Beverley (d. 721), bishop of Hexham 687–705 and of York 705–718. He
later retired to a monastery of his own building at Beverley, where he died. In 1037 he was
canonized. *DNB*, 29:435–36.

276. See Gibson, 743. A similar inscription was to be seen in St. Austin's Church at
Heddon a few miles away. Cox, 6:533.

St John had been Archbishop of York, & retir'd from thence, here to lead a Monastick life, & for his piety Athelstane had Such veneration that upon his account he made the town free & gave the foremention'd Stool to the Church. On the other end of the town Stands an other large Church built also Cathedrall wise to wch the Major & aldermen go.[277] In the town is a very famous free School[278] & 6 Almshouses and up to it is cut a Small channell out of the river Hull wch will bare boats of Small burthen. The cheif trade here is malting, flax, Tanning of leather & making bone lace. a mile from it is a Spaw Spring in a meadow, wch cures the Kings evill[279] and all manner of

Lonsburrow

Scabs & Scurfs. After dinner we went to Lonsburrow[280] a Small village where there is an Almshouse for 6 poor people founded by the old Ld Burlington,[281] who left here a Small brick Seat to his Son,[282] wch is neither bewtyfull on the outside nor in, having no gardins nor furniture, So we Soon were Sattisfy'd we came out of our way for nothing and came to

Pocklington

Pocklington a Small Market town. Here we took up our Quar-

---

277. St. Mary, begun in the twelfth century, though most of the present structure is somewhat later. Pevsner calls it "one of the most beautiful parish churches of England." Pevsner, *Buildings . . . Yorkshire . . . The East Riding,* 179.

278. The grammar school, purportedly founded by Edward VI. Oliver, 277.

279. Scrofula or tuberculosis of the lymphatic glands. The affliction was supposedly curable by the king's (or queen's) touch. The practice of touching for the King's Evil was continued from the time of Edward the Confessor to the death of Queen Anne. Wright, *English Dialect Dictionary,* 5:708. "About a mile from *Beverley* to the east, in a pasture belonging to the town, is a kind of Spaw; tho' they say it cannot be judg'd by the taste whether or no it comes from any Mineral. Yet taken inwardly, it is a great dryer; and wash'd in, dries scorbutick scurf, and all sorts of scabs; and also, very much helps the King's Evil." Gibson, 744.

280. Londesborough, Yorkshire.

281. Charles Boyle (ante 1674–1704), 2nd Earl of Burlington. Cokayne, *Peerage,* 2:431–32. According to Cox, it was Lord Burlington's mother, Elizabeth (1613–1691), Countess of Burlington, who founded and endowed "an Alms-house for twelve aged persons, being decayed Farmers, not far from her Seat." Cox, 6:542; Cokayne, *Peerage,* 2:430–31.

282. Richard Boyle (1694–1753), 3rd Earl of Burlington, arbiter of architectural fashion. Cokayne, *Peerage,* 2:432–33. The house (also called Londesborough) was pulled down in 1819. From Kip's engraving, it appears to have dated from the second half of the seventeenth century. Pevsner, *Buildings . . . Yorkshire . . . The East Riding,* 85–86.

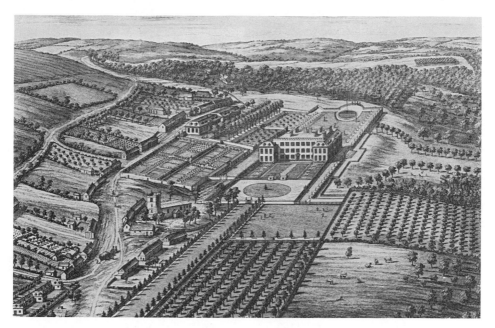

Londesburgh, Yorkshire. Johannes Kip after Leonard Knyff, c. 1700. Colonial Williamsburg Foundation.

ters for one night and the next day Set out for York wch is 10   26.
miles distant.¶
York is the 2^d Citty in England for dignity and the 4th in big-   York
ness. It gives the title of Ld Major^{283} wch none els but London
does. The Gentry here are very few thô in Winter time there
are allways enough to countenance Plays, balls &c. In this
Citty there are Severall good houses wch Stand to be lett, a
Sure Sign of the decay of trade in it & indeed it lives upon the
Small number of gentry wch resort to it. In former times here
were above 50 Parishes now there are not 30, & here are the
ruins of Severall Abbys & Colledges partiularly the Abby of
St Marys^{284} wch Stood a little out of the town upon the river

283. Lord mayor.

284. The Benedictine Abbey of St. Mary, York. Originally a convent dedicated to St. Olave, it was refounded and rededicated to St. Mary in 1089. The present remains are principally those of the church undertaken in 1270 by Abbot Simon de Warwick. Dugdale, *Monasticon Anglicanum,* 3:529–44; Pevsner, *Buildings . . . Yorkshire . . . The East Riding,* 112.

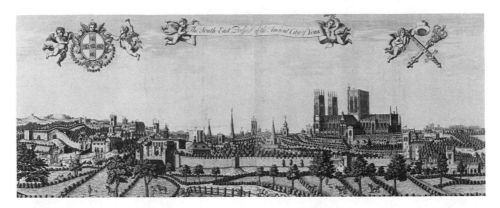

York, view from the southeast. Edmond Barker, 1718. Yale Center for British Art, Paul Mellon Collection.

Ouze. The monks of this place were inveterate enemys to those of S.[t] Peters,[285] now the Collegiat Church, and to this day the painted windows are preserv'd in w.[ch] were represented the monks of S.[t] Marys, Some like Apes & monkys some like hogs going in prosession[286] Religion Sure was at a very low ebb when it gave place to such mean pieces of wit & repartee. The Minster of S.[t] Peters is reccon'd the largest highest, & longest in England, its length is 524 foot, breath 222, & height from the top of the Lanthorn 213. The quire is very large and neat, behind which are the tombs of Severall Noblemen.[287] On

285. By 1262 there existed a college of vicars within the cathedral close, incorporated under the name of St. Peter's College. Dugdale, *Monasticon Anglicanum,* vol. 6, pt. 3, 1475.

286. ". . . a Canon called my attention to . . . a window of the Nave which is as ancient as the Church, where is a procession of monkeys, one of which carries the Archiepiscopal cross, another a bell to call the people; the four who follow each hold a lighted torch, after these one sees others who carry the Canopy and who are preceded by several surplices; under the Canopy is a monkey clad in priestly garments holding in one of his paws the Sacrament. One claims that this window was made at the time of the introduction of Transubstantiation, which was only accepted in this Church with very great difficulty and long delay." De Blainville, 21.

287. "The most beautiful marble tombs . . . are those of some Archbishops who had the management of this Church, they are represented in different fashions, but all sufficiently fine. The Mausoleum is that of Count Strafford, its craftsmanship is magnificent as much for its delicacy as for the quality of different marbles and for the inlaid work of which it is composed; Between the Count and the Countess who are there represented standing is an urn apparently destined to receive their heart; on the pedestal one reads their Genealogy." Ibid., 18–19.

one Side of the Ile Stands a table of the Founders, restorers, &
Benefactors of this Fabrick, wch. tells us that Edwin King of
Northumberland[288] first founded it in 627. The windows are
finly painted[289] & the Stone of wch. all is built, So good that on
the inside it looks as well as new. In the Vestry is a well call'd
by the name of S^{t}. Peter wch. is excellent comon water, but must
[have] be[en] Something more in time of Popery, when Devills
& diseases fled before it.[290] The Chapter house is very
remarkable for being a round room finly carv'd, & arch'd
atop without any pillar to Support the roof.[291] The builders
So valued their work that on one Side they wrote in gold
letters

    Ut Rosa flos florum, Sic est domus ista domorum[292]

The Roof is all leaded, & over it is a lanthorn 46 foot Square.
The first foundation of this Citty must have been very antient
for we find that Constantine the Great was here proclaim'd

288. Edwin (c. 585–633), king of Northumbria 617–633. Son of Aella, king of Deira. *DNB*,
17:134.

289. ". . . in the Minster there is the greatest curiousity for Windows I ever saw they are so
large and so lofty, those in the Quire at the end and on each side that is 3 storys high and
painted very curious, with History of the Bible; the painting is very fine such as was in Kings
Chapple in Cambridge . . ." Fiennes, 90–91.

290. "In the Vestry upon the left hand is a little Well of pure Water, called St. *Peter's-Well;* in
the times of Popery supposed to have been of great Virtue and Efficacy in charming Evil
Spirits, and curing of Diseases, but it may be his Holiness, since the Extirpation of his Papal
Authority in these Parts, hath laid an interdict upon its healing Faculty, since which time it
hath ceased, no doubt in Reverence to St. *Peter*'s Successor, from any such miraculous Opera-
tions." Brome, 157. "The relics of Papism are, a well to be found in the Sacristy, where those
entering are requested to drink a glass of its water, to the honour of St. Peter, to whom this
Church was dedicated before the Reformation; but either because I found this old practice but
a relic of superstition, or because moreover, I was not thirsty, I could not resolve to give myself
up to public devotions." De Blainville, 19.

291. The tierceron vaulting that covers the polygonal space is of wood, rather than stone,
eliminating the need for a center column. Among the "finly carv'd" enrichments were the
chapter seats with their individual canopies. Pevsner, *Buildings . . . Yorkshire . . . The East Riding,*
85–86.

292. "The chief of Houses, as the Rose of flowers." See Gibson, 721.

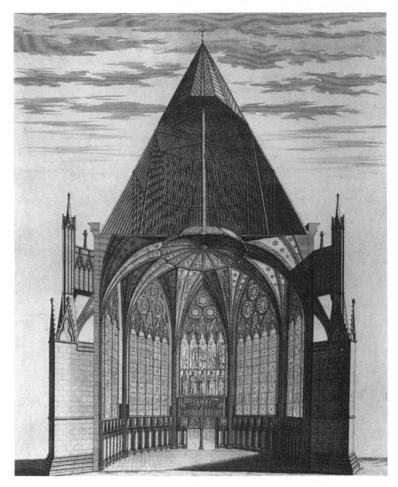

York Cathedral, interior view of the Chapterhouse. John Harris after John Haynes, 1736. British Museum.

Emporour & Severus,²⁹³ & Constantius Chlorus²⁹⁴ were here bury'd, wch shows that in those days it was no mean place; The walls sorounding the whole town add a great deal of bewty to it, and the Inhabitants are Still bound to keep them up, formerly the town was sorounded by a deep trench wth this wall wch was not Sufficient to keep it from the fury of the Danes who took it thô notwithstanding William the Conqueror built to it

293. Septimus Severus (A.D. 145–211), emperor of Rome 193–211. Bowder, 194.

294. Constantius I (A.D. 250–306), western emperor 293–306. Restored Roman control of Britain following the defeat of Allectus in 296. Ibid., 19–20, 69.

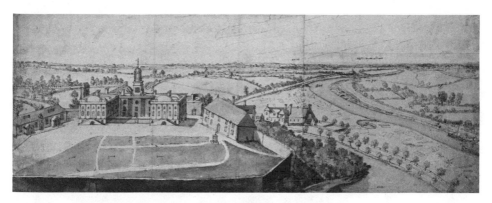

York, as seen from Clifford's Tower with the Sessions House, Prison, and Jury House shown in the foreground. Francis Place, 1710. British Museum.

a very Strong Castle. The Severall Roman Camps[295] neer the town are Sufficient to Show of what Import it was against the Inrodes of the Picts & Northern Inhabiters. within the walls of the Castle is now building a very noble Prison for debtors & Mallefactors, the cost is computed to 7 or 8 thousand pound[296] This Citty was made an Archbishoprick in 750 when Ulphus a Prince of YorkShire[297] gave much land to S.t Peters Colledge, & the horn he made use of at the Endowment is Still to be Seen. When any land was formerly given to a

295. York Castle, also known as Clifford's Tower. Built c. 1250–1275 on a large motte previously occupied by a wooden enclosure dating from the Conquest. The keep is a low tower built on a quatrefoil plan, with a large bailey, walled in stone. Pevsner, *Buildings . . . Yorkshire . . . The East Riding,* 130; King, 2:528.

296. Possibly designed by William Wakefield, this monumental structure was completed in 1705, anticipating the work of Vanbrugh and Hawksmoor. Pevsner, *Buildings . . . Yorkshire . . . The East Riding,* 130–31. "Every man who holds the usual idea that one forms of a prison would be without doubt astonished at the beauty of this one; at the entrance is a large courtyard spacious and orderly; on the right one sees a building fine enough where are the tribunals of civil and criminal judges; on the left is another building of the same symmetry as the first, where are all the offices which serve the use of the prisoners, such as the kitchen, the wash-house, the bakery, &c. in the centre one sees a wonderful building of freestone made up of three main buildings which one one might take rather for the house of a Peer of the Realm rather than a place of correction . . ." De Blainville, 20.

297. Ulf, son of Thorald, a wealthy Yorkshire thegn, described by Camden as having "govern'd in the west parts of Deira." Davies, 3; Gibson, 720.

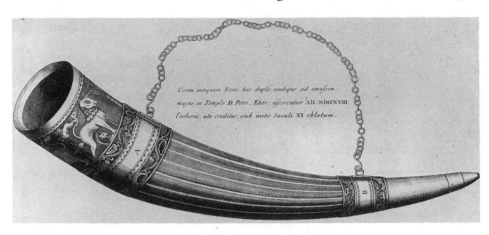

The Horn of Ulphus. George Vertue. British Museum.

church the manner was wth it to present a knife as King Athelstane did at Beverly, or a horn wch this Prince made choice of, who filling it with wine kneel'd down before the Alter, bestowing his land on God & St Peter Prince of his Apostles.[298] We din'd wth Dr Gale Dean of York[299] twice while we were here, and waited on his Grace the Archbishop of York[300] at his country Seat Bishop Thorp[301] two miles from the Citty.

Bishop } Thorp }

298. The parallel with Camden is striking: ". . . taking the horn wherein he was wont to drink with him, he fill'd it with wine, and kneeling upon his knees before the Altar, bestow'd upon God and the blessed S. *Peter*, Prince of the Apostles, all his Lands and Tenements." Gibson, 720. While touring with John and William Blathwayt in 1703, tutor P. De Blainville saw and described the horn of Ulf: "The Elephant's tusk has the shape of the horn of an ox, and is in the region of two feet long; it is hollow within and decorated on the outside with two rings of gilded copper; one claims that a Saxon King used it regularly for drinking, this was without a doubt a pleasant royal goblet . . ." De Blainville, 19. The metal mountings mentioned in De Blainville's description were added to the horn after "It was lost during the period of the Reformation, but was restored to the Dean and Chapter by Henry Lord Fairfax (into whose father's hands it had accidentally fallen) in 1675." Modern authorities accept as authentic the traditional association of this horn with Ulf's endowment. The horn itself is believed to be of Byzantine origin. Dugdale, *Monasticon Anglicanum,* vol. 6, pt. 3, 1175; Kendrick, 280–82; Davies, 1.

299. Thomas Gale (1635–1702), dean of York 1697–1702. *DNB,* 20:378–80.

300. John Sharp (1645–1714), archbishop of York 1691–1714; noted numismatist and antiquary. *DNB,* 51:408–11.

301. Bishopthorpe had been an archepiscopal residence since the thirteenth century, when

John Sharp, archbishop of York. Attributed to Sir Godfrey Kneller, c. 1691. Courtesy of the Rector and Church-wardens of St. Giles-in-the-Fields, London. Photograph: Paul Mellon Center for Studies in British Art.

it was purchased by Archbishop William de Gray. The present chapel appears to date from this period. At the end of the fifteenth century, the palace was nearly doubled in size by the addition of a large wing to the west of Archbishop Gray's building. Shortly after the Restoration portions of the older thirteenth-century building were remodeled by Archbishop Frewen. Wood, 566–67.

This is a Small brick House pretty old, to it is a handsome gardin w.th walks and good fish ponds.[302] My L.d treated us very curtiusly & carry'd us after dinner into his Studdy w.ch is compos'd of Select books. here he gave us a Sight of a very rich collection of all Sorts of medalls whether Grecian Roman, or modern ones. D.r Gale brought us acquainted w.th D.r Fall Precentor of the Church.[303] This is a Gentleman of excellent learning w.ch he not only improv'd but temper'd w.th civility w.ch he learn'd by being abroad Severall times. He Show'd us a copy of H:8.th letters to Anna of Bulloign[304] w.ch are Some English Some french, but very dull & ill Spellt even for the time they were wrote in. he Show'd us also Something more curious viz: a coppy of a prophecy made in that Kings reign w.ch by way of a picture foretold the downfall of Popery & the chance it had of rising again in the late King James reign. First was drawn in read lead the picture of H:8: pulling down Monasterys w.th his Scepter, then came Edw.6 confirming w.t he had done. After him follow'd Queen Mary, burning people and restoring that Church. next came Queen Elizabeth ruining all she had done. king James y.e:1: was the next in order who appear'd persisting on in w.t she had don, Then follow'd Ch:1: w.th his crown from his head, to Shew he should be beheaded, then came Oliver without any head to Shew he would not be king, but instead of that he was pictur'd w.th all manner of instrum.s of war, & being in armour Sorounded w.th Smoke & bloud. Ch:2.d was the next, who lay under a tree in a Sheapheards dress careless how the world went w.th a motto under him, he gives all away, after all came King James restoring Popery building Monasterys & alters. This was Carry'd to Rome above 100 years ago & kept in the Vatican there as a choice thing from whence D.r Fall by much importunity got leave to have it coppy'd.¶

Sep.t2:   On tewsday we left this citty & proceeded Northward to Bur-

302. The grounds had been the special interest of Archbishop Sharpe, who was probably responsible for much of the present garden layout. Ibid., 567.

303. James Fall (1647–1711), canon residentiary and precentor of York 1691–1711; archdeacon of Cleveland 1700–1711. Venn and Venn, 2:119.

304. Anne Boleyn (1507–1539).

rowbrigs,[305] a Small Market town, & wch. chuses Parliam^t men.
Neer this town we took notice of 3 large Stones call'd by the
country people the Devills bolts.[306] they are about 7 yards
round & 6 high. Whether [t]here was any Battle fought here, or
whether they were Set up in honour to the heathen Dietys Anti-
quarys can't determine, no more then they can tell wch. way they
were brought thither. Ime apt to think they were A compound
of Sand, lime, & vitriol left to time to harden into Stone, and
the rather because upon the throwing down the fourth, to make
a brige of, it shatterd all to peices. Neer this town lys Alburrow,   Alburrow
the oldest town in England, where have been found Severall
peices of Antiquity, as Urns, altars, coins, vaults &c.[307]¶
In the Afternoon we went to Ripon but took Sr Edward Black-
ets[308] house in our way. This house were it not So cry'd up
might pass for a very good one, but the name it has got of
being the finest in the North prepares travelers to expect a
much finer building.[309] The Case is of brick & leaded at topp.

305. Boroughbridge, Yorkshire.

306. The Devil's Arrows, three large, upright stone monoliths situated about a quarter-mile west of Boroughbridge. Standing nearly in a line, these stones are thought to be prehistoric sepulchral monuments. *Victoria History . . . Yorkshire*, 1:368–69. ". . . the *Pyramids,* call'd by the common people the *Devil's Arrows,* are most remarkable. That they are artificial, we have the opinion of Mr. Camden . . . A later Antiquary seems inclin'd to conclude them to be a British work; supposing that they might be erected in memory of some battel fought there, but is rather of opinion that they were British Deities . . ." Gibson, 733–34.

307. Aldborough, Yorkshire. "In the late Civil wars, as they were digging a Cellar, they met with a sort of Vault, leading, as 'tis said, to the river: if of Roman work . . . it might probably be a Repository for the Dead. The Coyns (generally of brass, but some few of silver) are mostly of *Constantine* and *Carausius* . . . No Altars are met with; but pieces of Urns and old Glass are common." Gibson, 734.

308. Sir Edward Blackett of Newby Hall, Yorkshire (c. 1649–1718), 2nd Baronet. Sheriff of Northumberland 1689–1690; M.P. for Ripon 1689–1690 and for Northumberland 1690–1700. Cokayne, *Baronetage,* 4:59. Blackett's seat was Newby Hall, a flat-roofed brick house of the late seventeenth century. Cornforth, "Newby Hall," 1802. ". . . His house is built with bricke and coyn'd with stone, with a flatt Roofe leaded, with Railes and Barristers, and a large Cupelow in the middle; you may see a greate way round the Country; the front Entrance is 3 gates of iron barres and spikes painted blew with gold tops, and brick work between the gates and pillars, with stone tops carv'd like flower potts, the pillars all coyn'd with stone; the middle gate is made large in a compass like a halfe Moone . . ." Fiennes, 97.

309. ". . . we viewed the house which consists of a main block with two detached buildings which stand at either end; taking into consideration the siting, the gardens, the prospect, the

Newby Hall, Yorkshire. Michiel van der Gucht after C. Hall, c. 1710. *Country Life.*

The inside is no finer then the outside haveing but indifferent furniture.[310] The finest part in it is a Staircase wch. is now painting, but it wants light.[311] The gardins are pretty good, & afford much fruit.[312] In this house we Saw the picture of an Ox wch. S^r. Edward Blacket had kill'd in 1692 wch. weighd 146 Stone & odd pounds.[313]¶

Ripon.   Ripon is a pretty new brick town, has Severall good houses in it & a very Spacious Marketplace,[314] & it chuses Parliam^t.

---

neatness, the walks, it can pass if not as one of the most spacious one of the most noble, at least as one of the most pleasant and most perfect that we ever saw . . ." De Blainville, 22.

310. "As for the interior of the house one can not say that the furnishings are luxurious; but they are clean, and the apartments very comfortable . . ." Ibid., 23.

311. De Blainville described a stair at Newby "so skillfully contrived that in the space of 8 to 9 feet in diameter it contains a flight of 24 stairs which comprise 130 steps so placed that one sees from the highest one the lowest one in direct line." Ibid., 23.

312. ". . . It is situated upon a hill which has 4 equal slopes all contained within the confines of the park; in front of the four facades of the building are 4 gardens to wit a flower bed, a kitchen garden, a stretch of fruit trees, and another lawn, which is adorned with a large number of life-sized statues, and all surrounded by breast-high walls and an iron balustrade . . ." Ibid., 23.

313. ". . . in the pantry hangs a picture of the dimentions of a large ox that was fed in these grounds with the account of its weight; this Gentleman breeds and feeds much Cattle in his grounds." Fiennes, 97. This picture was similar, perhaps, to that now seen in the kitchen at Burghley, depicting the butchered carcass of an enormous ox.

314. ". . . this little town is pretty and agreeable, its market place is the most beautiful and

men: In it is a Minster[315] founded by Wilfrid Archbishop of
York[316] about the year 678. and neer to it is a Colledge[317] for
a Dean Subdean, & 6 Prebends. This Minster Suffered much
in Olivers time & the great Storm w^{ch}: arose upon his Death
call'd Olivers Storm, blew down a very lofty Spire w^{ch}: beat
down a great part of the Church.[318] Since it has been repair'd.
Here is plenty of fish from two rivers w^{ch}: run by the town, but
neither are navigable. The Inhabitants did formerly drive a
great Woolen trade, but now they are only famous for making
Spurs. From hence we went to Salutation a lone house 10 miles   3.
from whence we Set out,[319] and after dinner came to Richmond. In our way we came over Nosterland Moor famous for
having (in the Saxons time) had a Council of Bishops held on
it They being in those times very fraid of witchcraft refus'd to
hold any under a roof, but all was done in the open air, because wizards could then as they thought have no power over
them. We came after dinner thrô Leeminglane to Richmond.   Leeming
This lane is part of the old Roman causway w^{ch}: beginning at   lane

---

the most orderly of those that we have seen on our journey; its shape is square, its houses well
built, its area very considerable, in the middle there is a tall freestone pyramid which is very
fine." De Blainville, 23.

315. Now Ripon Cathedral, formerly the parish church for Ripon. The present structure
was begun as the rebuilding of an earlier church in the late twelfth and early thirteenth centuries, concluding with the west front, a fine example of the Early English style. The nave was
subsequently altered at various times up to and during the sixteenth century, resulting in
"more of a mixture of styles than can please the eye." Pevsner, *Buildings . . . Yorkshire, The West
Riding,* 404. ". . . there is a good large stone built Church well carved they call it a Minster;
there is very fine painting over the alter it looks so natural, just like real crimson satten with
gold fringe like hangings and severall rows of pillars in isles on either side which looks very
naturall . . ." Fiennes, 95–96.

316. St. Wilfred (634–709), elected bishop of York in 664. *DNB,* 61:238.

317. The Collegiate Church of St. Peter and St. Wilfred, originally a Benedictine monastery,
but refounded about the time of the Conquest. Having been granted to lay patentees after the
Dissolution, it was again refounded by James I in 1604. Dugdale, *Monasticon Anglicanum,* vol. 6,
pt. 3, 1367.

318. According to Pevsner, the collapse of the tower occurred in 1615. Pevsner, *Buildings . . .
Yorkshire, The West Riding,* 405.

319. The village of Salutation stood four miles from Bedale in Kirkby Fleetham Parish,
North Riding, Yorkshire.

Richmond Castle, Yorkshire. Francis Place, 1674. British Museum.

Newport in the Isle of Wight is found again at Southampton & runs cleer to Edinburrow.[320]¶

Richmond.   Richmond is a fine large town, [*which*] Stands part on a hill. The houses are all of Stone & til'd. The Marketplace is very large, & in the town are 4 churches wth Steeples, but now only 2 have Service in them. Here was formerly a great Abby[321] & Severall religious houses and a Strong Castle on a rock wch was built in the Conquerors time to Secure the town against the danes.[322] There went a wall round the town wch was also

320. This was one portion of the main north road from York, connecting Aldborough and Catterick Bridge. Now part of the A1 motorway, the old causeway was two to three feet in height. Margary, 2:159–60, 91–92.

321. Probably the Benedictine priory of St. Martin's, founded 1137. Butler and Given-Wilson, 405.

322. Richmond Castle, begun c. 1070. Sited on a high bluff, the castle originally consisted of a main ward walled in stone. By 1180 a keep had been erected over the original entrance, incorporating the old gatehouse into its ground floor. Still other additions were made in the fourteenth century. The keep survives in an excellent state of preservation, along with portions of the outer walls and two towers. Pevsner, *Buildings . . . Yorkshire . . . The North Riding,* 292–94; King, 2:254.

defended by the rapid river Swale w^ch: is broad but not navigable The trade here is in woolen Stockins cheifly. The plenty of
Stones in the North are the cause of very fair briges & large
houses, of w^ch: the North is full. From Richmond we came to
Leesingthorn[323] where after dinner we past over the teese[324]
(a rapid Shallow river) to Durham. This is a Small Citty con-   Durrham
taining only 5 churches besides a Minster[325] founded in 995
when the See was remov'd hither by Bishop Aldwin.[326] The
Quire w^ch: is all new Since the rebellion of 41 is very neat,[327]
but evry part els of the Church is extreemly mean. Cutberd
the Patron of the Church lys at the East end[328] and in the west
end is the tombstone of old Bede,[329] w^th: this verse

Hac Sunt in fossa Beda venerabilis Ossa.[330]

The town lys on the Side of a hill, the Minster and Castle
being atop, but the rest encompast on all Sides by hills, thrô
w^ch: the windings of the river ware (w^ch: afterwards allmost

323. Leasingthorn, Durham, about five miles east of Bishop Auckland.

324. The river Tees.

325. Durham Cathedral, built primarily between 1093 and 1133. The cathedral is an unusu-
ally homogeneous example of Norman work, unadulterated by later additions. Pevsner,
Buildings . . . Durham, 79.

326. Aldhun (d. 1018), bishop of Durham 990–1018. The see had been moved from Chester-
le-Street, where Aldhun had erected a church to receive the remains of St. Cuthbert. *DNB*,
1:247.

327. Richly embellished choir stalls with "Gothic" canopies and tracery had been introduced by Bishop Cosin (see note 337) in 1663. Pevsner, *Buildings . . . Durham*, 108.

328. St. Cuthbert (d. 687), bishop of Lindisfarne. Having been moved repeatedly over the
course of four centuries, Cuthbert's remains were brought for the last time to Durham in 1104.
Following the defacing of his shrine in 1542, the saint's remains were buried under the floor of
the church. *DNB*, 13:359–62.

329. St. Bede (673–735), the noted scholar and ecclesiastical historian. Bede's remains had
been brought to Durham from Jarrow during the first half of the eleventh century. In 1541 his
sepulcher "fell prey to sacreligious greed" and his remains were dispersed. *DNB*, 4:98–105.

330. "In this grave lie the bones of venerable Bede." Brome wrote that ". . . innumerable
Pilgrims flocked hither every Year to visit his Sepulchre . . . over which hangs an old Parch-
ment, which containing a large Catalogue of his Virtues and Graces, and extolling his Person
with high Encomiums . . . doth at last put a period to all with this Epitaph, the Wit of that Age
consisting most in such jingling Rhimes." Brome, 168–69.

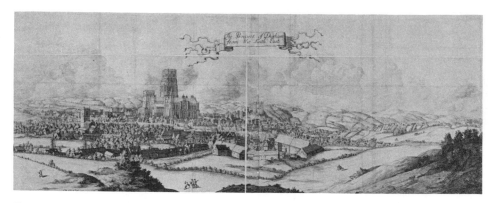

Durham, view from the southeast. V. Bok, c. 1680 [?]. British Museum.

Sorounds the citty) afford a very aggreable prospect. We took
an opportunity to See the Bishops Pallace wch was once a very
Strong Castle,[331] and is now good for nothing So much as the
prospect it makes a farr of[f]. The revennues of this Church
are the richest in England, for the Bishop[332] has 4000^li a year
besides fines upon renewances wch is allmost as much more,
and besides this as he is Count Palatine, he comands all the
temporall Offices of the County by wch he obliges his friends
& can either by Some temporall or eccliastick Office or Sta-
tion promote all his relations. The Deanery is worth 1500^li a
year, besides wch the present enjoyer of it Dr Monntague[333]

331. Durham Castle, also the Bishop's Palace. Begun about 1075, it grew by way of suc-
cessive enlargements in the twelfth, fourteenth, and sixteenth centuries. Still further additions
and improvements were made by Bishop Cosin (see note 337) during the period between 1661
and 1672. Pevsner, *Buildings . . . Durham,* 119. "The Castle which is the Bishops Pallace stands
on a round hill which has severall green walks round it with high bancks to secure them one
above another, and on the top are the towers; about the middle of the hill is a broad grass walk;
there are very stately good roomes parlours drawing roomes and a noble Hall but the furniture
was not very fine, the best being taken down in the absence of my Lord Crew . . ." Fiennes,
179. "The Episcopal Palace is very strong in its situation, for almost on every side it is on
precipitous rocks; one can still see there the towers and the terraces which are relics of ancient
fortifications which the historians relate have been made there at the time of the wars against
the invasions of the Scots . . ." De Blainville, 25.

332. Nathaniel Crewe (1633–1722), 3rd Baron Crewe of Stene, Northamptonshire. Bishop of
Durham 1674–1722. *DNB,* 13:79–81.

333. John Montague (c. 1655–1728), clergyman. Fellow of Trinity College, Cambridge
University; master 1683–1700; vice-chancellor 1687–1688; dean of Durham 1700–1728; preben-

has the care of an Hospitall 3 miles out of town,[334] the charity of wch is very extroardinary, for 30 poor are maintain'd half of whom have but 40p a year, and yet the Governours place is worth 500^{li} per annum. The 12 Prebends have each 3 or 400^{li} a year, and have 50^{li} amonth allow'd them in their turn to keep residence wch amounting to 600^{li} ayear, besides 100^{li} A year more to the dean, enables the Church to Keep a very noble table, to wch all Strangers are invited that come that way. While I was here I was very much obliged to Dr Adams, rector of Lincoln Colledge in Oxford[335] and to Dr Smith[336] both Prebends of this place for the civility the[y] Shew'd me. by them I got a Sight of the Bishops Library A large collection of curious books of all Sorts and Languages first founded and endow'd by Dr Cosens[337] Bishop of this Place. We also Saw the Church Library wch is a much nobler room but not So well Stock'[d] wth books as the former, yet it has a very valuable collection of Manuscripts and latly Severall peices of Roman Antiquity found at Lanchaster where there was a roman Camp,[338] have been reposited here. The Bishops Pallace

---

dary of Durham 1683–1700; fourth son of Edward Montague, 1st Earl of Sandwich. Venn and Venn, 3:202.

334. Sherburn Hospital, founded c. 1181 for the relief of sixty-five lepers. Montague had been appointed master of the hospital in 1680 and remained in that post until 1727. *Victoria History . . . Durham*, 2:115–17. ". . . they dined at the house of the Dean who after evening prayers escorted them to a Hospice two miles distant from the town, from which he receives 500 pieces for the office of master that he possesses as benefice; yet his house has nothing of note except the ancientness of its foundation . . ." De Blainville, 24.

335. Fitzherbert Adams (c. 1652–1719), clergyman. Rector of Lincoln College, Oxford University, 1685–1719; vice-chancellor 1695–1697; prebendary of Durham 1685–1719. Foster, *Alumni Oxonienses*, 1:5; LeNeve, 3:314, 318–19, 558.

336. John Smith (1659–1715), clergyman. Prebendary of Durham 1695–1715; treasurer 1699–1715; rector of Gateshead 1695–1704. *DNB*, 53:76; Venn and Venn, 4:102–3.

337. John Cosin (1594–1672), bishop of Durham 1660–1672. *DNB*, 12:264–67.

338. Lanchester Fort, lying one-half mile southwest of the village bearing that name. Erected c. 122 A.D., the fort remained in use until the end of the fourth century. The stones in the Chapter Library at Durham dated from the latter part of that period. Some of these had been collected by Dean Montague shortly before Percival's visit. Pevsner, *Buildings . . . Durham*, 179; De Blainville, 24n. ". . . we were made to view the Library of the Chapter which is not very well furnished with books but in recompense one finds there some very good ones either

Newcastle-upon-Tyne, view from the southeast. Samuel and Nathaniel Buck, 1745. Shown in the foreground are the keels used in loading the colliers anchored in the river. Yale Center for British Art, Paul Mellon Collection.

Newcastle
8.

makes a very entertaining landscip wth: the river ware running at its foot, wth: a woode on its banks. I cannot pass by this place without one remark that here are more poor then in any 3 places I came thrô, w^{ch}: may proceed from the number & riches of the clergy. From hence we Set out to Newcastle w^{ch}: is 12 Short miles from it. This is the most trading town in all the North, and contains 5 churches being very populous and rich. The Harbour is very comodious for Ships of great burthen But at Sheals[339] a Small village towards the mouth of the river, Ships of the greatest force may ride. The river tine[340] runs quite thrô the town w^{ch}: Stands very uneven, being built Some part above, and the rest at the bottom of a Steep hill. W:the:1 did Soround it with a wall & built a Strong Castle[341] w^{ch}: now Serves for a gail. Here are Severall handsome houses & a large

manuscripts or printed; one sees a number of inscriptions on freestone, that they claim have been placed there from the time of the Romans, the lettering is all of the same form and is as easily read as that which one finds engraved every day on the tombs of our cemeteries . . ." De Blainville, 24–25.

339. North Shields, Northumberland.

340. The river Tyne.

341. Founded in 1080; the earliest fortification consisted of a motte and bailey, now gone. Portions of a lofty, late Norman keep of 1172–1177 and a twin-tower gatehouse of 1247 are the principal remains. Pevsner, *Buildings . . . Northumberland,* 235–36; King, 2:339. ". . . there was a Castle in this town but now there is noe remains of it but some of the walls which are built up in houses, and soe only appears as a great hill or ascent . . ." Fiennes, 176.

exchange[342] and custom house.[343] The lead mines are 15
miles off, the iron, 4, and the coal pits 1 So that great quantitys
of these effects are transported, especially coal which is the
cheif trade, & employs neer 2000 Leg bullys or Collyers only
to Sail their keels.[344] Some Coal mines are 70 fathom deep
where the Labourers work from 12 a clock at night till twelve
the next day. The great quantitys lay'd up against winter are
preserv'd under Steelhs[345] or houses of wood, the roof of w^{ch}:
being flat have trap doors thrô w^{ch}: they shoot their coal out of
their wagons whos bottom is at the same time taken out. Then
when the coal is to be shipt the way is first to lade their lesser
boats or keels, and out of them the coal is thrown into greater
ships thrô holes made in the sides w^{ch}: afterwards are Stopt up
when they go their voyage. The yearly revennue of the town is
12000^{li} per annum w^{ch}: enables the Major to keep a constant
table, who from the first day of his reign, enters into a noble
house well furnish'd, & evry thing provided being Serv'd in
plate, & this he enjoys a year till the next be chose.[346] The
collyers have now voluntarily laid a tax on themselves for
building an hospitall for their widdows and children, & the
work w^{ch}: is quadrangular promises well.[347] ⟨ In this town lives

342. ". . . there is a noble building in the middle of the town all of stone for an Exchange on
stone pillars severall rows; on the top is a building of a very large Hall for the judges to keep
the assizes . . ." Fiennes, 176.

343. Probably the same building described by Celia Fiennes as a "lofty good building of
stone, very uniforme on all sides with stone pillars in the fronts both to the street and market
place and to the waterside; there is a fine clock on the top just as the Royal Exchange has . . ."
Ibid.

344. "The keel men are those who manage the lighters, which they call keels, by which the
coals are taken from the staithes or wharfs, and carried on board the ships, to load them for
London." Defoe, 535.

345. Possibly *stell*, usually connoting an open enclosure for cattle.

346. Mansion House, built 1691, continued in use as the mayoral residence until 1835.
Woodwork from the parlor of this residence is presently to be seen at Trinity House in
Newcastle-upon-Tyne. Hearnshaw, 106; Pevsner, *Buildings . . . Northumberland,* 23.

347. The Keelmen's Hospital, erected in 1701 at a cost of £2,000, raised primarily through
contributions of the keelmen themselves. It is a large quadrangular structure of brick, having
rather naive decorative detail. Hearnshaw, 106; Pevsner, *Buildings . . . Northumberland,* 261–62.
"Here is a large hospital built by contribution of the keel men, by way of friendly society, for

a Gentleman belonging to the Custom house who by accident
loosing quite his hearing, has by speaking to himself in a glass
made that an imateriall loss for he understands what any
man Says by the motion of their lips even the [Hardest
word?]. I could not See him, but the thing is certainly trew for
tis known to all the North and I was in company w^th: Severall
who all have made the experiment and assure me to be

trew⟩[348] Seven miles from the mouth of the river Stands
Tinmouth Castle[349] upon a rock. Tis not in any order at
present but it might be made a very deffensable & servicable
place in guarding the river. Tis Secure from any attack by sea
and by land there are drawbriges and redoubts ⟨besides a
Strong battery of 26 guns.⟩[350] It was once a Priory and there
are the remains of a very fine built Collegiat Church.[351] The
garison consists of 150 invalids who do duty under Capt:
Floy'd;[352] the governour is Coll: Villars.[353] At Sheals[354] w^ch: is
a mile higher up the river are Severall glasshouses, and Salt-
pans w^ch: latter pay yearly to the king 100000^li.[355] First there

---

the maintenance of the poor of their fraternity, and which, had it not met with discourage-
ments from those who ought rather to have assisted so good a work, might have been a noble
provision for that numerous and laborious people." Defoe, 535.

348. Marginal text, incorporated.

349. Actually Tynemouth Priory, a seventh-century foundation fortified during the Danish
invasions. Permanent works appear to have existed by 1095, when the priory withstood a two-
month siege. Following the Dissolution it continued to be used as a fortress. The barbican and
gatehouse of c. 1400 represent the only substantial remains of the medieval defenses. Church,
chantry, chapter house, and prior's lodgings constitute the primary remains. Pevsner, *Buildings
. . . Northumberland,* 300–304.

350. Marginal text, incorporated.

351. The Norman church was begun in 1090 and completed by 1130. Early English additions
begun c. 1190 are still evident in the chancel area. Pevsner, *Buildings . . . Northumberland,* 302.

352. Capt. Thomas Lloyd (d. 1710), commissioned captain of invalids at Tynemouth Castle
on 25 January 1695. His commission was renewed 3 August 1702. Dalton, 4:112.

353. Sir Edward Villiers (c. 1655–1711), knight marshal of the household and governor of
Tynemouth Castle. He was the son of Edward Villiers of Bartow, Cambridgeshire, and Richmond, Surrey. Venn and Venn, 4:302.

354. See note 339.

355. "Here are two articles of trade which are particularly occasioned by the coals, and
these are glass-houses and salt-pans; the first are at the town it self, the last at Shields, seven

are large iron basons about 7 yards long and 6 broad into
wch the Sea watter is lett in, then when these are full theres a
constant fire underneath wch boils the water till nothing remains but a little Seddiment, then the Sea is let in again and
this is done twice a week for 7 times, so that at last the pans
are fill'd wth the Settlement left by the Sault, wch being of a bay
colour is afterwards temper'd wth ox bloud wch helps to whiten
it and made use of by us on all occasions. Leaving this place
on the 10 we came to Hexam[356] having the River tine Still in
view. we past by a seat of the Ld Darwentwaters[357] where
there is a very large park a thing I did not expect to see in such
a Mountainous country. Hexam is a Small Market town chusing Parliam^t men. The Scituation is very pleasant Standing on
a broad river[358] wch with the river Tine and Severall others in
these parts Swell'd So high by reason of some great rains that
fell that it broke down Severall mills & Spoilt Severall Meadows of corn to the vallue of 5 or 6000^{li} Severall persons were
drown'd and it broke the high ways in many places So that we
were forc'd to break into grown'ds as we came. In this town
Stands an abby Church wch Suffred much by the Scotch[359]
and a Priory wch is now turn'd into a Seat of Sr William Black-
ets.[360] Here we lay a night & Set out next morning for Hart

miles below the town; but their coals are brought cheifly from the town. It is a prodigious
quantity of coals which those salt works consume; and the fires make such a smoke, that we
saw it ascend in clouds over the hills, four miles before we came to Durham, which is at least
sixteen miles from the place." Defoe, 536.

356. Hexham, Northumberland.

357. Edward Radclyffe (1655–1705), 2nd Earl of Derwentwater. Cokayne, *Peerage*, 10:224.
The Earl's seat was Dilston, a fifteenth-century tower-house, enlarged during the Elizabethan
era and again in the seventeenth century by the 2nd Earl. Pevsner, *Buildings . . . Northumberland*,
137; King, 2:331.

358. Devil's Water.

359. The monastic church of Hexham Priory, which survived devastating raids by the Scots
in 1296 and the decades following. The church was built c. 1180–1250 and substantially altered
during the Victorian era. Pevsner, *Buildings . . . Northumberland*, 171; Lloyd, "The Seat of an
Ancient Bishopric," 8.

360. Sir William Blackett of Newcastle-upon-Tyne, Northumberland (c. 1657–1705), 1st
Baronet. M.P. for Newcastle 1685–1690, 1695–1700, and 1705; sheriff of Northumberland
1688–1689. Cokayne, *Baronetage*, 4:135. Blackett's seat was the so-called Abbey House, incorpo-

II.   whistle,[361] a poor market town govern'd by Bailifs. In the Afternoon we came to Carlile[362] Crossing the famous Picts wall[363] at Thurlow Castle.[364] This wall beginning At the Sea 6 miles from Carlile crost the Country to Tinmouth Castle or there abouts. Tis hard to guess how high it was at first, but tis now found in some places to be 3 yards high, and where we past it it was two at least, & 5 or 6 broad having a Trench on the North Side, and we find that where there was lest need of any as one the Crags and Steep hills the trench ran on the South side, but in plain ground to defend the wall better it lay allways on the north. At each mile end we are told there Stood a tower[365] wch our guide confirm'd who living near, & being a Mason by trade had us'd many of the stones in building, and he assur'd us that the outsides of the wall was all of wrought Stones and thee filling up of whin Stone[366] harder then flint or marble[.] the story of a brass whispering pipe running thrô the wall be contradicted.[367]¶

---

rating fragments of Hexham Priory's early monastic buildings, added to by Sir Reginald Carnaby in 1539. Most of the surviving fabric, however, dates from the reconstruction that followed in the wake of a fire in 1818. Lloyd, 92.

361. Haltwhistle, Northumberland.

362. Carlisle, Cumberland.

363. Hadrian's Wall, built by that emperor 122–130 A.D. to secure Roman Britain's northern frontier. More than seventy miles long, the wall stretched from Solway Firth north of Carlisle to the river Tyne near Tynemouth Castle, situated over much of its length on an escarpment of volcanic rock. Pevsner, *Buildings . . . Northumberland,* 17–18.

364. Thirlwall Castle, a ruinous tower situated just north of Hadrian's Wall in a low-lying area of land near Haltwhistle between the South Tyne and the Fithing rivers. Supposedly dating from the first half of the fourteenth century, it was built largely with materials taken from the great wall. Ibid., 296; MacKenzie, 2:422.

365. At each mile interval were gates defended by garrisons quartered in small forts or "milecastles," roughly fifty by sixty feet in size. Between each of these were two signal towers placed at intervals of five hundred forty yards. Pevsner, *Buildings . . . Northumberland,* 17–18.

366. Whinstone. A term applied to various hard, dark-colored rocks as basalt, chert, greenstone, or quartzose sandstone. Only the ashlar face of the wall was laid in mortar, the rubble core being set in puddled clay. Ibid., 18.

367. "The Inhabitants tell you that there was also a Brazen Trumpet or Pipe (whereof they now and then find pieces) so artificially laid in the wall between each castle and tower, that upon the apprehension of danger at any single place, by the sounding of it, notice might be

Carlile[368] is a Small citty containing 2 Parishes There are sever- Carlile.
all good houses in it and the Streets are broad & well pav'd. Tis
Sorounded by a high wall and trench and defended by two Castles[369] and 2 or 3 rivers being a garison under the Ld Carlile.[370]
No boat can come within 3 miles of the town, yet here is a custom house for Scotch cloth and flax which pays the King some
years 6000^li. The Cathedrall make[s] now no great show, being
but part of a much nobler building ruin'd by the Scotch in the
troubles of 41.[371] The Quire is neat enough and there is to it
besides the Bishop a Dean 4 prebends a Chancelor and Arch
Deacon. We went on Satturday to Lanwharf a village within the 13.
borders of Scotland, to get to it we forded the river Salk famous
for Trout, wch river devides the 2 kingdoms. We found in this
place very good french wine for an English Shilling a quart, but
the rest of our entertainment was very indifferent.[372] The monday following we left Carlile & came to Cockermore[373] a neat 15.
Burgess town. Thrô it there runs a pretty large river but very Cockermore
shallow and rappid, and neer it Stands a Castle[374] belonging to

---

given to the next, then to the third, and so on." Gibson, 839.

368. See note 362.

369. The first of these two structures was Carlisle Castle. Built shortly after 1157, it consisted
of two wards with a keep situated within the inner ward. The second was a triangular gun-
castle built in 1541 by Henry VIII, incorporating a portion of the town wall. Only the base of
one tower remains, as the site is now occupied by Smirke's assize courts building of 1810–1811.
Pevsner, *Buildings . . . Cumberland*, 98, 101; King, 1:83.

370. Charles Howard (1669–1738), 3rd Earl of Carlisle. Cokayne, *Peerage*, 3:35.

371. Carlisle Cathedral, erected during the twelfth and thirteenth centuries. Only two of the
nave's original eight bays survive, the rest having been destroyed by the Scots between 1645
and 1652. Pevsner, *Buildings . . . Cumberland*, 88.

372. In a letter to Oxford schoolmate Digby Cotes, Percival gave a rather more detailed and
humorous account of this day's journey. See the Appendix, pp. 186–87, for the full text of this
letter. Until his visit to Lanwharf, Percival had planned to tour portions of Scotland as well as
England. To Cotes he wrote, ". . . my first days accomodations were So bad, that they deterr'd
me from advancing farther to Edinborrough as I first intended." Percival to Cotes, 18 September 1701, Add. Mss. 47025, 54v.

373. Cockermouth, Cumberland.

374. Cockermouth Castle. Consisting of two wards, the castle was built during the mid
thirteenth century, though what survives of the medieval work is of the period 1360–1370.
Pevsner, *Buildings . . . Cumberland*, 107.

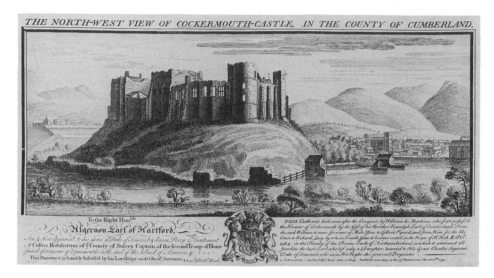

THE NORTH-WEST VIEW OF COCKERMOUTH-CASTLE, IN THE COUNTY OF CUMBERLAND.

Cockermouth Castle, Cumberland. Samuel and Nathaniel Buck, 1739. British Museum.

Whithaven

the Duke of Someset[375] where he comonly comes once a year.[376] Here is a free School[377] and a good market on mondays. In the Afternoon we got to Whithaven[378] a Seaport town being well Scituated for the Irish trade. This town is very well built the Streets being broad and regular and the houses very large and even. within 40 years ago there were not 40 houses now by their own industry & S.[r] John Louthers[379] help they have 6 or 700.[380] S.[r] John who has a Seat just without

375. See note 149.

376. In 1649 the castle buildings were stripped of their roofing and thereafter fell into decay. By 1676 only the gatehouse and a small portion of the north range were habitable. In 1682–1683, some limited repairs were made, possibly to render the castle fit for reception of the Duke on these annual visits. Jackson-Stops, 149, 210–11.

377. The free grammar school was founded in 1676 by Phillip, Lord Wharton, Sir George Fletcher, Sir Richard Graham, and others. *Cassell's Gazetteer,* [2]:69; Hutchinson, 2:116–17.

378. Whitehaven, Cumberland.

379. Sir John Lowther of Whitehaven, Cumberland (1642–1706), 2nd Baronet. Founder and patron of the town of Whitehaven. Hainsworth, 677.

380. The Whitehaven estate had come into the possession of the Lowther family early in the seventeenth century. Some time following the death of his father in 1644, Sir John Lowther began to develop Whitehaven, planting a new town just northeast of the old village. This was one of the earliest planned towns in postmedieval Britain.

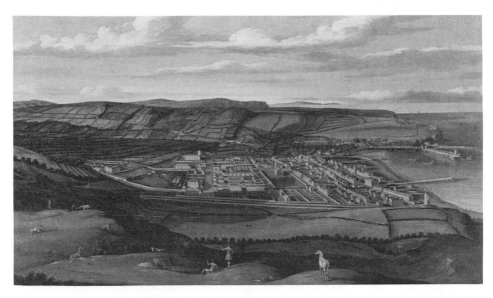

Whitehaven, Cumberland, view from the northeast. Matthias Read, c. 1732. Shown at the left is Flatt Hall, the seat of Sir John Lowther. Yale Center for British Art, Paul Mellon Collection.

it[381] built A Church[382] and free School[383] and owns most part of the town. The Harbour will hold neer a 100 Shipps and there are 70 belonging to the Inhabitants, who fetch great quantitys of tobacko from Virginia,[384] and transport to Ireland much coal & Iron Oar. One M.[r] Addison[385] who lives in the place and owns Some mines told us he has one a mile from the town the Oar of w.[ch] yeilds one third pure mettall,

381. Lowther's house, Flatt Hall, stood just southeast of the town, having been purchased from Sir George Fletcher in 1675 for the sum of £1,000. Hainsworth, 684.

382. St. Nicholas, built by Lowther in 1693. It was replaced by the present church of 1883. Pevsner, *Buildings . . . Cumberland,* 203.

383. In addition to a church and a grammar school, Lowther also built (or subscribed to the construction of) such public works as a customhouse, wharves, an inn, etc. Hainsworth, xxi.

384. William Byrd later sold tobacco through the Whitehaven mercantile firm of How & Kelsick. Tinling, 2:498–99.

385. Thomas Addison (b. 1641), Whitehaven merchant, officeholder, and iron smelter. For a period of time, Addison was in business partnership with Sir John Lowther of Whitehaven (see note 379). Hainsworth, 671.

tis carry'd in ballast to Ireland and there melted for wood is
here Scarce, but this Gentleman is certain of a way he has
found to do it wth. Sea cole.[386] The Ile of man Stands 9 leagues
from this Shoar and we could plainly See it from the top of a
hill neer the town.[387]¶

16.
17.
Cheswick

The next day after dinner we return'd to Cockermore and
the[re] after came to Cheswyck[388] a market town wch. Stands
very low, and is an unhealthy Scituation by reason of the
Standing waters neer it for there being no drayn to the great
quantitys of water that yearly pour down the hills wch. soround
it once in 6 or 7 years there rises pestilentiall vapours w.^ch.
bring a malignant fever and carry off Severall of the Inhabitants. Notwithstanding this, tis populous by reason of the
great trade drove in Saddles and bridles, wch. are Sent from
hence to Scotland and the West Indys. In the Afternoon we

Perith

came to Perith[389] a Small market tow[n] well inhabited and
very rich. Onn one side there Stand the ruins of an antient
Castle.[390] The next day we visited Mr Charles Howard[391] a
gentleman of good Sence and learning but a roman Catholick.

Greystock

He lives at Graystock[392] an old Castle of wch. Sort of building
all the North is full all Gentlemens Seats being no other by

386. Addison's experiments must have been among the eariest such efforts, as the first
successful use of coke in the smelting of iron ore was not recorded until 1709, in Broseley,
Shropshire. Even then, coke did not see widespread use in this application until much later.
Singer et al., 80–81.

387. Possibly the same hill from which Mathias Read took his view of Whitehaven in 1738.

388. Keswick, Cumberland.

389. Penrith, Cumberland.

390. Penrith Castle, a massive square structure built around an interior court, with two
projecting towers—one on the east range and one on the north. It appears to have been built
shortly after 1397, when William Strickland (later bishop of Carlisle and archbishop of Canter-
bury) was given a license to crenellate. Pevsner, *Buildings . . . Cumberland,* 175.

391. Charles Howard of Greystoke, Cumberland (d. 1713), 4th son of Henry Frederick
Howard, 25th Earl of Arundel. Gillow, 3:420; Cokayne, *Peerage,* 9:625–26.

392. Greystoke Castle, a fourteenth-century pele tower built by William, Lord Greystoke,
and destroyed by the parliamentary army in 1648. A later house built c. 1675 by the Howards
(that seen by Percival and Byrd) was altered beyond recognition in the late eighteenth and mid
nineteenth centuries. Pevsner, *Buildings . . . Cumberland,* 133.

reason of the frequent inroads of the Scots before king James
the first's reign. This Stands 4 mile from Perith & has to it two
Parks one four mile distant among the hills, tis terminated by
a lake 3 mile long and one broad call'd Hulls water,[393] tis in
some places 30 fathom deep, in it are taken very large trouts,
Perch, Chars[394] & Skellys[395] a fish that drives about in
Shoales[396] like Herrings, and are not much unlike them, neither do the[y] live longer when out of the water. Upon this
lake we had the diversion of hunting a [Perch?] w^{ch}: being hard
prest allways takes [this?] and then are drawn alive into the
boat. The next day we went to See Lansdale,[397] a new Seat of
the late L^{d}: Lansdales[398] building. The Stone of w^{ch}: it is built is
very bad Containing so much niter[399] that it has Spoilt some
excellent workmanship of Varios[400] by Sweating. The Hall
w^{ch}: is the first room we came into is all inlaid and as I Say'd
before the tryall of Hercules Alexander & Cæsar w^{ch}: was the

18.

Lansdale

393. Ullswater, situated along the border between Cumberland and Westmoreland.

394. A small, troutlike fish, *Salmo savelinus,* inhabiting lakes in the mountainous areas of the
North and Wales.

395. The gwyniad or fresh-water herring, *Coregonus clupeoides.*

396. A school of fish.

397. Lonsdale or Lowther Hall, built 1692–1695 for Sir John Lowther (see note 398). William
Talman is known to have provided a design for the house, though it is unclear whether this was
the scheme actually built. The house was destroyed by fire in 1718. Colvin, *Biographical Dictionary,*
805–6. "I went to it through fine woods, the front is just faceing the great road from Kendall and
lookes very nobly, with severall rows of trees which leads to large iron gates, into the stable yard
which is a fine building on the one side of the house very uniform, and just against it is such
another row of buildings the other side of the house like two wings which is the offices . . . these
are just equal and alike and encompass the two sides of the first court which enters with large
iron gates and iron palasadoes in the breadth; there is 4 large squares of grass in which there is a
large statue of stone in the midst of each and 4 little Cupids or little boys in each corner of the 4
squares; this is just the front of the house where you enter a porch with pillars of lime stone but
the house is the red sort of stone of the country . . ." Fiennes, 170–71.

398. Sir John Lowther of Lowther, Westmoreland (1655–1700), 2nd Baronet, later 1st Viscount Lonsdale. Cousin once removed of Sir John Lowther of Whitehaven (see note 379).
Lowther had died in July of the preceding year. Hainsworth, 678; Cokayne, *Peerage,* 8:131

399. Native sodium carbonate.

400. See note 114.

greatest man is painted on the walls wch. cost 500^{li}.[401] The
house is very convenient and has much gardening about it, thô
my L^{d}. had he liv'd would have greatly improv'd them, for he
had great designs that way. It Stands very high and every way
there is a delicate Prospect, and behind it is a terras 500 yards
long.[402] S^{r}. William Louther of Yorkshire[403] very civily
Shew'd us the house and Gardins and then we return'd to
Graystock by a Small seat belonging to M^{r}. Byrd a La[w]yer.[404]

401. Painted by Verrio during his employment at Lowther Hall, 1694–1698. This room was
celebrated in Tickell's poem "Oxford" (1707), addressed to the 2nd Viscount Lonsdale:

Such art as this adorns Lowther's hall,
Where feasting gods carouse upon the wall;
The nectar, which creating paint supplies,
Intoxicates each pleas'd spectator's eyes;
Who view, amaz'd, the figures heavenly fair,
And think they breath the Elysian air.
With strokes so bold, great Verrio's hand has drawn
The gods in dwellings brighter than their own.
Croft-Murray, 239.

". . . you are landed into a noble hall very lofty, the top and side are exquisitely painted by the
best hand in England which did the painting at Windsor; the top is the Gods and Goddesses
that are sitting at some great feast and a great tribunal before them, each corner is the Seasons
of the yeare with the variety of weather, raines and rainbows stormy winds sun shine snow and
frost with multitudes of other fancyes and varietyes in painting, and looks very natural—it cost
500£ that roome alone . . ." Fiennes, 171.

402. "The house is a flatt rooffe and stands amidst a wood of rows of trees which with these
statues and those in two gardens on each side (which for their walks and plantations is not
finish'd but full of statues) which with the house is so well contrived to be seen at one view . . ."
Ibid.

403. Probably Sir William Lowther of Marske, Yorkshire, and Holker, Lancashire (1670–
1705), 1st Baronet. M.P. for Lancaster 1702–1705. Cokayne, *Baronetage*, 4:171.

404. James Bird of Brougham Hall, Westmoreland (c. 1637–1714), attorney for Sir John
Lowther of Whitehaven (see note 379). Westmoreland gentlemen bearing this name were
admitted to Gray's Inn in 1674, and again in 1687. Hainsworth, 672; Foster, *Register of Admissions*, 318–19. By an indenture of 1676, James Bird had reunited the Brougham estate under the
Bird family for the first time in three hundred fifty years. Although rebuilt in the nineteenth
century, the house supposedly incorporated fragments of earlier structures dating from the
twelfth and fourteenth centuries. It was demolished in 1934. Nearby stand a number of rubble
outbuildings probably dating from Bird's time. Nicolson and Burn, 1:394–95; Royal Commission on Historic Monuments, 63; MacKenzie, 2:285.

This has Some good gardening and is So enclos'd wth wood
that tis a difficult matter to find it out.[405] On Monday M^r   22.
Howard carry'd us to see Sr Harry Fletcher[406] a very curtius
Gentleman, but has chang'd his religion when he was in
France.[407] His Castle is Holton[408] 3 miles from Graystock   Holton
and has a Park to it thrô wch are cut severall vistos. This Gentleman is a great lover of horses and has a very fine breed for
racing at this time. The same day we went to see one M^r
Fetherston[409] a Gentleman living 7 miles off at the ancient
seat of the Dacres.[410] A quarter of a mile from it are the

405. ". . . the hall . . . obtained the name of *Birdnest* . . . partly on account of his {Bird's}
name, and partly form the appearance of the house at that time, which was almost hid by the
trees . . . In the old part of the house the rooms have squared ceilings, ornamented with coats
of armour in stucco work, carved mantle pieces, with foliage, fruits and arms. The hall, which
is lofty, has five Gothic windows, each completely fitted up with painted glass, some of which
is the old stain, and has anciently been there . . ." Hutchinson, 1:303, 305.

406. Sir Henry (Harry) Fletcher of Hutton-in-the-Forest, Cumberland (1661–1712), 3rd Baronet. M.P. for Cockermouth 1689–1690. Cokayne, *Baronetage,* 2:83. In 1710 Fletcher settled his
estate on his "Popish Steward" and distant cousin, Thomas Fletcher of Moresby, Cumberland,
and retired to a monastery of English monks at Donay, in France, where he died in 1712.
Cornforth, "Hutton-in-the-Forest," 288.

407. According to one contemporary source, it was in Flanders that "some said he first lost
his religion, others that he only finished the foundation laid by some before, and though he did
not upon his return publicly declare himself a Papist yet he gave much cause to suspect it, to
his Father's great affliction." Soon after the death of his father in 1700, he made known his
change of religion, but would never "bear ye touching upon his (prsum'd) desertion of his
Protestant faith." Cornforth, "Hutton-in-the-Forest," 288.

408. Hutton-in-the-Forest. When the estate came into the Fletcher family in 1606, the house
consisted of a fourteenth-century pele tower and a later hall wing. To this, Sir Henry Fletcher
added a long gallery about 1640. Between 1675 and 1680 his grandson, Sir George Fletcher,
enlarged the living quarters and dressed the resulting pile in a new classical front. Ibid.,
233–35.

409. Timothy Fetherstonhaugh of Kirkoswald, Cumberland (c. 1658–1728), high sheriff of
Cumberland 1697. Described on his gravestone as "pious, upright, peacable, and inclined to
mercy." Fetherstonhaugh and Haswell, 223–25; Hudleston and Boumphrey, 111.

410. The College of Kirkoswald, founded in 1523 and purchased by the Fetherstonhaugh
family some years after the Dissolution. Most of the present stone building was erected during
Timothy Fetherstonhaugh's ownership, though earlier work is visible in the rear. While the
college itself was never actually occupied by the Dacres family, it did stand in the shadow of
Kirkoswald Castle (see next note), one of the family's Cumberland seats. It was only in this

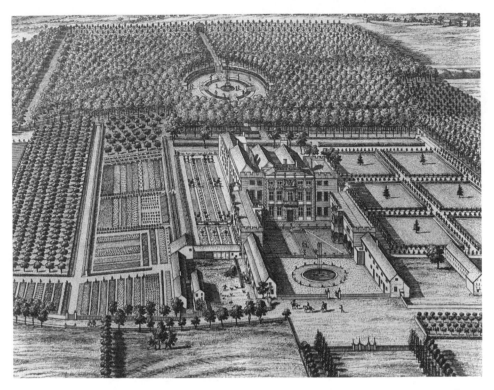

Hutton-in-the-Forest, Cumberland. Johannes Kip after Leonard Knyff, c. 1700. *Country Life.*

remains of an old castle wch. belong'd to the same family,[411] the walls of wch. are So thick, & ⟨the⟩[412] Moat to this day so deep that it must have been a place of considerable strength.

23.

We returnd in the Afternoon to Holton and the next day Set out for Kendall dining at Shop[413] a Small town of no remark Save for a rige of Stones near half a mile long wch. some have thôught an Artificiall work, but I rather beleive it naturally to

Kendal

be so Since the whole hill is of the same Stone & no cement

indirect sense that Fetherstonhaugh lived "off at the antient seat of the Dacres." Fetherston-haugh and Haswell, 196, 205, 216; Pevsner, *Buildings . . . Cumberland,* 150–51.

411. Kirkoswald Castle, a northern quadrangular castle, probably built in the fourteenth century and expanded c. 1500 by Thomas, Lord Dacre. Remains of three towers still stand, one of them quite large—possibly an early keep incorporated into later construction. King, 1:87–88; MacKenzie, 2:319.

412. Text struck through.

413. Shap, Westmoreland.

appears. At night we came to Kendal a Market town govern'd
by a Major 12 Aldermen & c. This is the County town for
Westmorland and is a Barony the title of which is affix'd to
the Royall Family & Prince George of Denmark now enjoys it.
It is Scituated on the river Kan[414] wch. is not navigable over
but there are 2 fine Stone briges over it. The town is neer a
mile long being all of tild houses. It drives a rich trade in
cotton, and woolen cloth & in Linnen & wosted Stockings.
Here is the broadest Parish Church I ever Saw Standing upon
4 rows of Pillars.[415] In it there is now an Organ about to be
Set up and an Allowance for Singing men & boys rais'd by
contribution. On one side of the river Stands an old Castle[416]
moated round but now ruin'd wch. was the birthplace of
Catherine Par,[417] on the town side is a Steep Mount cast up
sorounded wth. trenches, cast up very probably to batter the
Castle for tis within the retch of Cannon Shot.[418] We here got
acquainted wth. M^r. Crosby the Minister of the place[419] who is
a very ingenuous & well accomplish'd Gentleman, he confirm'd to us what we had read of a great fall of water of about
5 yards wch. at the approach of fowl weather makes but a
Small noise but in fair weather is heard very farr.[420] Here

414. The river Kent.

415. Holy Trinity Church, dating from the thirteenth and the late fifteenth–early sixteenth
centuries. The church is rectilinear in plan, having double aisles flanking either side of the
nave. Pevsner, *Buildings . . . Cumberland*, 253.

416. Kendal Castle, a twelfth-century earthwork and ditch encompassing a masonry curtain
wall with four towers, all dating from the thirteenth century. Ibid., 256.

417. Catherine Parr (1512–1548).

418. A large motte and bailey, known as Castle How, predecessor of the present castle.
Pevsner, *Buildings . . . Cumberland*, 258n; King, 2:492.

419. William Crosby (1644–1733), vicar of Kendall 1699–1733. Venn and Venn, 1:425. One
source credits Crosby with "an extraordinary character of sanctity, charity, and other amiable
qualities." Nicolson and Burn, 1:77.

420. "Lower in the river *Can*, there are two *Water-falls*, where the water is tumbled headlong
with a hideous noise; one at a little village call'd *Levens*, another more Southward near *Betham*
. . . From these the neighbours draw certain prognostications of the weather: for when the
Northern one has a clear sound, they promise themselves fair weather; but when the Southern,
rain and mists." Gibson, 805. See also Brome, 209.

25.
Lancaster

26.
Preston.

Haigh

plenty of Samon are cought, for leaping out of the water with intention to get over the fall the Fishermen are prepared wth: a long hook and then dexterously Strike them. On the 25 we came to Lancaster the County town of the Palatinate of Lancashire. This town Stands on the river Lone[421] w^{ch}: two miles afterwards falls into an arm of the sea. Tis Scituated on the side of a hill, on the top of w^{ch}: is a very large Strong Castle kept Still in good repair because in it is kept the Sizes, and Prisoners.[422] Neer it is a large Church[423] w^{ch}: is the only one in town. Here is little inland trade besides flax but its cheif trade lys outward towards Virginia, & Portugall. From hence we came the next day to Preston a neat market and Burrow town consisting of 3 broad streets besides lesser ones. The houses are many built of brick and are large and regular. So many gentry live in it & neer it that tis call'd little London Here is no manefacture only a little flax, nor no navigable river comes within a mile to it. Four miles from it Stands a handsome Seat belonging to S^r: Roger Bradshaih[424] w^{ch}: is to be seen at a great distance by reason of its high Scituation. This thô it Seems to Stand bleak is shelterd by the groves Sorounding it. There is nothing regular in the house it having been built at Severall time, when convenience was only consulted. From the top may be Seen 13 countys besides the Ile of

421. The river Lune.

422. Lancaster Castle, a quadrangular enclosure surrounding a Norman keep, with a gatehouse and three towers situated along its perimeter. The keep was completed by 1102. The largest of the towers and its connecting range of buildings were added during the thirteenth century, and the gatehouse was completed c. 1400. The complex is still used by the county's courts and prison. Pevsner, *Buildings . . . North Lancashire*, 156; King, 1:246; MacKenzie, 2:194–96.

423. St. Mary, originally the church of a Benedictine priory founded 1094. The present nave and chancel are predominately in the Perpendicular style of the fifteenth century, though earlier work from the Roman, Saxon, and Norman periods is visible. Pevsner, *Buildings . . . North Lancashire*, 153–54.

424. Sir Roger Bradshaigh of Haigh Hall, Lancashire (1675–1747), 3rd Baronet. M.P. for Wigan 1695–1747. Cokayne, *Baronetage*, 4:110. Sir Roger's seat, Haigh Hall, was a house of the late Elizabethan era, to which a large rear wing had apparently been added sometime during the seventeenth century. The house was demolished in 1827. Harris, 219.

man.[425] S.[r] Roger has a considerable part of his estate out of
Pitts of kennel[426] a Sort of cole of So fine a nature that it
keeps a constant flame till burnt to ashes. This does not dirty
if taken in hand, but is of a hard Substance resembling flint
and pollishes like jet looking like it in colour also when so
manadg'd.[427] In winter time poor people buy it to Serve
instead of candle. In these pitts are found vitriol Springs
where evry quart of water will yeild an ounce of Salt. a mile
from hence is Wigan a large Parish containing neer 900
houses. It is a Major town & drives a great trade in all Sorts of
bedding, Pewter, brass, & Iron work. It is worth 500.[li] a year
to the Bishop of Chester[428] who holds it with his Bishoprick,
& to which it is to be anex'd. I had the honour to be made a
Burgess while I was here of this corporation.[429] Severall Gentlemens Seats Stand here about as M.[r] Standishes a romanist[430]
where we din'd on the 28, M.[r] Ashurst[431] where we din'd the

Wigan

425. "The hall is a stately edifice of brick, faced with stone, with three semi-circular pro-
jections in front. Over the door are the arms of Bradshaigh, quartered with Stanley. Placed
near the summit of a high hill . . . the house commands a view of 13 counties, of the Irish sea,
and the Isle of Man; and by the liberality of the earl, the publick are admitted almost without
limitation." Baines, 3:553.

426. Cannel. A bituminous coal that burns with a very bright flame, now used extensively
in the manufacture of coal oils and gas.

427. "In *Haigh* near Wigan, in the grounds of Sir *Roger Bradshaigh*, there are very plentiful
and profitable mines of an extraordinary Coal. Besides the clear flame it yeilds in burning, it
has been curiously polish'd into the appearance of black marble, and fram'd into large Candle-
sticks, Sugar-boxes, Spoons, with many other such sorts of vessels; which have been presented
as curiosities, and met with very good acceptance both in London and beyond sea." Gibson,
802.

428. Nicholas Stratford (1633–1707), bishop of Chester 1689–1707. *DNB*, 55:33.

429. The corporation was empowered to admit nonresident and honorary burgesses to vote
in elections without limitation. In 1802, one hundred such burgesses were made to obtain an
outcome unfavorable to the Duke of Portland. *Victoria History . . . Lancaster*, 4:73.

430. Probably William Standish of Standish Hall, Lancashire (1618–1705). Foster, *Pedigrees*,
vol. 1. His seat was Standish Hall, a moated house, noted for its traditional association with the
Lancashire plot of 1694. Baines, 3:505.

431. Probably Thomas Henry Ashurst of Ashurst, Lancashire (1672–1744), high sheriff of
Lancaster 1694. Foster, *Pedigrees*, vol 1, {f.5}; Baines, 3:557. Ashurst Hall, a house of the mid

day following, & M.ʳ Dickison[432] where we also din'd, a Romanist also.¶

We had the honour while we were at S.ʳ Roger Bradshaighs to
be elected Burgesses for the town of Wiggan After which we
were complimented by the Major who told us we were the
honestest Burgesses in the Corporation as haveing hitherto not
falsify'd the oath we took upon our election.[433] On the 6 of
Oct. we Set out for Winnyck[434] Say'd to be the richest Par-
sonage in England w.ᶜʰ M.ʳ Finch[435] to whose house we went
now enjoys.¶

In the way 2 miles from Wiggan is a burning well So nam'd
because it will burn like brandy. the method to make it do so
is first to empty the bason & afterwards Stiring the mud to put
a candle to it, & presently there will be a flame all over it.[436]¶
In this town there is nothing very remarkable, but neer it is
dug a very rich marl, with w.ᶜʰ a feild that lys not far from the
Church was 84 years ago Strew'd. Since that time it has never
been marld, yet it has bore every year a large crop, So that it
has rais'd an estate of 400.ˡⁱ per annum to the owner. The
nature of this marl is that unless the Earth is almost quite
dispirited twill work no effect. M.ʳ Finch Shew'd me while I
was here, a walking Stick made out of an oak dug up from

Oct.
6
Winick

seventeenth century, was situated in Dalton. Pevsner, *Buildings . . . North Lancashire,* III; Baines,
3:557.

432. Probably William Dicconson of Wrightington Hall, Lancashire (1655–1743), a promi-
nent Catholic and zealous Jacobite. Dicconson spent much time in the court of the exiled royal
family at St. Germain. Gillow, 2:60–61.

433. See note 429.

434. Winwick, Lancashire.

435. Henry Finch (1679–1728), prebendary of Ely 1690–1714 and York 1695–1704; rector of
Winwick, Lancashire, 1692–1725. He was the son of Heneage Finch (1621–1682), 1st Earl of
Nottingham. Venn and Venn, 2:138.

436. "Within a mile and a half of *Wiggan,* is a Well; which does not appear to be a spring,
but rather rain-water. At first sight, there's nothing about it that seems extraordinary; but upon
emptying it, there presently breaks out a sulphureous vapour, which makes the water bubble
up as if it boyl'd. A Candle being put to it, it presently takes fire, and burns like brandy. The
flame, in a calm season, will continue sometimes a whole day; by the heat whereof they can
boyl eggs, meat, *&c,* tho' the water itself be cold . . . The same water taken out of the Well will
not burn; as neither the mud . . ." Gibson, 802.

underground in the Ile of Man. Thrô long lying there it is
become black & will pollish like ebony. In this Country are
many large fir trees dug out in the Same manner which are of
better use to the poor then candles, for when cut into that
Shape, they keep a constant flame and dont melt as candles
would do when they peap into their ovens & Pitts wth: them.
One thing to be noted in these trees is that they are found to
lye all one way w^{ch}: is an argum^t: for the deluge.437 Being but 2
miles from Warington438 wc went on the 9th: thither. Tis a
large Market town containing 2 principall Streets. making of
pins employs the poorer Sort of people. Here is a fair Stone
brige wth: 5 arches that joins Lancashire to Cheshire over the
river Mersey. On the Spring tides this river is very troublesome filling the roads and neighbouring feilds often times in a
year, So that people are often drown'd. In this town we Saw a
Strange production of nature wth: the help of art, An Alderman
and Appothecary of the town has found out a liquor to Steep
corn in, w^{ch}: having done himself & afterwards Set produc'd
Some roots of 162 Stalks. each being Strong & large. while the
corn was yet green a cow cropt it, but the remaining Stubble I
had in my hand. Since one root can come but from one grain
& this liquor is very cheap, this experim^t: may turn to very
good account.¶
Within 5 miles of this town is a very great Salt work439 w^{ch}: thô
not many years past discovred has had Such vent that the

9.
Warington

437. ". . . there is no reason to admire, that so many Trees in places of this nature throughout England, but particularly in this County, should lye overwhelm'd, and as it were buried in
the ground For when the roots of them were loosen'd by reason of too great moisture of the
earth, 'twas impossible but they should fall, and so sink and be drown'd in such a soil. The
people hereabouts . . . dig them, and use them for firing. For they burn clear, and give a light
as good as Torches . . . And for this reason, [t]he vulgar think they have been *Firr-trees;* which
Cæsar denys to have grown in Britain. I know the opinion generally receiv'd is, that these have
remain'd here ever since the Deluge, being then beat down by the violence of the waters . . .
But as for these points, we may expect more light into them from the curious Philosophers of
this age." Ibid., 789.

438. Warrington, Lancashire.

439. Percival probably referred here to the works at Marbury near Northwich where rock
salt was found in 1670. Ormerod, 1:71.

Leverpool

owners have 60 yards underground clear'd a cave resembling a Cathedrall for its highth & extent being Supported by Pillars very regularly cut. In the Afternoon we came to Leverpool[440] So call'd from Lavar a Small bird w^{ch}: frequented a pool neer the town. it was about the bigness of a magpy being all black but the bill w^{ch}: was very large & red as were the legs w^{ch}: were like those of a duck. This is a large Market & Burgess town Stands on the Mouth of the river Mersey & gives a fair passage to Ireland. It is neer 3 quarters of a mile long & as broad, containing 2 Parishes thô but one Church,[441] but there is now a very fine one building after the patirn of St Andrews at London[442] w^{ch}: will cost 5 or 6000^{li}. The cheif trade of this town is in the importation of tobacko, & exportation of Salt w^{ch}: is made here in great quantitys. Here is also a large Sugar work for refining the worser Sort & making it into loaf.[443] In the managing this day is made use of w^{ch}: being wet to cover a pot of this Sugar drives down the groser parts of it into a receiver So that w^t: remains becomes hard & white. To this Port belongs neer a 100 Ships, but many of them have been damag'd by a late Storm, (w^{ch}: we were Sensible of when at Haigh) there never was known So violent a one before. had it happen'd on a Spring tide it had drown'd all the town, but as it was it drove the vessells close to the houses, broke down the Key wall & washt away much timber w^{ch}: lay ready for building. The Damage is computed to 3 or 4000^{li} to this town only.

440. Liverpool, Lancashire.

441. St. Nicholas, the parish church for Walton Parish, of which Liverpool was a part. Built c. 1360 and destroyed during World War II. *Victoria History . . . Lancaster,* 4:25; Pevsner, *Buildings . . . South Lancashire,* 151.

442. Owing to the rapid growth it had experienced during the latter part of the seventeenth century, Liverpool was cut off from the parish and provided with a new church, St. Peter, which was consecrated in 1704. *Victoria History . . . Lancaster,* 4:45. "The new church built on the north side of town is worth observation. 'Tis a noble, large building, all of stone, well finished; has in it a fine font of marble placed in the body of the church, surrounded with a beautiful iron pallisado. There is a beautiful tower to this church, and a new ring of eight very good bells." Defoe, 543.

443. Possibly the sugar-house built c. 1668 in Redcross Street by one "Mr. Smith, a great sugar-baker at London." *Victoria History . . . Lancaster,* 4:23, 23n.

There happen'd at this time a very extroardinary peice of
providence. A Ship then riding in the river at Anchor was
forc'd loose and beat to peices; 2 boys who accidentally Stay'd
aboard Seeing the danger clim'd up to the mast head in hopes
to prolong their drowning. they hung by this mast Some time
till at last a Sudden gust of wind blew the Ship quite on one
Side wch. Swung the boys off, & mircaculously they fell into the
Ships boat wch. was forc'd from her Side & lay floating neer it.
Very fortunately the tyde Soon went out & left the Boat upon
the Sand, where accidentally they found an old oak with w^{ch}.
when the next tyde came in they guided her to a point where
they both landed Safe. In the town live Severall rich Merchants
who have very noble houses, & the free Schooles[444] Custom
house & exchange[445] are very handsom building[s]. The King
last year receiv'd 60000^{li} without drawbacks & indeed the
town is very populous, & thô it has lost 50000^{li} by the last war,
yet has it within this 13 years got as much more. Here is an old
Castle[446] of which my L^{d}. Macklesfeild[447] is Governour but tis
of no manner of use. The only thing here wanting is water w^{ch}.
must be Sent for half a mile and yet tasts brackish. One thing
peculiar to this town is that who ever is free of it is at the Same
time free of Waterford & Wexford in Irland, & Bristoll[448] and
while we were here the Major forc'd us to accept the honour of
being made freemen. We Set out from hence on the 11 for   11.
chester crossing over the river which is here about 2 miles

444. A free grammar school was founded in 1515 through the bequest of John Crosse, vicar
of St. Nicholas, Fleshambles, in London. In 1673 the school was quartered in the Chapel of St.
Mary del Key, close by St. Nicholas Church. Ibid., 2:593, 4:43.

445. A new town hall was built in 1673, being "plac'd on pillars and arches of hewn stone,
with the publick Exchange for the Merchants underneath it." Ibid., 4:23; Gibson, 801.

446. Liverpool Castle, a small structure having five towers, two of which formed a
gatehouse. Built in the thirteenth century (with the addition of one tower 1431–1433), it was
partially demolished in 1663. What remained of the castle was pulled down in 1720. King,
1:248; MacKenzie, 2:199.

447. Charles Gerard (c. 1659–1701), 2nd Earl of Macclesfield. Cokayne, *Peerage*, 8:330–32.

448. This passage appears to have been inspired by Bishop Gibson's additions to Camden,
which state that ". . . such as are free of this town have the benefit of being Free-men also of
Waterford and *Wexford* in that Kingdom [Ireland], as also of *Bristol* in this." Gibson, 801.

Chester.

broad. The passage is on any high wind very dangerous &
frequently passengers are drown'd. On this Side westward is
the famous bay Hylock[449] held to be the largest & most comodious in England, twas where the English Army encamp'd
before they went to the Boin in Ireland.[450] from Leverpool
Chester is distant 12 miles whither we got at night.¶
The Citty of Chester is of its Self a County Palatine and famous for its Antiquity. The River Dee runs by it wch tis
thôught was once navigable for Ships of the greatest Burthen
but now only Small Barks can come up. Yet there is a Project
on foot of restoring it to its former depth.[451] In the Citty are 9
Parish Churches beside the Cathedrall[452] an old pile of building but not very good. The town is populous cheifly for the
favourable passage it affords to Ireland upon account of which
it is allways well Stock'd wth Gentry. The Inhabitants trade
outwardly very little thô the king receivs yearly about 6000^{li}
for tobacko & other imported goods. The town is sorounded
by a wall wch is kept up in good repair So that 2 or 3 may walk
a breast upon it.[453] Within it Stands an old Castle[454] where a

449. Hoylake Bay at the mouth of the river Dee.

450. The Battle of the Boyne, 11 July 1690, in which James II was defeated and driven from
Ireland.

451. Silting of the Dee had resulted in the decline of Chester as a port and the diversion of
much trade to Liverpool. In 1698 agreements were drawn up with London merchant Francis
Gell for making the river Dee navigable for vessels up to one hundred tons. By 1700, local
members of Parliament were promoting a bill embodying these arrangements. *Victoria History
. . . Chester,* 1:131–32.

452. Chester Cathedral, a Benedictine abbey church until 1540, when it was elevated to
cathedral status by Henry VIII. The present structure was erected in a number of succeeding
phases, mostly in the Decorated and Perpendicular styles, now heavily restored. Pevsner, *Buildings . . . Cheshire,* 136. "The great church here is a very magnificent building, but 'tis built of a red,
sandy, ill looking stone, which takes much from the beauty of it, and which yielding to the
weather, seems to crumble, and suffer by time, which much defaces the building." Defoe, 393.

453. These walls form a circuit nearly two miles in length. Averaging five to six feet in
width, they provided a sort of elevated walk that was maintained throughout the eighteenth
century for its value as a pleasant promenade. Pevsner, *Buildings . . . Cheshire,* 154. ". . . the
town is walled all aboute with battlements and a walke all round pav'd with stone; I allmost
encompass'd the walls . . ." Fiennes, 157.

454. Chester Castle. Founded in 1070, the castle was a powerful stone edifice of two wards,
erected on an earlier earthwork. Beyond the remains of one tower, very little survives of the

company of 150 invalids are maintaind, but tis not defensible,
& only is of So much use as to keep the town in Auw. The
Citty is Serv'd wth water from the river by a very ingennuous
Engine set up about 2 or 3 years since.455 In the Market place
has latly been erected a very noble Exchange by the Contributions of Severall Gentlemen.456 It Stands upon 3 rows of
Pillars, is 125 feet long, 42 broad, & 85 high. above is a very
noble room where the Major & Aldermen keep Court. The
form of this Citty is irregular, the houses very old, & for the
most part built upon Posts advanc'd into the Street So that
people may walk dry under these Piazas call'd Rows in the
worst of weathers.457 Severall large & new brick houses a
Scatter'd about the town, & Severall coaches are kept by the
gentry living in the Citty. On Thursday we sat out for Hoom
Church458 where we got at night. We past thrô Darly459 a
Market town, where there is a very fair Church, & thrô Midle-
wych460 another Market town famous for its brine pitts.
These are Salt Springs that issue out 50 yards underground,

16.
Hoom Church

Midlewych.

medieval defenses. King, 1:67.

455. "When I was formerly at this city, about the year 1690, they had no water to supply
their ordinary occasions, but what was carried from the River Dee upon horses, in great leather
vessels . . . But at my coming there this time, I found a very good water-house in the river, and
the city plentifully supplied by pipes, just as London is from the Thames; though some parts of
Chester stands very high from the river." Defoe, 394.

456. Construction of the exchange began in 1695 and was completed in 1698. The building
was destroyed by fire in 1865. Ormerod, 1:363. ". . . there is a new Hall building which is for
the assize and it stands on great stone pillars which is to be the Exchange, which will be very
convenient and handsome; the Hall is round, it is built of bricke and stone coynes, there are
leads all round with battlements and in the middle is a tower; there ballconies on the side and
windows quite round the Cupillow that shews the whole town round . . ." Fiennes, 157.

457. "These Rows are certain long galleries, up one pair of stairs, which run along the side
of the streets, before all the houses, though joined to them, and as is pretended, they are to
keep the people dry in walking along. This they do indeed effectually, but then they take away
all the view of the houses from the street, nor can a stranger, that was to ride through Chester,
see any shops in the city; besides they make the shops themselves dark . . . dirty, and uneven."
Defoe, 392.

458. Hulme Church in the parish of Sandbach, Cheshire, four-and-a-half miles northeast of
Middlewich. Now called Holme Chapel.

459. Darley, Cheshire, formerly about two miles south of Winford.

460. Middlewich, Chester.

17.

and the water being convey'd by pipes into pans is then boild to a very fine white Salt. From Hoom Church we got to Buxton passing thrô Macclesfeild for Shortness [Manfeild?] a large Major town. tis famous for button making. In the Church which was formerly a Colledge,[461] the Earle of rivers[462] has a place where his Ancestores ly bury'd, the late Earle[463] who dy'd in 1695 has a very fine tomb where he lys in at length under a Canopy Supported by 2 pillars all of Marble.[464] In the wall on one side of him is fix'd a coper plate wherein a pardon is writ to—Leigh for 26000 years & 26 days.[465] From hence we directed our course with the help of a guide to Buxton passing over the hills wch divide Cheshire from DarbyShire. We Stopt half a mile Short of Buxton to See Pools hole[466] the 1st wonder of the Peak of which there are

Buxton

461. St. Michael (formerly All Hallows), the parish church for Macclesfield. The College of Macclesfield, actually a chantry of secular priests, was founded c. 1508 and a chapel built on the south side of the church by Thomas Savage, bishop of London. Besides this chapel, little of the medieval structure remains. Dugdale, *Monasticon Anglicanum,* vol. 6, pt. 3, 1448; Pevsner, *Buildings . . . Cheshire,* 265.

462. Richard Savage (1654–1712), 4th Earl of Rivers. Cokayne, *Peerage,* 11:28–29.

463. Thomas Savage (1628–1694), 3rd Earl of Rivers. Ibid., 11:27.

464. "Above a large altar tomb is a recumbent figure in a flowing robe and large wig, under a canopy supported by four marble Corinthian pillars. Over which are the arms and crest of Savage, with the supporters, a falcon belled Or, and a Unicorn Argent. Over the Pillars are also the Earl's Arms impaled with those of his wives. Over the figure is inscribed

here lyeth the body of the
viscount Colechester & Savage of Rocksavage,
baron of Darcey of Chich, who died
the 14th day of September 1694,
at his house in Great Queen-street,
within ye parish of St. Giles in the Feilds, in the
the 14th day of October following,
in the 67th year of his age.

Ormerod, 3:755.

465. The so-called "pardon brass" of Roger Legh (d. 1506), which proclaims that the pardon for five Paternosters, five Aves, and one Creed is twenty-six thousand years and twenty-six days. Pevsner, *Buildings . . . Cheshire,* 267.

466. ". . . another of the wonderless wonders of the Peake. The wit that has been spent upon this vault . . . had been well enough to raise the expectation of strangers, and bring fools a great way to creep into it . . ." Defoe, 469.

A. the Entrance into *ye* Cave. *B.* the representation of Plants in Rocks of a black Bituminous Substance. *C.* the figure of a Lion *D.* the Queen of Scots Pillar. *E.* the fig. of a Human Corps. *F.* the Sparry globe call'd *ye* Font. *G.* a Sparry Substance call'd Cottons Haycock. *H.* the Plitch of Bacon. *I.* the Chair *K.* the Needles Eye. All these are form'd by dropping of Water from the Rock of a Sparry matter call'd Stalactites.

Pool's Hole. Illustration from *The Genuine Works of Charles Cotton . . .*, London, 1715. Michiel van der Gucht. Colonial Williamsburg Foundation.

Pools hole

Seven,[467] & Sent our horses forward to the town. This hole is at the foot of a hill where multitude of Lime Stones are dug & burn'd. about it are Severall Small Cottages wch afforded us guides into it. At the entrance we found it so low that we were forc'd to bend double to proceed about 20 yards after which the roof So enlarg'd it Self that we were able to walk upright and thus it continu'd to widen evry way till we came to the middle of the hole. Our passage was very troublesome by reason of the great Stones we were necessitated to go over which lying very thick and uneven, & being moreover Slipery with the water wch drops continually from the top made us advance but Slowly. In this cave are Severall large Stones resembling haycocks made by the petryfying water which drops from above. with the help of candles we could descern others which our guide Shew'd us like a Lyon, a pair of Organs, a lanthorn, a man lying at length and a flitch of bacon hanging down from the roof, but fancy must make out what nature has left imperfect in these figures.[468] About midway we met wth the Queen of Scots's Pillar to wch place that Queen who was beheaded after by Queen Elizabeth advanc'd & gave name.[469] Here we let off a pistoll wch made a louder noise then a Canon would above ground.[470] Farther in we met with

467. The seven wonders of Derbyshire's Peak district. Publicized by the poems of Thomas Hobbes and Charles Cotton, these "wonders" were the object of great curiosity among early travelers.

468. ". . . the dripping of the water wears impression on the stones that forms them into severall Shapes, there is one looks like a Lyon with a Crown on his head . . . another place lookes just like the shape of a large Organ with the severall keys and pipes one above another as you see in a great Cathedrall; there is another rock looks like a Chaire of State with the Canopy and all . . ." Fiennes, 108–9. "As to the several stones called Mr Cotton's, Haycock's, Poole's Chair, Flitches of Bacon, and the like, they are nothing but ordinary stones; and the shapes very little resemble the things they are said to represent; but the fruitful imagination of the country carls, who fancy to call them so, will have them to look like them . . ." Defoe, 471.

469. "I was as farre as the Queen of Scotts Pillar, which is a large white stone and the top hangs over your head like a canopy, all great white stones and in spires or large iceickles, and glistring as the other . . ." Fiennes, 109. ". . . it is a piece of stone like a kind of spar . . . a pillar of which almost every body that comes there, carries away a piece, in veneration of the memory of the unhappy princess that gave it her name." Defoe, 471.

470. "Now you arrive at the Queen of Scots' Pillar, clear and bright as Alabaster . . . Near the Pillar we fired a Pistol, which redoubl'd like the noise of a Cannon . . ." Leigh, bk. 3, 43.

nothing but ascents & descents over the rocks if I may call
them so that ly within the Cave. Some times we could walk
Streight, Sometime were forc'd to go on all 4, & Sometimes we
waded over brooks w^{ch}: run thrô & cross the hole, & by reason
of the turnings & windings of the Cave make a noise like
thunder as they pass along. We went to the farther end, w^{ch}: is
a good quarter of a mile from the Entrance and return'd a
different way to See Pools bedchamber & kitchen w^{ch}: are
lesser caves leading into the greater onc.[471] Having visited
these we return'd some part of the same way, till we fell into
the first passage where we enterd, & So creeping as we did at
first, we came at last to daylight & the enjoym^t: of fresh air,
both which were very welcome to us. At the Caves mouth
Stood Severall people some to beg, & others with basons of
water & herbs, for us to wash & cleans us from the dirt we had
contracted while we were in.[472] After this we went to Buxton   Buxton
a Small vilage Seated in a very barren & hilly part of the
County, yet much resorted to in Sumar times for its baths &
waters.[473] The wells here are the 2^d: wonder of the Peak. There

471.
"Of this *Infernal Mansion*, you must see
Where Master Pool and his bold Yeomanry
Took up their Apartments, which do lye
Over the narrow pass you enterrd by,
Up an Ascent of easie mounting, where
They shew his *Hall*, his *Parlour, Bed-Chamber*,
Withdrawing-Room, and *Closset*, and to these,
His *Kitchin*, and his other *Offices*
And all contriv'd to justifie a Fable,
That may indeed pass with the ign'rant Rabble,
And might serve him perhaps a Day, or so
When close purs'd; but Men of Sense must know,
Who of the Place have took a serious View,
None but the *Devil* himself could live there *Two* . . ."

Cotton, 68.
472. ". . . when we came out we were met by some poor Woman, who live near to it, with
Water and Herbs to purifie and cleanse our selves from any filth or dirt we might have contracted by creeping along that darksom Cavern." Brome, 94.
473. " 'Tis inclosed in a fair Stone-Building, erected by the Earl of *Shrewsbury*, and the
Water, by its Operation, being of a neat Affinity with that in the Cross-Bath, draws hither in
the Summer, a great Concourse of People, of all Ages and Degrees, here being Lodgings

are in all 4 Springs, one is cold, and excellent drinking water but not medicinall, the 2:^{d} close by is milk warm, & diuretick, the 3:^{d} is tepid, & fills 2 large basons where lame and diseas'd persons bath, & find much Benefit,[474] the 4:th is a very Strong chalybeat water Stronger then That at Tunbrige & is free for any one to drink of. We left Buxton the next day early in the morning that we might See the remaining wonders and be at Chatsworth the Duke of Devons[475] House before night The third wonder is Tydeswell[476] w^{ch}: is the only one we did not See by reason it lay 10 mile out of our way. This well ebs & flows wth: the Sea & when tis level wth: the ground, it will Some times rise a quarter of a foot & cover 10 or 12 yards of the Earth about it. The fourth wonder is Elden hole[477] w^{ch}: is on the side of a hill two miles from Buxton. The mouth of this is about 15 yards wide and M:^{r} Cotton[478] tells us he plum'd it

18:

Tydswell

Elden hole

---

prepared on purpose, proportionable to their Quality, or Condition." Ibid., 93.

474. "I must . . . give it the praise due to the medicinal virtue of its waters; for it is not to be denied, but that wonderful cures have been wrought by them, especially in rheumatic, scorbutick and scrofulous distempers, aches of the joints, nervous pains, and also in scurvy and leprous maladies." Defoe, 468.

475. William Cavendish (1641–1707), 1st Duke of Devonshire. Cokayne, *Peerage*, 4:343.

476. Tideswell, "a Flowing and Ebbing Well which ceases its miraculous motion but on great raines which raises the springs, and then the man which was with us told me he had seen it severall tymes in the winter when the springs were high to Ebb and Flow severall tymes in an hour . . . so that its likely when the springs are high the water from the sea may have a quicker flux and reflux thro' the Channells of the Earth but this is a good distance from the sea of ebbing and flowing rivers." Fiennes, 111. ". . . the basin or receiver for the water seems to have some other receiver within the rock, which, when it fills by the force of the original stream . . . the air being contracted or pent in, forces the water out with a bubbling noise, and so fills the receiver without . . . if any person were to dig into the place, and give vent to . . . the contracted space within, they would see Tideswell turned into an ordinary running stream, and a very little one, too." Defoe, 474.

477. ". . . a frightful chasm, or opening in the earth . . . directly down perpendicular into the earth, and perhaps to the centre . . . twenty foot over one way, and fifty or sixty the other; it has no bottom . . . What Nature meant in leaving this window open into the infernal world . . . we cannot tell. But it must be said, there is something of horror upon the very imagination, when one does but look into it." Ibid., 477–78.

478. Charles Cotton (1630–1687), author of "The Wonders of the Peak" (1681), a descriptive poem written in imitation of Hobbes's earlier work "De Mirabilius Pecci" (1636?). In the poem Cotton described his own sounding of the hole: "But I my self, with half the Peake

884 yards yet could find no bottom. Severall poor people
brought up Stones to fling in, & laying my ear close to the
ground I could hear them Some times a minnet falling, re-
bounding from one side to the other as the[y] hut against the
sides & makeing a noise like thunder as they fell.[479] After this
we went to Casleton[480] riding over the hills where are multi-   Casleton
tude of Leadpitts. we past by Mamtor[481] the 5.th wonder of w.ch   Mamtor
Hill tis reported that thô it is continually mouldring down yet
dos it not wast in the least by Reason of some new Supply of
matter, but this is fals as any one may plainly discern by
Stones w.ch in Severall places are left bare. 3 years ago a Lond-
oner attempted to climb up this dangerous rock, but failing in
his attempt fell down above 500 yards to the bottom yet receiv'd no hurt. Casleton is a Small town Seated at the foot of a   Casleton
high rock on the top of w.ch are the ruines of an antient &
Strong Castle,[482] So Strong by nature that no art could ever

surrounded, / *Eight hundred fourscore and four yards* have *sounded.* / And though of these *fourscore*
return'd back wet, / The *Plumment* drew, and found no Bottom yet: / Though when I went
again another Day, / To make a further, and a new Essay, / I could not get the *Lead* down half
the way." Cotton, 278. This work seems to have been standard reading for those touring the
Peak district during this early period. Celia Fiennes and Daniel Defoe also allude to Cotton's
sounding of Elden Hole. Fiennes, 109; Defoe, 477. According to one account, a "Rustick that
was let down with Ropes and Candles, to give an account of this Avernal Pit, and by his diving
too far into the Bowels of the Earth, was drawn up Senseless . . ." Brome, 92.

479. ". . . if we threw into it a Stone of any bigness, when we laid our Ears down close to the
side of the Pit, the Ratling which it made by its fall would be very distinct and audible for a
long time together, until it was got beyond our sphear of hearing." Brome, 92–93.

480. Castleton, Derbyshire.

481. ". . . Mam Tor, or, as the word in the mountain jargon signifies, the Mother Rock,
upon a suggestion that the soft crumbling earth, which falls from the summit of the one, breeds
or begets several young mountains below . . . Here the pretended wonder is formed, namely,
that the little heap below, should grow up into a hill, yet the great hill not be the less for all that
has fallen down; which is not true in fact, any more than, as a great black cloud pouring down
rain as it passes over our heads, appears still as great and as black as before, though it continues pouring down rain over all the country. But nothing is more certain than this, that the
more water comes down from it, the less remains in it; and so it certainly is of Mam Tor, in
spite of all the poetry of Mr Cotton or Mr Hobbes . . ." Defoe, 471–72.

482. Peveril Castle, built on a strong defensive position soon after the Conquest. The small
inner ward and the outer earthen enclosure appear to date from this period. In 1175 a keep was
built within the inner ward. This structure remains largely intact, though the castle had become

take it in the time twas built. it Stands on the point of a Steep
& craggy rock half a mile to the bottom, & there was no other
way to come to it but by a draw brige layd over as Steep a rock
wch is within 3 yards of that on wch the Castle Stands.[483] There
was a passage from this Castle underground to the town Ive
reason to think because the floor Sounded hollow, & in the
town I Saw a hole artifically made to wch I could Perceive no
end, & this no doubt was the entrance. Under this Steep rock

Devills
ars

is the cave call'd the Devils Ars.[484] The mouth is a perfect
arch neer 30 yards wide & as high. Within this mouth are
severall poor cottages where people live secure from rain or
Snow, & make a perfect village underground.[485] on one Side
of this Cave runs a brook wch issues out of the mouth wth Such
force that it drives Severall mills. On the other Side is a Sandy
entrance for neer 50 yards at wch distance the Hole lessens So
that there is a necessity of Stooping to proceed. But having
already Seen Pools hole and this being of the Same nature we
thought it not worth our while to advance any farther. Our
guides inform'd us that it continues for neer 600 yards that
there are two brooks to cross when a third puts a ne plus ultra
to any mans proceeding.[486] But Mr Cotton[487] who was in

---

ruinous by the seventeenth century. Pevsner, *Buildings . . . Derbyshire*, 200–201; King, 1:110.

483. ". . . the Castle in the *Peake* . . . seems to have been impregnable by its Situation upon a high and dangerous Rock, which is so steep, and craggy, that there appears but one way, by which there is any access to it." Brome, 90.

484. ". . . notwithstanding the grossness of the name given it . . . there is nothing of similitude or coherence either in form and figure, or any other thing between the thing signified and the thing signifying . . . on the steep side of a mountain there is a large opening very high, broad at the bottom . . . this being all wild and irregular, cannot be said to be an arch, but a mere chasm, entering horizontally the opening being upwards of thirty foot perpendicular, and twice as much broad at the bottom at least." Defoe, 472–73.

485. ". . . you enter a great Cave which is very large, and severall poor little houses in it built of stone and thatch'd like little Styes, one seemed a little bigger in which a Gentleman liv'd and his wife that was worth above 100£ a year which he left to his brother choosing rather like a hermit to live in this sorry cell . . . now none but very poor people live there which makes some small advantage by begging and by lighting strangers into the Cave . . ." Fiennes, 110.

486. ". . . We passed still on, till at length we were stop'd by the Water, which . . . cry'd, a *Ne Ultra* to us, though, as they say, 'tis usual, not only to wade over this with great facility, but another current likewise, which runs along the Cave some ten or twelve yards distant from this

severall times is of oppinnion that the hollow continues by
reason the arch does not contract. After we had refresh'd our
horses at Castleton we proceeded to Chatsworth wch is from
hence 5 miles, and we arriv'd thither in very good time, send-
ing our horses to an Inn in the Vilage, & repairing our selves
to the Dukes Pallace where we lay that night & the sonday
following.¶

The scituation of Chatsworth[488] is between two high hills in a   Chatsworth:
vally which affords a prospect of 20 miles lenght. One of these
rocks is very Steep & craggy & terminates the Park, the other
being of a more gentle declension affords very good pasturage
for Cattle, & contains a large warren. The river Darwent[489]
runs at the foot of the gardins & yeilds plenty of fish. About
the House are Severall groves & Small woods. It is not half
finish'd being design'd Square with a Court in the middle but
as yet only 3 Sides are finish'd.[490] The Stone of which tis built
is brought but two miles & is white & very lasting.[491] The best
Artificers of all Sorts have been employ'd upon this noble

---

to a third, which is impassable." Brome, 91.

487. See note 478.

488. The original house was built around an interior courtyard c. 1557 by Sir William
Cavendish and his redoubtable wife, Bess of Hardwick. The 1st Duke of Devonshire (see note
475) rebuilt this Elizabethan house between 1687 and 1707, assisted by architects William
Talman and Thomas Archer. These changes resulted in the house as it appears today. Lees-
Milne, *English Country Houses,* 70, 75–76. "It is indeed a palace for a prince, a most magnificent
building, and . . . the very obstructions and . . . disadvantages of its situation, serve to set off its
beauty, and are, by the most exquisite decoration of the place, made to add to the lustre of the
whole . . . The Front to the garden is the most regular piece of architecture I have seen in all
the north part of England . . ." Defoe, 475.

489. The river Derwent.

490. Actually only two of the sides, William Talman's east and south fronts, had been fully
completed. Work on the west front was well along, however, having begun in August 1700
when the old Elizabethan west front was demolished. Not until 1705 was the north front rebuilt,
presumably under the supervision of Thomas Archer. Lees-Milne, *English Country Houses,*
75–76; Lees-Milne and Cornforth, "Chatsworth," 17–19.

491. Nearly all the stone used in the building was obtained locally. Gritstone came from
Beely Moor and Bakewell Edge; finer stone from Roche Abbey; marble from Calver; and
blackstone from Sheldon Moor—all within a few miles of the estate. Lees-Milne and Cornforth, "Chatsworth," 5.

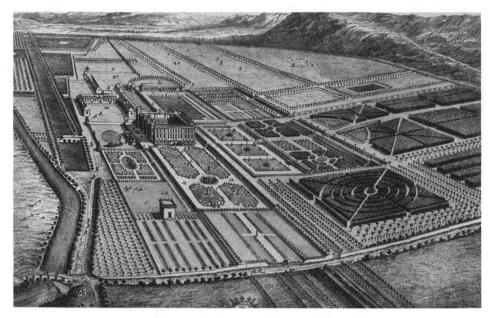

Chatsworth, Derbyshire. Johannes Kip after Leonard Knyff, c. 1700. British Museum.

building where there is the best of carving, Architecture,
painting Tappistry &c. The front to the gardins is 186 feet
long, & 82 high, containing 12 Sash windows in a row the
pains of which are 20 inches broad, & all of looking glass.[492]
The great Staircase is of Stone, 17 feet broad, & consists of 34
Steps which after the manner of that at Hampton Court support one another.[493] Up these Stairs goes an Iron rail of very

492. "These *Looking Glass* Plates are ground smooth and flat, and Polish'd. They are sometimes used in Sashes, or Sash-Windows. But tis a dear sort of *Glass;* for they ask 4s. a foot for
Such Squares, and if they are large, 'tis much more." *Builders' Dictionary,* vol. 1. ". . . in the front
is 7 large windows the glass is diamond cutt and all off large Looking-glass, the panes bigg 4 in
a breadth 7 in height . . . . all the windows the squares of glass are so large and good they cost
10s. a pannell . . ." Fiennes, 105–6. "And all these Glories glitter to the Sight / By the advantage
of a clearer Light. / The *Glaziers* Work before substantial was / I must confess, thrice as much
Lead, as Glass . . . / The Windows now look like so many Suns, / Illustrating the noble Room at
once." Cotton, 298.
    493. Percival referred here to the great stair that ascends from the ground floor to the
King's Guard Chamber at Hampton Court. ". . . there is another fine staircase all stone and
hangs on its self, on the outside, the support is from the wall and its own building, the stone of
the half paces are large and one entire stone makes each . . ." Fiennes, 106.

fine work painted & guilded.494 On the roof are painted
Europe, Asia, Africa & America w^th: Ceres the mother of
Plenty in the middle by Vario,495 & on the sides Stand the
Statues of Apollo Pallas and Lucretia all of marble in Niches.496
These stairs lead up to a gallery w^ch: hangs half way over, the
floor of w^ch: is only 3 great Stones weighing 300 tun and a half
each.497 From these Stairs one Sees thrô into the great Hall a
very Spacious room, on the opposite Side of w^ch: is painted at
length the murder of Julius Cæsar in the senat house, & on
another side Augustus Shutting the Temple of Janus. The
remaining sides are Fresco work. The whole ceiling is taken
up with the Description of Julius Cæsar Deify'd w^th: all the
Gods about him, done finly by Laguar.498 Up one pair of
Stairs is a gallery 86 feet long, 24 broad, & 18 high.499 I never
saw so finish'd & bewtyfull a room. On the right hand as you
enter is painted the History of Pastor Fido,500 & on the left
are collumns, & the finest carv'd work. The Cæling is very
finely fretwork'd501 room being left for the 7 liberall Arts,
Appollo & muses, Mercury & the [Sorpenies?]502 3 pictures

494. In 1691 this iron railing had been installed by the noted smith Jean Tijou after he
received a payment of £250 for its fabrication. Lees-Milne and Cornforth, "Chatsworth," 10.

495. Painted 1687–1689. Ceres is depicted attending Cybele in her chariot. Croft-Murray, 237.

496. Executed by the noted sculptor Caius Gabriel Cibber. Lees-Milne and Cornforth,
"Chatsworth," 10.

497. ". . . on the top of the stairs the space leading to the roomes are 3 large Stones, the
Stones cost 20£ a piece, so large and thick, you would wonder how they should be raised up so
high and be supported by its own arch without any pillars on the outside . . ." Fiennes, 106–7.

498. Louis Laguerre (1663–1721), decorative painter. Among his other commissions were
Burghley, Petworth, Blenheim, and Hampton Court. Working with his assistant Ricard,
Laguerre completed painting of the hall at Chatsworth in 1694. DNB, 31:397; Lees-Milne and
Cornforth, "Chatsworth," 9.

499. Now the library, remodeled by the 6th Duke.

500. Il Pastor Fido (The Faithful Shepherd), Battista Guarini's pastoral play first published in
1590 and subsequently popularized in many English editions. The paintings, done c. 1700 by
Louis Cheron, are now set in the ceiling of the theater. Croft-Murray, 245.

501. The gallery ceiling of gilded stucco was executed by England's leading plasterer,
Edward Goudge. Lees-Milne and Cornforth, "Chatsworth," 11.

502. The identity of the "Sorpenies" remains uncertain. The two principal figures (Muses?)
shown with Mercury clearly represent the arts of painting and sculpture, being depicted

of Varios work: The other pictures are of the best masters, and the room is fill'd with Severall fine Statues of marble & flower-potts guilded. At the farther end of this gallery is a door that leads you into a great Dining Room whose height as well as that of all the floor is 22 feet. It is Sett off wth: carv'd work[503] & Statues of great value, and on the ceiling is painted Vertue banishing Vice by Vario for the work of w^{ch}: with that of another room & closset he was paid 600^{li}.[504] Out of this room you see thrô 6 more whose doors answer one another[505] & their cælings are finly painted & Sides hung with tappestry or wainscoted & addorn'd with carv'd work. Their floors are also all inlayd. Thrô all these rooms you look into the chappell which is the noblest I ever was in. it is 32 feet high 45 long & proportionably broad. On the right hand are painted the miracles of our Savior, On the left the Vertues. On the roof is the Ascencion wth: the 4 Evangelists at each corner.[506] The Alterpeice is all of marble wroght wth: steps of the same going up to it & on each side Stand two statues of Justice & char-ity.[507] The floor is allso pav'd with black & white marble, & the sides where there is no painting wainscoted with cedar inlay'd. Tis impossible to describe the bewtyfull appearance it makes, the Ornam^{ts}: of the pulpit & Alter are of velvet im-

respectively with pallet and bust. Verrio painted these ceiling roundels in 1697. Croft-Murray, 237.

503. The carving was begun in 1692 by Samuel Watson, Joel Lobb and William Davis. Lees-Milne and Cornforth, "Chatsworth," 14.

504. The dining room or great chamber had been painted by Verrio in 1691, for which he was paid £500. Croft-Murray, 237.

505. Percival clearly refers here to the state apartment running along the south range of the house. The mention of six rooms is puzzling, however, unless it included the suite of "rooms" seen in the mirrored doorway as described by Celia Fiennes: ". . . at the end of the dineing roome is a large door all of Looking-glass, in great pannells all diamond cutt, this is just opposite to the doores that runs into the drawing roome and bed chamber and closet, so it shews the roomes to look all double . . ." Fiennes, 106.

506. Painted by Laguerre and Ricard 1689–1693. Croft-Murray, 251.

507. The altarpiece of alabaster and black Ashford marble was designed by Cibber, who also seems to have carved the figures representing Faith and Justice. Lees-Milne and Cornforth, "Chatsworth," 6.

broaderd w:th gold and Silver. On the right hand of this chappell is an Appartment where Mary Queen of Scots was
detain'd prisoner 7 years.[508] The rooms of this like the rest
are painted all on the top, & either hung w:th tappestry, or Set
off with pictures & Prints. Here is a pretty Studdy of books
thô the greater part are at another Seat of this Dukes call'd
Hardwick[509] in the same County. I have not time to describe
w:^t remains of this noble Pallace as its Bagnio all of italian
Marble,[510] its Chimney peices of marble brought from Egipt
&c. The carv'd work of wood about this house cost 2600^{li}. Ile
pass to the gardins w:^{ch} are already as fine as the House, thô
they are not half finish'd. Behind the House is a Menagery a
long row of building in w:^{ch} are preserv'd patriges, Pheasants,
Heathpouts & outlandish birds. This is devided into 3 parts
w:^{ch} hath each its court & Fountain in the middle. On the right
hand of this upon a higher ground is a Greenhouse 150 feet
long & 22 broad well fill'd w:th plants & greens. before this is a
Canal 100 yards long & half as broad, in the middle of which is
a fountain that plays to a great Height. Farther on is a wilderness & in the middle an artificiall tree of leather out of evry
leaf of which comes a Stream of water.[511] This is sorounded

508. Mary Queen of Scots was kept at Chatsworth at various times between 1569 and 1584.
This was owing to the marriage of Sir William Cavendish's widow, Bess of Hardwick, to
George Talbot, 6th Earl of Shrewsbury, who had been appointed Mary's custodian by Eliz-
abeth I. Thompson, 16.

509. Hardwick Hall, Derbyshire. Hardwick had come into the family through the issue of
Sir William Cavendish and Bess of Hardwick.

510. ". . . within this is a batheing roome, the walls all with blew and white marble the
pavement mix'd one stone white another black another of the red rance marble; the bath is one
entire marble all white finely veined with blew and is made smooth, but had it been as finely
pollish'd as some, it would have been the finest marble that could be seen; it was as deep as
ones middle on the outside and you went down steps into the bath big enough for two people;
at the upper end are two Cocks to let in one hott the other cold water to attemper it as persons
please; the windows are all private glass . . ." Fiennes, 106.

511. Actually the tree may not have been of leather. In his *Natural History . . . ,* Charles
Leigh remarked on this same tree, "exactly resembling a Willow, made of Copper, of which
(by the turning of a Cock) every leaf continually distils Drops of Water, and so lively represents
a Shower of Rain" (bk. 3, 44–45). According to Celia Fiennes the tree presented a very realistic
appearance: ". . . the leaves and barke and all looks very natural . . . the roote is full of rubbish

by 8 Fountains of different make; between this wilderness &
the Canal I mention'd is a Cascade of 45 Steps, at the uperend
lye two Nereids[512] with urns which Send out a torrent of
water wch. falling down all those Steps loses it Self in a large
Bason at the bottom.[513] Neerer the House is a green terrace
753 yards which is the length of the gardin at present thô tis
[to] be inlarg'd considerably. In the gardin are 5 descents
wch. lyeing on a Slope from the foot of the rock declines gradually to the river side. To make room for the new designs a
great rock wch. Stood within the compass of the gardin has
been levell'd, & in its place is a canal making 322 yards long 25
broad, & 4 feet deep wch. will directly front the House.[514]
Beyond this is an iron gate thrô which one may see a rude
prospect of rocks, woods & the river Darwent running at their
feet for a great way.[515] At the end of this canal next to the
house Stand two large Statues of Flora & Aphitrite[516] one of

---

or great stones to appearance . . ." Fiennes, 105.

512. In classical mythology these were the fifty daughters of Nereus and Doris, among
whom was Amphitrite (see note 516). They were the attendants of Poseidon. Zimmerman, 174.

513. Apparently, Celia Fiennes saw this feature before it had been enlarged: ". . . beyond
this is a bason in which are the branches of two Hartichocks Leaves which weeps at the end of
each leafe into the bason which is placed at the foote of lead steps 30 in number; on a little
banck stands blew balls 10 on a side, and between each ball are 4 pipes which by a sluce spouts
out water across the stepps to each other like an arbor or arch; while you are thus amused
suddenly there runs down a torrent of water out of 2 pitchers in the hands of two large Nimphs
cut in stone that lyes in the upper step, which makes a pleasing prospect, this is designed to be
enlarged and steps made up to the top of the hill which is a vast ascent, but from the top of it
now they are supply'd with water for all their pipes so it will be the easyer to have such a fall of
water even from the top which will add to the Curiositye." Fiennes, 105.

514. ". . . to make a clear vista or prospect beyond into the flat country, towards Hardwick
. . . the Duke . . . removed, and perfectly carried away a great mountain that stood in the
way . . . This was so entirely gone, that, having taken a strict view of the gardens at my first
being there, and retaining an idea of them in my mind, I was perfectly confounded at coming
there a second time . . ." Defoe, 475.

515. Such "rude" scenery was later to become an essential element in English gardening.
Significantly, the denigrating attitude of earlier writers toward this sort of landscape is absent
in Percival's account of Chatsworth and Derbyshire.

516. In classical mythology, Amphitrite was goddess of the sea and wife of Poseidon.
Zimmerman, 20.

marble, & tother of a fine white Stone. These are parted at Some distance from 2 others in the other part of the gardin neerer the House by an iron rail of very fine workmanship guilded & Set with Urns on the top.[517] On the right hand of these upon another descent is a large bowling green, & at the upper end of that a Summer House[518] Standing upon Pillars, & painted on the top wth the History of Castor & Pollux.[519] Below this Green is another gardin in wch is a fountain that plays 30 or 40 pipes. Tis an oval bason wth a Neptune in the middle and on each side of him a sea Nymphs.[520] Under the door of the front of the house is a grotto where the water runs continually[521] on each side of which you goe up Stairs into the House. The gardins now at work upon contain 96 acres of ground. Below the House towards the river is a very long canal, & fishponds wth walks & groves but these are now neglected for makeing far better above. These gardins and the ground the House Stands upon take up 130 acres. I Say nothing of the Out Houses where there is nothing yet finish'd but two Stables divided by the gate House, each of wch are made to hold 40 horse. The iron work in and about the House has cost a prodigious deal of mony one single gate of wch fronting the Building cost 600^{li}. Ile attempt no further to describe this Pallace least I do it injustice. We left this place on the 21 and came to Darby.[522] This is the cheif town of the County & the only one wch sends members to Parlim^t. In it are 5 Parishes, & the Church of St Anns is remarkable for its towr being 60

21.
Darby.

517. This was the iron clairvoyée fabricated by Jean Tijou and William Marshall and erected c. 1687 on the west side of the house, flanked by stone pylons bearing Cibber's winged Sphinxes. Lees-Milne and Cornforth, "Chatsworth," 5–6.

518. The bowling house, dismantled c. 1755 by the 4th Duke and re-erected in its present location at the northern end of the east parterre. Thompson, 24.

519. The Dioscuri, twin sons of Zeus and Leda, worshipped as protectors of seamen and identified with the constellation Gemini. Harvey, 148.

520. ". . . there is one bason in the middle of one Garden thats very large and by sluces besides the Images severall pipes plays out the water, about 30 large and small pipes altogether, some flush it up that it frothes like snow . . ." Fiennes, 105.

521. This is the grotto beneath the steps of the west front.

522. Derby, Derbyshire.

yards high & fine carv'd.[523] Here are many neat new built
Houses, and the town is very populous & rich being great
Mal[t]sters & dealers in lead & tin whereof very rich mines ly
within 8 mile of the town. In it are 2 handsome almshouses for
12 poor each,[524] & a very large free schoole.[525] We left this
place on wednesday & came to Litchfeild which Stands in
StaffordShire. We past thrô Burton a well built town where
there was formerly a Castle[526] & monastery,[527] & is a Col-
legiet Church.[528] Here is a famous brige of 30 arches or more.
between this and Litchfeild on the right hand is the great
forrest of Needwood.¶

⟨Litchfeild⟩[529] Is a Citty containing 3 Parishes besides a
Collegiate Church.[530] This Cathedrall is not very large but the
neatest of any I ever Saw. It was first built in 656 by Oswy
King of the Northumbers.[531] In the wars of 1641 it was ruin'd
yet by the industry of Bishop Hacket[532] it is restored to its
first bewty on the inside, thô the Statues of the Kings of

*22.
Burton*

523. Percival almost certainly meant All Saints or All Hallows Church (now Derby Cathedral), "most famous for its height and architecture." Cox, 1:428. In 1723–1725 James Gibbs
rebuilt the church, allowing the sixteenth-century tower to remain intact. Pevsner, *Buildings . . .
Derbyshire,* 112.

524. The Countess of Shrewsbury's Almshouse, founded c. 1560, and Wilmot's Almshouses,
ten small dwellings for individuals, built by Robert Wilmot and endowed by him in 1638.

525. The Derby Grammar School, founded c. 1160. In 1554 it was refounded under a
charter granted by Queen Mary. A building erected by the corporation to house the school
dates from this period. *Victoria History . . . Derbyshire,* 2:208, 216–17.

526. Burton Castle, mentioned in the Domesday survey, now completely vanished. King,
2:452.

527. Burton Abbey was a Benedictine monastery (St. Benedict and All Saints) founded c.
1103. *Victoria History . . . Stafffordshire,* 3:199–200.

528. The Church of the College of Christ and St. Mary, Burton-upon-Trent, previously the
Abbey of St. Mary and St. Mowden. Ibid., 3:297.

529. Lichfield, Staffordshire. Marginal text, incorporated.

530. A college of secular canons was founded at Lichfield c. 1140 by Bishop Roger de
Clinton. Dugdale, *Monasticon Anglicanum,* vol. 6, pt. 3, 1241.

531. Oswy (612–670), king of Northumbria 651–670. *DNB,* 42:333.

532. John Hackett (1592–1670), bishop of Lichfield and Coventry 1661–1670. Hackett's
repairs to the cathedral extended over a period of eight years between 1661 and 1669. *DNB,*
23:418–20.

Mercia wch Stood on the west side are miserably defac'd; It
Shows it Self at a great distance by 3 lofty & well wrought
Spires; it has 32 Prebendarys a Chancelor & other Officers, &
the Quire is good not only as to its ornamentall part, But for
its musick. The town is employ'd in no manefacture besides
making woolen caps for Seamen, but the gentry living in it are
its cheif Support. Tis divided by a Standing Pool over which
are 2 briges. In the upper division Stands the Cathedrall,533
Bishops Pallace534 & Prebends Houses wch look fairly at a
distance being Sorounded by a wall & ditch.535 The lower part
is cut out into large Streets & is very populous. From hence we
Set out on Fryday & came to the citty of Coventry where evry
thing is toll free besides Horses & this they obtain'd at the
ernest seuit of Godniva a Lady who was forc'd in 1050 to ride
naked thrô the citty on horsback to free the Inhabitants from
Sore taxes lay'd on them by Her husband Leofrick first Earle
of this place,536 & wch he would remit upon no other condition In memory of her there is Still once a year held a pros-
sesion before wch is carry'd a skin painted white, but formerly
the picture of a Naked Lady. The Scituation of this citty is
low, & Sorounded wth woods, formerly it was Sorounded by a
fine high wall, but King Charles the 2^d dismantled it for hold-

24.
Coventry

533. Lichfield Cathedral. The present structure represents the rebuilding of a Norman
cathedral in the thirteenth century. It suffered extensively during the Civil War. Pevsner,
Buildings . . . Staffordshire, 174–75. ". . . the Minster is a stately structure but old, the outside has
been finely carv'd and full of Images as appears by the nitches and pedistalls which remain
very close all over the walls . . ." Fiennes, 112.

534. An ashlar-faced building of seven bays and two stories, built 1697–1698 by Edward
Pierce, one of Wren's craftsmen. Pevsner, *Buildings . . . Staffordshire,* 188; Hill and Cornforth,
184–85.

535. Lichfield Close. "The Close is so call'd because it is enclosed round with a Wall . . . In
this Close stands the Cathedral Church, a goodly and beautiful Fabrick . . . In the same Close
are the Palaces of the Bishop and Dean, with the Houses of the Prebendaries, in a Court on the
Hill, all of them almost new, and very handsome." Cox, 5:4–5.

536. Leofric (d. 1057), Earl of Mercia. *DNB,* 33:61. ". . . *Leofrick,* the first Lord of this City,
being much offended, and angry with the Citizens, oppressed them with most heavy Tributes,
which he would remit upon no other Condition, at the earnest Suit of his Wife *Godina,* unless
she would her self ride on Horseback Naked through the greatest and most inhabited Street of
the City, which she did indeed, being covered only with her fair long Hair . . ." Brome, 73.

ing on the Parliaments Side against his father:[537] Some remains of it notwithstanding appear, & the 12 gates are Still
kept up over one of which is hung the Sheild bone of a vast
large boar that after he had wth his Snout turn'd up a pond
now going by the name of Swineswell[538] is reported to have
been Slain by Guy of Warwick.[539] In this Citty are 2 Parishes
the Churches of which are the largest & neatest I have ever
Seen.[540] one is a 100 yards long & 45 broad, the middle Ilse
being 45 foot broad & the Pillars Supporting the roof very tall
& Slender.[541] Both Churches have Spires to them of a great
heigth & rare workmanship,[542] & are well fill'd thô the major
part of the Inhabitants are quakers Anababtist & Presbiterians wch latter have got the Governm^{t} into their hands, &
make themselves very odious by their absolute proceedings.
The Cathedrall[543] is quite ruin'd having Suffred with 27

537. ". . . on the 22 day of July [1661] came the E. of Northampton . . . and several
others, who caused the Walls and Towers to be thrown down around the City. They began
to make the first breach at *Newgate*, where the Wall began to be built." Dugdale, *Antiquities,* 1:153.

538. ". . . at *Gatford-Gate*, there hangeth up to be seen, a mighty great Sheild-Bone of a wild
Bore, (or rather of an Elephant, being not so little as a yard in length) which some believe *Guy*
of *Warwick* slew in Hunting, when he had turn'd up with his Snout a great Pit, or Pond, which
is now call'd *Swansewell*, but *Swines-well* in times past." Brome, 74.

539. Guy of Warwick, a romantic hero, "almost wholly a creature of fiction." Reputedly the
son of Siward of Wallingford, he is best known for his supposed slayings of the Northumbrian
dragon and of the Danish giant Colbrand. *DNB*, 23:386–88.

540. Holy Trinity and St. Michael's.

541. Holy Trinity, a large Perpendicular church with a lofty crossing tower and spire,
dates primarily from the fourteenth to sixteenth centuries, having replaced an earlier thirteenth-century structure. Pevsner, *Buildings . . . Warwickshire,* 259. See note 543 for St.
Michael's.

542. ". . . the spire and steeple of one of the Churches [Holy Trinity] is very high and is
thought the third highest in England, in the same Church yard stands another large Church
which is something unusuall, two such great Churches together, their towers and the rest of the
Churches and high buildings make the town appear very fine . . ." Fiennes, 113. "The tall and
beautiful steeple; which, for its excellent workmanship and height is inferior to none in
England, was more then XXII years in building; being begun in *Anno* 1373 . . . and finished
Anno 1395." Dugdale, *Antiquities,* 1:166.

543. The parish church of St. Michael, elevated to cathedral rank in 1918. Built in several
phases between the thirteenth and early sixteenth centuries, it was partially destroyed in 1940.

religious houses in this town w:ch H: y^e: ^{8}: pull'd down at one
time. This is a very populous & trading place having a manefacture of Stuffs & broad cloth. The buildings here are all old,
& here is nothing very remarkable besides the market cross
w^{ch}: is very high & neatly work'd.544 From hence we came thrô
Rugby a market town to Northampton w^{ch}: gives name to the   Northamp
County in w^{ch}: it Stands. Here the sizes are kept and the gov-
ernm^t: is under a Major & Aldermen &c. The Scituation is
upon a Small hill from w^{ch}: one may see a great part of the
Country w^{ch}: is flat about it. Here are the ruins of a Castle545
& wall w^{ch}: went quite round the town at the foot of w^{ch}: the
river nen546 Slides gently along & joins another Small Stream.
In the town are 4 Parish Churches the cheif of which All
Hallows547 is Very bewtyfull and magnificent wth: a cupola
atop, being built Since the fire which on the 3^d: Sep^{br}: 1675
burnt down the greatest part of the town.548 Since that time it
has been So well rebuilt that for bewtyfull houses large Streets,

---

Pevsner, *Buildings . . . Warwickshire,* 249–50. "Here is no cathedral, as some have falsely said,
neither is the great church, so called, either collegiate or conventual. In King Henry 8th's time,
the priory being dissolved, the church which they would have called a cathedral, was reduced
to a private parish-church, and continues so to this day." Defoe, 404–5.

544. ". . . the Cross is noted and the finest building in England for such a thing in my
phancy it very much resembles the picture of the Tower of Babel, its all stone carv'd very
curiously and there are 4 divisions, each being less than another, to the top, and so its Pira-
midy forme; in each partition is severall nitches for statues quite round it where are Kings and
Queens, and just on each side before each statue is their arms and the arms of England and the
town, and so its adorn'd with coullours and gilding in their proper places, as in the garments
and Crowns or Coronets and finely carv'd with Angels and Cherubims and all sorts of beasts
birds flowers in garlands and leaves, thus in every division, there is variety quite up to the top
which is finely carv'd and gilt." Fiennes, 113.

545. Northampton Castle, built in the late eleventh or early twelfth century. Only fragments
of what appear to have been a motte and bailey walled in stone now survive, along with a
semicircular outwork dating from the Civil War period. King, 2:317.

546. The river Nene.

547. All Saints or All Hallows, rebuilt 1676–1680 following the fire of 1675, possibly to the
design of Henry Bell of King's Lynn. Pevsner, *Buildings . . . Northamptonshire,* 317.

548. Actually the fire occurred on 20 September 1675, destroying more than half the town
in twenty-five hours. *Victoria History . . . Northamptonshire,* 3:31.

The Sessions House at Northampton, watercolor, Thomas Eayre, c. 1721. British Museum.

Market place[549] Church and Session house[550] tis the best Country town in England.[551] Within and about it live many gentry who are the Support of the town notwithandsing which the Inhabitants are poor thô they drive a great trade in Shoos & childrens Stockins. The drapery Street is very Spacious and the houses very lofty and regularly built concerning w^{ch}: there runs a verse

> A new Church old Steeple
> Fine houses but very poor people

for the Steeple of the old Church having escap'd the fury of the flames it was left Standing and the Church added to it.[552]¶

549. In 1712 one observer remarked, "The Market Hill is lookt upon as the finest in Europe; a fair spacious, open place." Ibid., 3:25.

550. The Sessions House was built 1676–1678, with interior plasterwork by the noted plasterer Edward Goudge. Pevsner, *Buildings . . . Northamptonshire,* 326.

551. According to Thomas Baskerville, the town had "Phoenix like risen out of her ashes in a far more noble and beauteous form." *Victoria History . . . Northamptonshire,* 3:33.

552. The tower dates mostly from the fourteenth century, though its base may be earlier. In the seventeenth century, repairs were made to the upper portion and a balustrade added. Pevsner, *Buildings . . . Northamptonshire,* 317.

On monday we left this place and came to Dunstable passing
thrô Newport pagnell in BuckingamShire and Ouvre⁵⁵³ in
BedfordShire both Market towns, the latter being famous for
fullers earth.⁵⁵⁴ This town of Dunstable is a Small market
town consisting of 4 Streets wch point directly to the 4 quarters
of the world. This place is famous for Capons⁵⁵⁵ & larks, and
for making all sorts of Strawork as womens hatts &c. in each
of these Streets is a pool of dirty standing water in which the
Otlers⁵⁵⁶ wash their horses these thô not 2 feet deep are never
dry in the hottest Sumer, yet no Spring feeds it, for they are
forc'd to dig 20 fathom for to make their wells. Within 3 miles
of this town is a Small village call'd hockly in the hole⁵⁵⁷
which gives name to an infamous lane wch in Winter is very
deep & full of holes, and had been allmost impassable for us
were it not for a causway wch is thrown up only for horse men.
From hence we past over a Steep chalky hill to Dunstable.
Whence after we had Stay'd one night we departed, and came
to St Albans a large and ancient town Scituated on the side of
a hill on the top of wch Stands a Cathedrall Church⁵⁵⁸ wch formerly belong'd to an Abby⁵⁵⁹ built in 793 by King Offa,⁵⁶⁰

553. Woburn, Bedfordshire. See note 554.

554. Fuller's earth. A hydrous silicate of alumina, used in the cleaning of cloth. "More to
the South-west, is *Woburn*, not far from which there is dug up great store of *Fullers earth*, com-
momly call'd from the place *Woburn*-earth . . ." Gibson, 291.

555. A castrated cock.

556. Ostler. A stable hand or groom.

557. Now Hockliffe, Bedfordshire. ". . . along by Hockley in the hole, a dirty road extreme
troublesome to travellers in winter it must be impasable . . ." Gibson, 288. ". . . we came to
Dunstable over a sad road called *Hockley in the Hole* as full of deep slows, in the winter time . . ."
Fiennes, 117.

558. St. Alban's Cathedral, built in an unhappy mix of the Norman and Early English styles
with a Victorian west front. Construction began c. 1077. Pevsner, *Buildings . . . Hertfordshire*,
295–96. ". . . the great Church which is dedicated to St. Albans is much out of repair; I see
the places in the pavement that was worn like holes for kneeling by the devotes of the Religion
. . . but the whole Church is so worn away that it mourns for some charitable person to help
repair it . . ." Fiennes, 118.

559. The Benedictine Abbey of St. Alban, founded 793 by King Offa (see next note).
Dugdale, *Monasticon Anglicanum*, 2:177.

560. Offa (d. 796), king of Mercia 757–796. Builder of Offa's Dyke from south of Wye to
the mouth of the Dee. *DNB*, 42:2.

the Abbot of which place was the first in England made by the pope,[561] tis remarkable for its Butchers market. From hence we came to Barnet famous for its market of Sheep, hogs, and

higate

Oxen. Here we made no Stay but passing thrô Highgate the highest peice of ground in Midlesext we arriv'd At London on the 28th. of Octr finishing a progress of 14 weeks just, wch. we made both to our pleasure and improvment.

561. About 795 Willegod was made abbot by Offa, who had gone to Rome to obtain the canonization of St. Alban. Dugdale, *Monasticon Anglicanum,* 2:179.

Appendix of Related Correspondence

Sir Robert Southwell to Sir Hans Sloane, [undated]

Having had many Tryalls of your [Freindshipp], an[d] your acquaintance in the world being soe Generall, Lett me request you to think, where I may find a fitt Companion for my Nephew Sr John Percivale, who is taking a progresse about England. Mr Bird was of the mind to partake herein, as well for his owne Recreation, as to obleige me. And I had prepar'd Horses and every thing for the purpose. And I was extreamly rejoyc'd in my mind to have him. but by an accident that hath happen'd, Mr Bird cannot now stirr from the Towne. Wherefore pray range over all your Bead-Rolls; for that your Successe herein will highly obleige

S.^r your most affec.^t friend
and Servant
Robert Southwell

Copy received by addressee.
British Library, Sloane Mss., 4061, f. 38.

Francis Parry to Sir John Perceval

S.^r   24. June 1701

    Knowing with what care and prudence your Education has hithertoo been manag'd, and that tis now thought necessary for the applying that Stock of School and University learning with which you are more than Sufficiently furnisht, to the use it was design'd; and your conversation be enlarg'd, & that you acquaint your Self with Men of all Countrys & Degrees, their Tempers, modes of living, and Employments; give me leave in gratitude to that person by whose wise Conduct & fatherly concern you have attain'd all those externall as well as internal advantages, that may render you capable of the highest dignity & Station, to recoṁend Some observations to you, relating to your own Country which in no wise you ought to be a Stranger to, when you launch out into foreign parts. For as it is very præposterous for a Man to Speak another language better than his own, So it is for him to be better acquainted with the affairs of another

Mr Parry's
Directions to me
in my Travelling

Country than of his own. For all knowledge of other Countrys that is not usefull to a Man's own is but insignifficant curiosity.¶

The first Notions therefore of behaviour and business ought to be taken in at home; for these making the greatest impression, all other Notions will be made to conform to them, for which reason it is, that many of our young Gentlemen Travellers return worse qualified for any Service of their Country than when they went abroad, and learn nothing in their Travells but what must be unlearn'd, if ever they design to live like Englishmen.¶

In Order therefore to lay a good foundation for the conduct of your whole life, you are now going to Survey England, and because you begin at that Port where I have lately been, I presume to give you what remarks I there made, that I think may be usefull to you.¶

From Salisbury you go to Christ-Church, between which places the River is by Act of Parliament made Navigable; concerning which you may enquire at whose charge it was done? and what the cost might have been? of what burthen the boats are that it carries? how many Men go in a boat? how long She is going up & down? what are the Comodities carryed to & fro? and what advantage this water carriage may be to the Neighborhood.¶

Christ-Church is a Port town, & tho of little trade, yet here I Shall mind you of Such enquirys and remarks as you ought to make at every Port you come to viz. Concerning the capacity & Security of the Port. The number of Ships belonging to it. What Comodities are thence exported & to what place, & what Comodities it imports. Concerning the number quality perquesites & Sallarys of the Port Officers, you may have from him who was the occasion of giving you these hints. And it cannot be amiss for any Gentleman who wou'd understand the Interest of his Country, and previous to it the trade therof, to know as well the publick charge as the publick advantage of Trade.¶

Not far from Christ-Church at Limington is a very great Salt work, which is worth your Seing.¶

Pool is the next Port Westward, where you may See the making of Copperas; and to a Gentleman of So much curiosity as is bred and instill'd into you, none of the works of nature, beneficiall ones especially ought to be unregarded. Not-withstanding the abundance of Salt that is made So near as Limington, & that the Duty of foreign Salt is double that of English viz. ^{s}6:^{p}8 p bushell, yet here are great quantities of french Salt imported. Yet none of it is us'd here, but brought in for the advantage of the drawback of the Duty; for Bond is given at importation for payment of the Duty in 6 months, in which time 'tis either exported to Newfoundland to cure fish there, or Sent to the more Western Ports for the curing of Pilchards or herrings or Some Cod & Hake. And the advantage of the Drawback for what is exported beyond Seas ly's in this, that the bushell is measured inward by lumping, & outward by Shivering, which is 10^t p cent difference.

West of England

Christ-Church

Limington

Pool

And for what is us'd for curing of fish at home, the allowance for Exportation is near as much as the value of the Salt with the duty. In So much that
the duty upon Salt is the greatest encouragement that ever was or can be to
the fishing trade.¶

From Pool it is but a Step to the Isle of Purbeck, where I have been in-   Isle of Purbeck
form'd there is a very good house belonging to [*blank space*] and the ruins of
an old Castle are visible to one travelling on the road, and I think the
nearest way to Weymouth thro this Isle.¶

From Weymouth you may Step to Portland, which furnishes Stone for all   Weymouth
our noble fabricks.¶   Portland

From thence you have a Small journey to Dorchester, wch is famous for   Dorchester
nothing but being the County Town. Therfore it may be better to go from
Weymouth to Abbotsbury, where is the finest Swannery in the World   Abbots-bury
belonging to Coll. Strangways. and thence thrô Bridport you go to Lyme.¶   Lyme

But if you have a mind to See Some of the best of that Country So cry'd up
for Hunting, you may go from Pool to Dorchester and See the house where
the great Duke of Ormond past the retired part of his life, & go from
Dorchester to Weymouth. The Riches of Dorsetshire consist chiefly in
Sheep, of wch a prodigious number is Sold every year at Michlemass at
Wayhill near Andover, which Supplys Wilts, Hants, Sussex, Surrey, Middlesex, London & the Countys about it.¶

From Lyme I know nothing can retard you from making the best of your
way to Exeter, for I know no place or thing very remarkable that Should
Stop you. But the whole County of Devon is enrich'd by the Manufacture
of Serges, Saies, Perpetuans, and the like woollen Manufactures. Half a
days journey on this Side Exeter you pass by a new built House of Sr Walter
Youngs which is worth Seeing. And there may be more houses that may
draw you very deservedly out of y^r way to See. Of which I have no knowledge, nor had time when in those parts So much as to enquire after.¶   Exeter

Exeter is a gentile & rich City and a considerable Port; tho hithertoo no
Ship cou'd come up to it, but they all unladed at Topsham, from whence in
boats the goods were brought up to Exeter, where the Custom house is, and
where the chief Officers of the Customs live. But of late having obtain'd an
Act of Parliament to make the River Navigable to Exeter, & having rais'd a
considerable Sum of Money, and labour'd dilligently to effect it, you will by
this time See whether it be feasable or no, and will answer the trouble &
charge.¶

From hence you may go to Torbay, and by a Short passage Strike over to   Torbay
Dartmouth, a little but very Secure Port.¶   Dartmouth

Your next Port is Plymouth, a populous Town being of great Trade. Here   Plymouth
you may rest your Self a little, and the fatiguing way between Dartmouth &
this wou'd require it if nothing else wou'd.¶

But you must not leave this place without Seeing that curious Tower that is built upon the Eddy Stone Some leagues off to Sea. And to take a just account of the new Dock is a good days work. And you were best to go thither by water to See what forts or block houses are or may be made to Secure the Passage that goes out of the Sound into the River where the Dock is, & where the Kings whole fleet may ly.¶

M.r Edgecomb's

You must also allow your Self time to Step over to Mount Edgecomb, which King Charles Said was the pleasantest Seat in the World. The royall Fort is also worth your Sight; & you must observe how Safe & comodiously the Merchant Ships ride in Cat-Water.¶

Cat Water

Loo

Fowey

The next Western Port from Plymouth is Loo, & not far from thence ly's Fowey, Secure Ports for Small Ships, & very proper & convenient for fishing.¶

Truro

M.r Boscowen's

Thence you go to Truro, whither all the Tin of this part of the Country is brought to be Sealed & exported. A little down the River ly's M.r Boscowens Seat worth your going to, not for the Sake of the house, but to See the various Inletts of Water, which afford most convenient places for the Smugling of foreign goods; as Clements River a mile below Truro, where a Small Vessel may run two miles up into the Country; Tregony River, a mile below the other which runs up 3 miles; Carman river a league below that, and Several other Creeks; all which you may observe if you go from Fowey to Truro by water which I wou'd advise you to do if you can get a conven.t passage, the pleasure whereof will more than answer the charge, & your horses you Send by land.¶

Penryn

Falmouth

Penryn is your next Port, which is impoverisht by Falmouth which ly's nearer the Sea, & upon the Bay, which is capable of recieving any number of Ships of no greater a bulk than a 3.d rate Ship, for a Ship that draws more Water than Such a Frigat can Scarce get over the Bar; and the Port is, or may be well Secur'd by Pendennis Castle. The most Western Port on the South Side of Cornwall is Penzance, which Stands in Mounts Bay, which is a very dangerous Bay, if the Wind blow fresh Southerly, & little Security is to be had at Penzance. Upon a Rock in this Bay is built a Castle call'd S.t Michaels Mount belonging to S.r John S.t Albans.¶

Penzance

S.t Ives

Hence you cross to S.t Ives, a Short passage, and very good way till within a mile of the town. And when you are about Midway you may See both Seas. S.t Ives is very much incomoded & damaged by the Sands, and has a great resemblance of a decay'd Spanish Port, and you must walk near a mile down to it.¶

fishing on y.e South Coast of Cornwall

Upon all the Southern coast of Cornwall and at S.t Ives is the great fishing for pilchards & for Hake & Some Cod; & if you come there at the fishing time, as possibly you may, it will be worth your while to observe the Manner of catching and curing all these kinds of fish. A Virtuoso may herein find Something of Nature to Philosophise upon; for at S.t Ives open a Cod that had 3 crabs each as big as my hand in his belly.¶

From hence you must go back again to Truro takeing Redruth in your way,   Redruth
near which place you may See a great many Tin and Some Copper Mines.¶
The next Port is Padstow, whence are Shipt the best Cornish Slate, and   Padstow
thence you may make your way to Launceston the chief town of this   Launceston
County; concerning which you may wondor how it comes to pass that it
Sends more Burgesses to Parliament than any other County in England;
and in your journeying you may enquire after the reason or occasion of it,
which tho I cou'd not, yet you may meet with it.¶
Not far from hence is a house of the Earl of Bath's building which is Said to
be very magnifficent, and fit to be Seen for itself, tho possibly not for its
Situation, nor for any thing that I can hear about it.¶
What else is remarkable till you come to Biddiford I know not, but this   Biddiford
Port is worth Seeing, for being more comodious than Barnstaple it draws
the trade from thence. For tho Barnstaple be a better Town, and better   Barnstaple
Situated in itself, yet because no Ship can come up to the Town, but all the
Goods thither bound are forced to unlade at Instow 5 miles down the River,
the trade runs to Biddiford, where Ships of good burden may come up to
the Key.¶
The next town you are to have your eye upon is Minhead, and I know   Mine-head
nothing to draw you out of the direct road thither; but that I can't prescribe
to you because my business call'd me from town to town as well little as
great, without any regard to Roads.¶
This Port you may believe to be considerable, because there is an Act of
Parliam.ᵗ pass'd this Session for the recovring Securing & keeping in repayr
the harbour of Minehead, for the benefit & Support of the Trade & Naviga-
tion of this Kingdom. Adjoining to Minhead is Dunster Castle belonging to   Dunstar Castle
Mʳ. Lutterell, where you will certainly be treated if Sʳ Jacob Banks chance to
be there, & knows of your coming to town.¶
Going hence you cannot but Step to Taunton, a large Town, & of great   Taunton
Trade. And that you may let no Port in this Channel escape you, you must
go from hence to Bridgwater and thro Wells to Bristoll.¶   Bridgewater
From Sᵗ Ives to Bridgewater ther's as great fishing for Herrings as there is   Bristol
in the Southern Channel for pilchards; and great quantitys of white Her-   Herring fishing
rings are usually carry'd for France, not in barrels, as they are carry'd to
Portugal Spain & Italy, but in bulk or loose in the hold of the Ship. For the
French will admit no Herrings to be imported into their Country by the
English, but what are cur'd with french Salt, and they are not Satisfyed with
yᵉ oathes of the Masters of the Ships that they are So, but they will have
them brought loose, that they may See them to be So cured.¶
More, and more usefull observations in these Countrys you will undoubtedly make who travel them for an other purpose than I did or cou'd do,
who had my head fill'd wᵗʰ the daily renew'd clamours & complaints of or
against the Excise Men. And if any thing that is here offer'd may help to the

Improvment of your knowledge in home affairs, I Shall think my labour
well bestow'd, and your kind acceptance of it a Sufficient requitall to S.[r]

Y.[r] most faithfull hum.[bl] Serv.[t]

Francis Parry

Letterbook copy.
British Library, Add. Mss. 47025, ff. 42v-45v.

Peter LeNeve to Sir John Perceval

Peter Le Neve Esq.
the Herauld's
directions to me
in my journy
round England.

S.[r]   24. June 1701

Essex
Suffolk
Norfolk
& CambridgeShire
Giddey Hall

Mr Ambrose

Writtle
Chelmsford
New Hall
Colchester
Wytham

Falkborn hall
Coggshall
Fælix Hall

Harwich

Ipswich

After passing over Bow bridge, and thro Stratford turn up the road on
the left hand to the green Man in Epping Forest to view Wansted house &
Park late S.[r] Josiah Childs Baronet, now Bernard Child's Esq. his 2.[d]
Son: Then into the road again at Ilford: thence to Rumford, a mile beyond which
is an old Seat call'd Giddey Hall, formerly possess't by S.[r] Thomas Cook K.[t]
on the road Side; So towards IngatStone, nigh which on the left Stands an
odd built house of an octagonall figure, but call'd the round house, now
belonging to M.[rs] Ambrose, widow of . . . . Ambrose who being Melter of
the Mint during the time of recoining the Money, got money, but lost his
Life, Said to be worth the viewing on the inside, because the rooms are well
proportion'd, which can hardly be Supposed by the outward form. Then if
worth while, See the Seat of the Lord Petre at Writtle, So to Chelmsford and
New-Hall, whereabouts Mr Owsley is best able to direct. Thence to Colchester, but perhaps may think it worth while to visit Wytham a market
town where was an old Camp. ¶
Falkborn Hall the Seat of Edward Bullock Esq. Coggshall and Fælix Hall by
Kelvedon formerly the Estates And Seat of Sr Robert Southwell Kn.[t] your
Ancestor in the time of Hen: 8 Mr Owsley will inform whether Maldon,
Braintree, Thaxted, Dunmow Gosfield, or any Seats thereabouts are worth
going out of the way to view 10 or 15 miles on the right hand, or worth while
to go to Harwich or Landguard Fort. ¶
From Harwich you must perhaps ferry over the river Stower, parting the
two Countys into Suffolk, wher Arwarton presents itself on the left, An old
Seat of the Ancient Family of Parker, ⟨My Brother Parkers Seat⟩[1] lately S.[r]
Philip Parker's Bar.[t] of the Same Stock wth the late Lord Morley, which
passed by Heires females from the familys of De Avillers & Bacon to them,
without any Sale from the time of Will.[m] the first. ¶
Being arriv'd at Ipswich, Christ Church presents itself without the town,
where Cardinal Wolsey designed to erect a Colledge, but his possessions
being Seized on by K. Hen.8. it came thro other hands to the family of

---

1. Marginal note, incorporated.

Wythiple, & by the daughter & Heir of Sᵣ Willᵐ to Devereux Viscᵗ
Hereford.¶

It ought to be now determin'd whether the road to Yarmouth is to be taken,
or that to Scole Inn, & So to Norwich. For the 1ˢᵗ I once travell'd it & found
it very pleasant, being full of Towns, & Several Gentlemens Seats on each
Side the road. To the other I am a Stranger. I will therfore describe the road
to Yarmouth: between Ipswich & Woodbridge I do not remember any Seat.
On the left out of the road Stands Playford another Seat of Sᵣ Tho. Feltons.
At Woodbridge was formerly a Priory (now only ruins) wherein the chief
Gentry of these parts were buried, especially the Uffords & Paytons, who
had their names from Ufford & Payton Hall.¶

On the road a little beyond Woodbridge may be made an Excursion to
Orford (vyeing in the Season wᵗʰ Colchester for Oysters) & Alborough, 2
Port towns perhaps worth Seeing (but I know not) And in the way to
Alborough from Orford, Sudborn formerly belonging to Sᵣ Michael Stan-
hop, after the Wythepole's & the Viscᵗ Hereford, where are Some Monu-
ments in the Church of that family.¶

Thence if you come into the road at Glemham parva may be Seen a neat
house & gardens in the middle of a Park now belonging to Thomas Glemham Esq. a Gentleman endow'd with great civility as inheritor of the
Vertue & Estate of Sᵣ Sackville, Sᵣ Thomas & Sᵣ John Glemham his Ancestors. If Sᵣ John will be pleas'd to use my name with my Service, I Shall take
it as an honour, having never Seen yᵉ Gentleman, but I am Sure you Shall
be welcom to him for the Sake of my Brother Oliver Le Neve of great
Wichingham in Norfolk, they having married two Sisters the daughters of
Sᵣ John Knivet of Ashwell Thorp in Norfolk, Knᵗ of the Bath, & Coheirs to
their Brother Thomas Knivet Esq.¶

Stratford is the next town, beyond it lys Benhale, a house & Park of Sᵣ John
Dukes Barᵗ Thence yᵉ road continues to Saxmundham a pretty market
town: After, Yexford presents itself, near which is Cockfield Hall where
lives Sᵣ Charles Blois Barᵗ a Member of Parliamᵗ and every way a Gentleman. next you come to Darsham House & park, inhabited by the Lady
Knivet, Relict of the aforesaid Sᵣ John Knivet daughter of the Lady Bed-
ingfield lately deceas'd, who in the Old house here continues the Same
hospitallity Hereditary to the 2 family's. Bliborough & Westwood Lodge
Stand both in the road, but further to the Sea on the right. Dunwich may be
thought worth the Seeing for the Antiquity. This I am Sure of that at
Henham Hall and Park by the road Side, the lovers of Antiquity will find
occasion of Contemplation, when they recollect that the famous Charles
Brandon Duke of Suffolk in Hen: 8. time lived here; & before him the
Family of Kederston whose Estate devolv'd by Heires female to Tho.
Chaucer Esq. a Descendant of the famous Poet of that name, and his
daughter & heir marry'd to Delapole Earl of Suffolk. This Mannor among

Woodbridge
Playford

Orford
Alborough
Sudborn

Glemham, yᵉ
Seat of Tho.
Glemham Esq.

Stratford
Benhale, Sᵣ
John Duke's Seat
Saxmundhum
Coxfield Hall,
Sᵣ Ch. Blois's
Seat
Darsham,
the Lady Knivet's
Seat

Bliborough
Dunwich
Henham Hall
Sᵣ Jⁿ Roys's Seat

the rest being convey'd from the Crown, after the Attainder of that family, to the Said Charles Brandon with the Title of Duke of this County, & it is Said, S.ʳ John Royse Bar.ᵗ the worthy possessor hereof has an original picture of that Duke.¶

Southwold

More to the right may be Seen Southwold, & the Bay commonly call'd by contraction Sold-Bay, famous for the fight between the English and Dutch in the late reign of King Charles the 2.ᵈ Of which fight the present Fr. King Said, that no Nation but the English wou'd endure beating 3 days together.¶

Satterly hall,
S.ʳ J.ⁿ Playter's
Seat

Not 2 miles from the road to the right on a rising ground Stands an ancient Seat call'd Satterly Hall, having Possessors called there from, and in the time of Edward the fourth purchass'd by the family of Playter, whose lineal Descendant S.ʳ John Playters Bar.ᵗ is the present Inheritor: where if S.ʳ John will be pleas'd to call, he will find a piece of mutton and other honest Country fare, S.ʳ John having married a relation of mine.¶

Beccles

Rose hall, S.ʳ R.
Rich's Seat

Thence to Beccles, the last Town of Suffolk on the great road; without the town on the Marsh Side is Rose-Hall, which had old possessors of the Same name, & after by purchasse came to the family of Garnish, who had very large Inheritances in this County & Norfolk; & have Still very good footing in both: but this was long Since Sold, acknowledging S.ʳ Rob.ᵗ Rich Bar.ᵗ latley deceas'd as Lord thereof. The House is old fashion'd, built with brick, and the great Hall of an Antique make.¶

Gillingham,
S.ʳ Edmond
Bacons Seat

Lake Linthing

Somerly Hall
S.ʳ Rich.ᵈ
Allen's Seat

I must now advise my ingenuous Traveller to leave the ordinary road to Yarmouth, after having Seen Gillingham in Norfolk S.ʳ Edmond Bacon's Seat and return'd back to Beccles, to visit Somerly, going into the Peninsula over Mutford bridge, where he will meet with a Sight Something Surprising Scitt. the lake call'd Linthing, which is within a Stones cast of disemboguing itself into the Ocean, but is there Stop'd by a bank of Sand. The waters recoiling make a long course round the Island. Thence to Somerly Hall the Seat of S.ʳ Rich.ᵈ Allen Bar.ᵗ whose true name is Anguish. But haveing this Seat with other Revenues devised to him by S.ʳ Tho. Allen the younger, Bar.ᵗ his Unkle, he has lately assum'd his name without any warrant from the King preceding, or other Authority than that of his being call'd by y.ᵉ name of Allen without any alias by the King in the letters Pattents for the creating him to that dignity, w.ᶜʰ may make a moot case for the Heralds to dispute upon, whether there being no Such person as Richard Allen then in life, the Patent is not void. But to return to our Itinerary. Here the Spectator may view a noble Royalty (He being Lord Paramount of this whole Hundred or Island call'd Lothing land) a fair Park, formerly celebrated Gardens when in the possession of S.ʳ J.ⁿ Wentworth, Several large Broads, (a word used here & in Norfolk for a poole, or where a River Spreads itself over the adjacent ground) Several Decoys, & a Warren. For these reasons this Gentleman is reckon'd to have a great advantage over his Neighbours in

Speedy & cheap providing for his Sudden Guests within his own
Jurisdiction.¶

Being So nigh Leistoff ought to be view'd, once a poor fisher town, but by   Leistoff
the decay of Yarmouth in a better Estate than formerly. Thence to Yar-
mouth is a very pleasant road for about 6 miles on the Beach by the Sea
Side. You ride by Copton or Hopton lights, in which a Smith works all   Hopton lights
night, the fire of whose forge is a guide to the Ships under Sail, and before
you enter Yarmouth by Gorleston famous for nothing but the Seamens   Gorleston
mistresses here inhabiting, and the ruins of the Monastry. You may ride to
Burgh Castle on the left hand, of wch Cambden and all our old Historians
take notice, the ruins whereof are hardly to be Seen.¶

And So we bid adieu to Suffolk.¶

Thus Safely arriv'd at Yarmouth, where the fort, the Key, the Bridge, the   Norfolk
Gates, Walls & the Church are all worth notice, the last built by the Same   Yarmouth
Bishop who translated the See from Thetford to Norwich, & built that
Cathedral.¶

Yarmouth Capons are here eaten in perfection (Scitt. a red herring;) Most
persons who come hither take a boat to go off to Sea, & upon Braden
within less than a mile, where three Rivers meet, & make a great broad
Water. And take a Curry (whereon they draw their goods, the Streets being
narrow which cross from one part of the town to the other) to See the Fort
which is of no force, & the Peer, wch is maintain'd at great charge by
Several Acts of Parliam^t After having Satisfy'd your curiosity here, the next
Town towards Norwich in the road, is Castor, where may be Seen the   Castor
Ruins of a once Stately house, but now inhabited by a Farmer, & made use
of for his corn &c. Of this Town was Lord, Sr John Falstaff K^t of the Garter   Sr J^n Falstaff
in the Reign of K. Hen: 6. famous in the Reign of Hen: 5th his Father in the
French War, with whose name a little varied Shakespear the late Poet has
made bold in his Play call'd Hen: the 5th & the humours of Sr John Falstaff,
much to the prejudice of this once great Man. But the Pile of building
aforenam'd was I think erected for a Colledge of Priests by S^r . . . . . Paston,
to whom it came after his death.¶

You ride by or thro Manteby & Filby, where nothing worth remark to the 2   Manteby, Filby,
Burrows; Towns of a like obscurity, thô Manteby (being never Sold Since   The two Burrow's
the time of William ye 1st) had long Since a Seat belonging to Sr John de
Manteby the Heir generall, uniting it by mariage to the Earl of Yarmouth's
Family where it now continues: it's a low Country hereabout call'd Flegg,
divided into 2 Hundreds, wherin are Several broad waters, the road lying
on the Causeway thrô them. The Earth here easily yeilds to the labour of the
husbandman, for which they have a proverb, that they plow their ground
without Man or horse, viz. a Mare or 2 wth a boy.¶

There is nothing observable on the road, till you arrive at Ludham the   Ludham

Bishop of Norwich his Country Seat, tho mean & let to Farm, which with many Mannors here about belonged to the Abbot of St Bennet in the Holme Situate on the other Side of the Water by the River's Side turning on the left hand a little out of the way to view the ruins thereof. The Posses-sions of this Abbey were in Hen: ye 8th time exchanged with the Bishop of Norwich, The old Estate of the Bishoprick being given to the King, and the Bishop accepting of the Revenues of this Abbey; Willm Rudge the Abbot of St Bennets being then made Bishop of Norwich, his Successors were Still reckon'd Abbots of that Monastery.¶

Hence you cross the River at Wrehxam, & when you come to Rackeath, may turn off on the right to See Rackley Hall Sr Horrace Pettus's Seat, So to Spixworth & Horsham St Faiths, the Seats of the family of the Southwells, whence making a little round riding thro Attlebridge, & turning towards Norwich imediatly on your left, after you are over the bridge to Morton-Hall al: Helmingham (where liv'd in Queen Eliz. time Thomas Southwell Esq. & in K. James's reign Sr Hen. Southwell K.^t, of the privy Councell to the last, wch in my poor opinion is as pretty a Situation as any hereabouts or in the County, the House being built by Thomas Southwell Esq. In the Church lyes buried Katherine Audley Widdow of . . . . . . Audley of Bear Church Essex, & a Southwell by name who had it for life. The present Owner Nicholas Helwis Esq. if you please to use my name will Shew the inside of his House.¶

Thence a mile or two to Ringland the Estate of my Grandfather, who Sold it to a Kinsman of mine, & another Kinsman Mr Francis Neve has lately rebuilt the old house which Shews itself a neat little piece of Architecture.¶

So to Cossey the Stone habitation of Sr Francis Jernegan Bar.^t, whose Ancestor in the reign of Q. Mary Master of the Horse & Privy Counsellor had it of her gift. This Gentleman's family have always profess'd the Romish Persuasion, which hinder's not from being every way a Gentleman, are Said to be descended from the Danes, and a 2.^d Branch of them who liv'd at Somerlay Town Suff. The Mannor is one of the best in the County, having Several Towns round it held therof; and was long Since belonging to the old Earls of Britanny in France, & Richmond in England, & has like-wise been Settled in joynture on Several Queens. Hence there is nothing worth Seeing to Norwich, whether thô accounted but 12 Miles directly from Yarmouth, yet by this circuit it will be a good days journey. In Norwich, the

Cathedrall, the Dukes Pallace, & garden, the Chappell in the Field House, the Castle, (of the Same form & I think dimensions with that you will See at Rising by Lynne) the Market place, the Hall thereby built of Flints, and the publick buildings, with the ruins of the Religious houses may be worth Seeing, especially the Steeple of the Grey Fryers built by Sr Tho. de Erpingham a K.^t & Warriour in great favour with Hen. ye 5th he having his Arms thereon. The persons to whom I can best recomend you, are D.^r

Prideaux Arch Deacon of . . . . & one of the Prebendaries; a Searcher into
the Antiquities of the Cathedrall Church & City. Robt Davy Esq Record^r
and one of the Members for that City in the present Parliam^t And Alderman Fr. Gardiner, who has neither Spar'd his time nor Mony to collect
curious Books. Some of these Gentlemen are able to advise what Seats may
be worth the view about that City besides Sprowston. Sr Charles Addam's
Bar^t & Rackheath nam'd before, Sr Horatio Pettus's Bar^t The first descended from his Grandfather Sr Tho. Addams Lord Mayor of London,
The other, from Sr John Pettus Mayor of Norwich.¶
Spixworth & St Faith's are the two next towns. At the first liv'd Tho.
Southwell jun^r 2^d Son of Richd Southwell of St Faith's Esq. eldest Son of S^r
Rich^d of Woodrising K^t At the 2^d Rich^d the father, & Rich^d the Son, Father
of Anthony, father of Sr Robert now living where the Said Anthony was
born. At this Town of St Faiths is the greatest Fair kept for live beasts in the
3 Counties just before Mich^{ss}¶
Next is Staining Hall, where John Harbord Esq. built not long Since a neat
House, living Sometimes there, otherwhiles at Gunton nearer to the Sea, &
more out of your way. Oxnede deserves your thoughts, the Seat of the R^t
Hon^{bl} the Earl of Yarmouth, to be Seen for the Situation, Park, neat Church
& monuments in it, the House & cabinet of Rareties. When you design for
Lenne if you have not Seen Cossey, Ringland & Morton Hall before, your
way must be to Mile Cross, taking the left hand road, it carries you to
Attlebridge, where you cross the River wch runs thro Norwich. Taking the
right hand 2 miles further, you cross it at Lonwade bridge again &c. But if
you have not Seen Cossey & Morsen, thither go to Ringland Morton &
Wichingham, & just beyond . . . . . . bridge be pleas'd to turn into the
Inclosures on the right, to accept the civility to be found at Wichingham
Hall from my Brother Oliver le Neve Esq. where I will engage you a kind
wellcome, who if you think it worth while will wait on you to Repham a
market Town, where may be Seen 3 Churches, one decayed, in one Church
yard, but nothing else worth Seeing, & Salle a mile beyond, one of the
neatest Churches in the County, built by one of the Bruces Lords here, So to
Melton Constable, a fine Building just finish'd in a Park by Sr Jacob Astley
Bar^t of Hilmorton. likewise in Warwick Shire, one of the Knights of the
Shire at this time for the County, of the Same family with the Barons Astley
of Pateshall in StaffordSh: & the late Ld Astley of Reading (whose Heir he
is) famous for his Military Exploits in the late Wars A.D. 1640.¶
In the Church are Several neat Monuments. The town has the addition of
Constable from a family who were So call'd, as being Constables to the
Bishops of Norwich; for then every great Lord & Bishop lived in Such State
wth his Several Officers about him at his Court, as the King at his, with the
Constable, Marshal, Sewer, Steward &c.¶
Editha the Sister & co-heir of Peter de Melton at other times call'd Peter le

Arch-Deacon
Prideaux now
Dean of Norwich
(1721)

Sprowston Seat
of S^r Ch. Addams

Spixworth, & S^t
Faith,
The Southwells

Staining Hall
Seat of J^n
Harbord, Esq.

Oxnede, y^e
Seat of the
E. of Yarmouth

Mile Cross

Attlebrigg

Lonwade
bridge

Wichingham
Hall Seat of
Oliver le Neve
Esq.
Repham

Salle

Melton-
Constable Seat
of Sr Jacob Astley

Constable marry'd to Sr Jacob's Ancestor in the time of Edward ye 1st fixt them here where they have increas'd their old Inheritance by the addition of divers lands.¶

Hence thrô Fackenham a pretty Market Town to Reynham the magniffi- cent Habitation of the R.^{t} Hon.^{bl} Charles Visc.^{t} Townsend Ld Lieu.^{t} of the County, Custos Rutolor. &c. His Ancestors having liv'd here in great Splendor Since the time of Edward the 4th. when Sr Roger Townsend K.^{t} Sergeant at Law, Attorney Gen.^{ll} & one of the justices of the Comon Pleas. Horatio late Ld Visc.^{t} Townsend was the first of this family made a Peer, his Grandfather being created a Bar.^{t} This Gentleman being very gouty, con- triv'd his Staircase So, & an Engine in it, that he cou'd convey himSelf up to any floor of his house. The present L.^{d} being of great natural parts has So polisht them with learning, & his Travells into Italy, France, Germany, Holland &c. that he is fit for the greatest Employments in the State; but that his innate modesty forbids Such ambitious thoughts . . . .¶

Now Rising Castle about 6 or 7 miles further appears Situate on a hill, & deserves for Antiquity one of the first places, which I have in part already describ'd. The Castle being built by Will. de Albany Earle of Arundell, is very like that at Norwich & a large Ruine. It was call'd the Honor of Castle Rising attending for Some time that family, till an Heir female convey'd it to the Montalts, the last of whom Settled it in reversion on Edward the 3^d Being after that given to Several persons, & reunited to the Crown again, at length it fixt in that of the Dukes of Norfolk, until within these few years it was Sold by the last Duke to another of the family Scil: to Tho. Howard Esq. deceas'd, Son of Sr Robt Howard K.^{t} Auditor of the Exchequer.¶

It is govern'd by a Mayor & Alderman. Here is a fair Alms house (Said to claim your Sight) for a Governess & 12 poor Widdows, founded by Tho. Howard Earl of Northon in the time of K. James the first. And the Succeed- ing Dukes were to be Patrons thereof. The most comon tradition of this County is that Lenne arose to the present greatness by the decay of this place. but your Self will be a judge whether ever Rising cou'd be So well Situated for a Sea Trade.¶

I must take notice of 2 things: 1. The Chase, the only one either in this County, Suffolk, or Cambridge Shire, where the Deere are as Secure as within the Fortification of the Park Pale: For being Lords of a great parcell of barren ground, and the whole Hundred being in possession of the Albanies, they had the Royaltie of hunting & hawking &c all hereabout. The 2^d is, that it is the 5th town in this County, which Sends Members to Parliam.^{t} thô one of the largest Countys in England, & as populous, when a little County in the West Sends almost four times the number; which putts me in mind of an answer to a complaint of a Gentleman, who "told a North and West Country Member, that it was very "hard that the East Shou'd pay So excessivly to the

"Taxes, and the North & West So little, who desired him
"to Say no more, that it was very well they did not pay
"all, Since those parts Sent So many Members to outvote
"them at any time.¶

But I hasten to Lenne: the River the Church and Several other things may
be observable here, to which you may be directed by M.ʳ Bell Alderman, if
you please to use my name, he being an ingenuous Architect. It was the best
Town which the Bishops of Norwich had till the exchange of their lands in
Hen: 8ᵗʰ time, as I have before taken notice. For 'till then, the Bishops had
the Seignory thereof. Thô the May.ʳ & Burgesses had Several Charters of
privileges from K. John, and almost all the Succeeding Kings, yet Still they
own'd y.ᵉ Bishops as their Lords (who had a Palace where they often resided
at Gaywood just without the Town) being call'd Lyme Bishop till King
James 1ˢᵗ alter'd the name to Lyme Regis, renew'd their Charter, & added
many & great priviledges. If you please to view the town wall, you will find
the ruins of an odd Sort of Chappell in the wall as ever I Saw, which I
guesse to have been dedicated to S.ᵗ Margaret the Virgin, the old Patroness
of the Town.¶

I question with my Self whether I Shall advise my Travellers to ferry over, &
ride to the washes only to See them, tho they come back again.¶

If your curiosity leads you out of the way So far, you will ride thrô a flat
Country without a Stone, yet well built Churches with lofty Spires, So that it
was not only to the Ladies but the Churchmen formerly that the proverb of
Far fetcht and dear bought might be applied.¶

I think you ride by Firrington Church, where they Shew you the Tomb (as
they Say, & it may be true) of Sir Frederick Tylney K.ᵗ who liv'd in the time
of K. Rich.ᵈ 1ˢᵗ & was at the Siege of Acon in Palestine. They'l tell you a long
Story of one Hica-thrift fighting with a Gyant w.ᶜʰ is trite among the Boys,
the foundation whereof might be Some matter of fact, that Some one of the
ordinary Sort of persons maintain'd the right of Comon against a Man of
Estate & Power in the Country. This part may be compared to Holland
(except for the Riches & Industry of the Inhabitants,) for here the Sea is
kept from overflowing it at a vast expence, & by many By-Laws, Some of
w.ᶜʰ may be Seen on Record in the Rolls of the Kings Bench of the 3.ᵈ year of
Edward 3.ᵈ It was inhabited long before y.ᵉ time of William the 1ˢᵗ for all the
parishes are mention'd in Dooms-day Book. As to the Story that no Mice
nor ratts breed here, it is altogether false, to be proved by this instance
among Many.¶

An Attorney, none of the honestest, being employ'd by an Owner of a
Mannor here to get & keep possession for him, & after, to recieve his
Rents: When the business was over, the Rents recieved for Some time, the
Gentleman finding for Several reasons he was abused, desired his Receiver
to account w.ᵗʰ him, who cou'd only give him an extravagant gross Sume of

Lenne &
Gaywood

The Washes

Firrington
Church

expenses equalling that of his Receipts; but after urging for particulars, he produc'd a parcell of eaten pieces of paper which he Said he thought he needed not to have brought to have confirm'd the truth of his Acc.ᵗ, for he might plainly See it was *ratified* already. It was formerly one Hundred with that of Fresh-bridge in which Lynne Stands, & paid a proportionable 12.ᵗʰ part to all publick Payments.¶

So much for Lynne & Marshland.¶

Middleton ancient Seat of the L.ᵈ Scales

In the pursuance of your journey you ride by Hard-wick to Middleton, where may be Seen by the Rivers Side in a low ground the Skeleton of the Porch of the old Mannor place belonging to the Lords Scales formerly Owners hereof, who[*se*] Inheritance after it had continued 5 descents or 6,

rise of y.ᵉ Howard Family

reverted to the 5 or 6 Issue of 2 daughters, one marryed to . . . . . Howard, the elder Branch of the Duke of Norfolks Family, which had there first rise from S.ᵗ John Howard K.ᵗ a Judge in the latter end of Edw.ᵈ the 1.ˢᵗ, whose Father, nor any before him had not enlarg'd their Estates much further than to the bounds of the Parish of Wigenhale, a town just by this where

Wigenhale

they were Lords of a Mannor call'd Wigenhale Howards.¶

Pentney-Abbey

From hence I must direct your course to Pentney Abbey well worth Seeing, built of Stone, & leaded on the top w.ᵗʰ but little variation from the old

Narburgh. a Seat of the Spelmans

Structure whilst an Abbey. The next Town in your Road is Narburgh, whereof Cambden takes notice. Here is the Seat of the family of Spelman whereof S.ᵗ Hen: Spelman was the Glory in the last Age.¶

Swaffham

Swaffham a market town on a hill parcell of the Honor of Richmond in this County presents itself next to your view. Here they tell you a Story of a Pedler, who built the Church & enlarg'd it, beyond the bounds of Truth. The Spurrs made here are famous, tho not to that degree of those of Rippon.¶

South-Pickenham a Seat of S.ᵗ Ed. Atkins

Thence thro South-Pickenham (where I am told S.ᵗ Edw.ᵈ Atkins K.ᵗ lately

Watton, Sculton, Woodrising Seat of y.ᵉ Bedles, once of y.ᵉ Southwells

deceas'd has built a pretty House) to Watton another Market Town of good Note, and from hence thro Sculton to Woodrising, about 4 miles, the place w.ᶜʰ So long entertain'd the Family of the Southwells, till S.ᵗ Tho. Southwell K.ᵗ Sold it to S.ᵗ Francis Crane with many other Mannors as Carbroke, Craneworth, the Hundreds of South Grenho & [Grimsthow?] &c. & from that family to Rob.ᵗ Bedle Esq. whose Son now lives here.¶

Merton, Seat of W.ᵐ DeGrey Esq.

Your curiosity being Satisfy'd here, your next course is to Merton, which House I never Saw, yet am of opinion you may cast your eye thereon. This is one of those Estates which has made but one change, Since the time of the first William call'd the Conqueror, for in his time in Dooms-day book it is recited to be parcell of the possessions of Baynoird, and by a daughter & heir of a younger branch of that family, about the time of Ed. 2.ᵈ it was convey'd to that of De Grey, who have ever Since in the Male Line continued the possession. Will.ᵐ de Grey Esq. is now Lord thereof.¶

From hence the next place well worth your riding out of the way to See is

Bukenham House & Park, lately built after a very neat Model by Sr Sam: Vincent of London deceas'd having many things worth view in the inside there of.¶

Bukenham, house of Mr Vincent

Now your road ly's directly over the heath to Thetford, without passing any Town except Croxton or . . . . but the Park which was parcell of the possessions of the late Duke of Norfolk.¶

Croxton

The next Town to Thetford tho out of your road on ye right, is Sandy-downham, which you will hardly think worth your while to view, tho it is noted in print for the Shoals of Sand lately issuing out of Small holes in Such quantities that it drown'd houses, & almost overwhelm'd ye Church. Of the particulars whereof if you think not fit to be an Eye wittness, the report may be Surprising. One Mr Wright was lately Lord of this Town, an eminent Antiquary in his time.¶

Sandy-downham

Mr Wright an Emin^t Antiquary

As for Thetford, the observables here are the high Mount, the ruins of the Abbey, the Town house built by Sr Joseph Williamson K^t &c.¶

Thetford

If Euston was not Seen before, now is the time, as well worth Seeing as any thing Since you left London. Culforth next, where the gardens and Canals lately made by the late Ld Cornwallys. Ampton is truly worth notice for the Entertainment dayly given to all gentlemen who are pleas'd to visit the possessor thereof . . . Calthorpe Esq. of a younger branch of Sr Chr. Calthorpe K^t.¶

Euston

Culforth Seat of my Ld Cornwallis Ampton house of Mr Calthorpe

Then Hengrave a fair Seat of great Antiquity: it boasted of Gentlemen to which it gave name. Now S^r . . . . Gage Bar^t has a just Title to it.¶

Hengrave Seat of S^r . . . Gage Bar^t

Thence to Bury is about 4 miles. Several observables are in this Town: the Abbey ruins, once the most wealthy in the County, the Churches, & other things; the Recorder both a good Lawyer & facetious in conversation, & Mr Maynard Second brother of Banister Ld Maynard who has the Estate at [Hoxon?] formerly Sr Robt Southwells, are the only persons to whom I have the honour to be known here. But at a little distance of 3 miles lives Sr Richd Gipps K^t of Whelnetham, who for the Sake of Sr Robt will wait on you 6 miles.¶

Bury

Welnetham house of Sr Richd Gipps K^t

But out of your road to Cambridge to Stowlongtoft is the library of the late famous Sr Symonds Dews Bar^t Grandfather of Sr Symonds Dewes the present Proprietor, if your curiosity will lead you thither.¶

Stowlongtoft Seat of Sr Symonds Dewes, a library there

I am told Rushbroke, where the family of the Germins have long been Lords, now the R^t hon^{bl} Tho. Ld Germin is worth Seeing. When you design for Newmarket &c, the County is open till you come to Kenetford, of which nothing more is to be Said than over the heath on your right hand to Chippenham, built first by Sr Wm Russell K^t & Bar^t Treasurer of the Navy to K. Ch: the Ist; His Successor Sr Willm Russell Bar^t convey'd it to another Treasurer of the Navy Scit. Edw. Earl of Orford, who has Scatterd Some of the loose corns of his great gains upon the new buildings &c I am told likewise that Cheevly above Newmarket the Seat of the R^t Hon^{bl} Hen: L^d

Rushbroke Seat of ye Ld Germin

Chippenham, Seat of the E. of Orford

Cheevly Seat of the Ld Dover

Dover 2ᵈ brother to the Lᵈ Jermyn is well built & furnisht, tho the Mob
were pleas'd in the year 1688 to gutt it, as the term then was.¶

New-Market

After having taken the diversion of New-Market if any thing there to Stay
you out of riding time, except the Parson of one of the Parishes a most
pleasant companion, no Hater of Clarret tho not a lover of it to excess, Mʳ
Fisher by name, who will give you all the direction his Company can afford,
if you please to wheel out of the comon road, after you have past the
ditches, comonly call'd the Devils two ditches, to the left, proceed to

Horseth Hall, Seat of . . . Brumley Esq.

Horseth Hall, lately built by the Lᵈ Allington deceas'd, & more lately Sold
to . . . . . Brumley Esq.¶

Berklow

Linton

Thence to Berklow where was a fight between the Saxons & Danes, & 2 of
the Tumuli Still remaining by yᵉ Church. To Linton a neat well Situated
Market Town, in the middle of which you will observe a little new built
Box.¶

Walden

From this Town the way to Walden is to be enquir'd 4 Miles thro HadStoke
& little Walden; all wᶜʰ wᵗʰ Several other Mannors own'd the Family of the
Howards Earls of Suffolk for Lords.¶

Audley-End, the Seat of the Earls of Suffolk

At Great Walden the ruins of the Castle & the Church may be Seen.
Audley-End is within the Parish about a mile beyond, built on the ruins of
Walden-Abbey, founded by Geoffry de Magnaville Earl of Essex: a vast
building begun & finish'd by that Earl of Suffolk who was Lord high
Treasurer of England in the time of K. James the 1ˢᵗ If you please to ride up
to the Warren house on the top of the Hill, you will See a foursquare
Encampmᵗ (as I guess) but it may be only the ditch cast up when they made
the Warren.¶

Little-bury

Mʳ Winstanleys house

Then if you please take the great road to Little-bury the next town, in which
lives Mʳ Winstanley, builder of the light house on the Eddistone by Plymouth, & the ingenuous contriver of the water works by Hide Park Corner. I
will not undertake to describe the Several pretty diversions you will meet
with in this house & gardens, that will but anticipate your curiosity, for you
will find great diversion in the view, the charge not much.¶

Chesterford

Ikelton

Wymple
Earl of Radnors
fine gardens

From thence the Cambridge road is thro Chesterford; 2 miles between that
& Ikelton is an old Roman Camp, described in the addition to Camden:
here must turn off on the right hand to go to Wymple cross the Country, if
you have a mind to See the fine gardens lately made by the Rᵗ Honᵇˡ the
Earl of Radnor, I am told worth riding 20 miles out of the way to See.¶

Badburgam, Seat of Sʳ Richᵈ Bennet

Gogmagog Hills

Thence I would Steer your course to Badburgham, lying under Gogmagog
Hills, a neat old Seat & good gardens; Sʳ Richᵈ Bennet Barᵗ decᵈ had lately
the comand thereof, & before his Grandfather, it acknowledg'd Sʳ Horatio
Palavicini of Italian extraction for its owner.¶

From this place riding over the aforesaid Hills on the top of them you must
observe an inclosure with a double Rampier (whereof our Chorogrophers

make mention) and here you will See a pleasant Prospect of Cambridge &
the County round them.¶

From thence 4 or 5 Miles to Cambridge, whether, and during the rest of   Cambridge
your journey I wish you health and pleasure as being

S^r

Y^r most hum^{bl} Servt

Peter Le Neve

Letterbook copy.
British Library, Add. Mss. 47025, ff. 45v-53r.

William Byrd II to Sir Robert Southwell

Harwich ye 17th [*July*] 1701.

Sir

        I envy'd Sr John the pleasure of writeing to you every
time, and therefore we have agree'd to take it by turns. This waits upon you
from the Sea-Side, whither we are got at the time prescrib'd with Safety
pleasure an[d] a whole Skin. The first day we past thro Bow, Stratford,
Ilford, Rumford, and dind at Brentwood, and from thence we past thro
Ingatston to Chelmsford. Here we met Mr Oesly a great master of the
Antiquitys of Essex, but peaks himself chiefly in genealogy. He was very
civil, and favour'd us with a pretty deal of information. He conducted us to
New-hall, which in the days of old has been very magnificent, but has now
nothing remarquable except a Streight Shady walk of a mile long, that leads
from the entrance of the Park to the house, but the view is intercepted by a
riseing in the middle; there is besides this a grove of firrs the finest I have
Seen in Eng^d From hence we proceeded towards Witham, (where our
Antiquary left us,) and thence to Keldon. After dinner we rid to Felix Hall
now in ye possession of Sr Anthony Abdy, a gentleman whome the Spleen
has made very untractable. The house is Something irregular but great part
of it new; tis finely Scituated in the center of a good park. Before Mr Oesly
left us, he gave us to understand that besides this Felix Hall, there was
another Seat and an extraordinary Park about Seaven miles distant, belong-
ing to Sr Robt Southwell in K: Harry the 8^{th's} time. From Viewing this we
rode to a pretty Seat about 4 [*miles?*] off call'd [B]rackly lodge, belonging to
Mr Whitcomb a freind of mine, where we quarter'd, and met with good
entertainment. The next morning we made a Shift to get [a]way time
enough to arrive by 11 a clock at Colchester, where we met with [a] pretty-
many observables, but we beg leave to reserve particulars til we have the
honour to See you, and desire you in the mean time to expect onely y^e

Skeleton of our travels. From Colechester we made a long Stage of 22 miles
thro Manningtree to Harwich, and above half the way had a prospect of
Manningtree-river, which for 12 mile is very broad. The journey hitherto
has been without any misfortune, & attended with a great deal of Pleasure.
Sʳ John is perfectly well, and (which you will be pleas'd to hear) he is
likewise very jovial. I cant percieve any tincture of melancholly in his
temper, but the gravity he Sometimes puts on is nothing but thinking,
which unless it engross him too much is a very great virtue. I will not Say
how many good qualitys I discover in him, because he is to See the letter,
but I am of opinion that youll live to See him a credit to your instructions,
and a great ornament of his Country. We have begun to read Sʳ Thomas
Smith's Republique of England, which we enter upon first, because it
contains the most general information. When we have masterd that, twill
be time enough to descend to particulars. We talk french Sometimes, &
Sometimes Sʳ John Sings, but I have a very good reason to let him do that
by himself. Our horses are not over-rampant, So that there is like to be no
ill consequence from their high-mettle. The Sumpter-horse performs very
well tho at first he was a little uneasy. All our affairs are in good Scituation,
and variety makes every thing pleasant to us. I am with all the Respect in yᵉ
world

                          Sir   your most faithfull Servᵗ
                                                                WByrd.

We Send our complements to the Ladys.

Copy received by addressee.
Collection of Mr. Paul Mellon, Upperville, Virginia.
Photocopy, Virginia Historical Society.

William Byrd II to Sir Robert Southwell

                                                  Norwich yᵉ 26 July 1701.
              Sir
                      I am Sorry it is our fate to date a Second letter to you
from Norwich, where we have been arrested by the illness of the Groom
ever Since wednesday last. The poor fellow began to complain of a pain in
his Side about a week ago, and was let bloud for it, which we concluded
woud cure him. We traveld Slowly on his account, imagining his distemper
woud wear off, but instead of that it is now turnd to a feaver. The ablest
Physician in Town has been Sent for to him, and all other care has been
us'd to recover him, and there is Some reason to hope that he is passt all
danger. But if he do recover, it will be Some time before he is fit for
travelling, and therefore we have got another groom to Supply his place as
far as Cambridge, where we Shall tarry 3 or 4 days, and if by that time

George can get Strength, he may follow thither. In the mean time care is taken that he want nothing to finish his recovery. Thus Sir our Progress has been interrupted by this accident, and if we meet wth many Such, we must dispair of Seing Scotland. Tomorrow morning we Set out towards Thetford, & in our way Shall See Euston Hall. It has been the less regret to us to tarry here So long, because tis a large City, and affords a great many remarques, and besides we have by mentioning Mr Haughtons name, fallen into the acquaintance of Mr Whitefoot, a Clergyman of very great civility & under-standing. and he again has made us known to an old acquaintance of yours, Dr Pridaux, who is Sub Dean here, and master of abundance of learning; He values himself particularly upon his Skil in Arabique, by virtue of which he has convers'd more with the Alcoran and the comments upon it, than Some other Doctors have with the Bible. We far'd not So well at Ipswich by Mr Haughtons recommendation, for there his correspondent Mr Stystead protested he did not know him. We are not negligent in our observations, but lay about us for matter to put into our journall. One remarque I have made here, is, that their clove-Gilliflowers are exceeding large, and they use Some art to make them So. They Shelter the top of the flower wth a thin board from the dew (wch they call capping of it) and by this precaution it thrives much the better. Besides they hang a Sheeps-hoof on the top of the Stick that Supports the flower, into wch the worms & Earwiggs creep in great numbers, and So may be destroyd. On tuesday next at the Duke of Norfolks Pallace will be a Solemnity they call the feast of Flora, where will be a collection of the finest of these flowers that the Country affords, but we Shant be tempted to Stay to see it, not tho all the old divertisments of Flora's feast were to be seen there. I am

Sir

your most faithfull Servt
WByrd

Sr Robt Southwell. Sr John Sends his Service

Copy received by addressee.
Collection of Mr. Paul Mellon, Upperville, Virginia.
Photocopy, Virginia Historical Society.

William Byrd II to Sir Robert Southwell

Cambridge ye 5th August 1701.

S^r

Since our arrival at Cambridge I have had the honour of one letter from you, and Sr John has recievd two. We have been ever Since wednsday Surveying the university, and we owe a great deal of our knowl-edge of this place to the information and Convoy of Mr Colebatch. He is a

man of distinction for learning and knowledge of the world, and we had the
happiness of haveing abundance of his company. He desird me to let you
know, that he is under great concern, that he cant dispatch ye affair you
were pleas'd to commit to him, with So much expedition as he promis'd.
We din'd yesterday at Mr Vice-chancellour's, where Philosophy flew about
the Table faster than the wine. Sr John begins to make good discoverys of
himself in company. We took a journy on Saturday last to Audley Inn,
about 12 miles from hence, which has ye name of being the largest house in
Eng^d In our way we call'd at a house of Mr Winstanlys, that built the lighthouse call'd Eddy-Stone off Plymouth. Here are Several of his contrivances,
wch like the greatest part of modern philosophy, relish more of whimsy
than advantage to mankind. Amongst other things there's a Perpetual
motion, performd by a brass ball, that runs by a gentle declension down
Several Spiral ledges, til comeing to the bottom tis instantly drawn up by a
Pully, and So repeats its tour again. From hence we proceeded to Saffron
Walden, where we met with a man very expert at planting & cureing y^t
commodity. You will not doubt but we took notes of So usefull a Process,
and I can assure you that Ireland is threatend with the propagation of it. In
returning hither at night, we were overtaken by a Shower that found the
way to our Skins, and we deservd it, for not observing the Spanish advice
concerning our cloaks. We have great variety of amusement here, and are
So excessively full of questions, that I wish it dont plunge us into a habit of
being Something impertinent. I fore-See that our journals are like to Swell
into a Volume, and we begin to prefer our performances to those of the
florid Mr Brome already. Tomorrow we quit Cambridge and go to Ely, and
from thence we Shall proceed to Stanford, where I hope we Shall meet the
groom, who we understand is recoverd. The Horses Stand very well, and
the Sumpter performs as well as the best of 'em. If we do not visit Scotland,
it will be for want of time, and not for fear of the Itch, for we have met with
a Nostrum for that desease. And least it Shoud come over the mountains
into Glocester-Shire, pray please to take part of our Remedy. Take as much
fine Sifted Brimstone as will lye upon a Six-pence, Drop into it 3 or 4 drops
of Sallet-oyl, & haveing this composition in one palm, rub it hard against
t'other til it be all rub'd in, go to bed immediately upon it, and keep warm,
wch if repeated 5 or 6 nights together must prove infallible. You must
forgive me that I put this Recipe in the 2^d person, for tis hard to be a
Doctor and a Courteour at the Same time especially at the Unviersity, but
in all capacitys I shall never forget to be

    Sir   your most faithfull Servt
           WByrd.

Sr John & I Send our Respe[cts]
  to the Ladys.

Copy received by addressee.

Collection of Mr. Paul Mellon, Upperville, Virginia.
Photocopy, Virginia Historical Society.

William Byrd II to Sir Robert Southwell

York ye 27th of Augst 1701.

Sir

At Lincoln I had the entertainment of yours which made
me forget the fategues of the fore-going day. We had come from Nottingham, which is Set down in our books to be but 24 miles from Lincoln,
but they prov'd very good measure, and gave us reason to observe that we
were travelling in the north. At Lincoln we fell into the hands of Mr Pollen a
freind of mine, that made much of us for 2 days. There is hardly any thing
very remarquable in this decay'd City, but a Tomb-Stone in the Minster of
Dr Honywood, upon which it is recorded that his Grand Mother livd to See
367 persons of her legitimate posterity namely 16 children 114 grandchildren, 228 great-grandchildren, and nine of the 4th generation. This City
is extreamly impaird, and from haveing 50 parish Churches it has now but
15, and but 4 of those in which besides the Minster, divine Service is
performd. From hence we passt by Brig a Town of Smal consequence, to
Barton, where we embarqu'd our Selves and horses to cross the mouth of
the Humber which is 5 miles over, to Hull. It blew fresh, and was rough-
water, but for all that we coud not be sick, tho we thought of all the nasty
Images in the world to provoke us to it. In a little more than an hour by the
favour of a good wind we ferryd over, and arrivd Safe at Hull. This is a fine
Town, with a great many good buildings, and inliven'd by a very good trade
to Holland Hamborough and the northern Countrys, insomuch that the
Kings Customes amount yearly to about 20000 pounds. The want of the
french Trade has done this place Some prejudice, for whereas they us'd to
reacon above 200 Ships belonging to it, they now cant pretend to more
than 150. It is very advantagiously Seated for forrein commerce, and
besides, the River Humber divideing it Self into So many branches affords
it water carriage into many parts of the Country to distribute their goods
round about. The Citadel is in a poor condition, it never haveing been
duely fortifyd, and it is well for us that our Ships protect us and render all
our land-fortifications unnecessary. In Trinity house which is an Hospital
for 28 poor Seamen, or their widdows, there hangs up the Effigies of a poor
Laplander, that almost 100 years ago was taken up with his little boat by a
Greenland Ship, and in those dark times was taken for a mereman & by
most people is Stil believd as Such.¶
I had almost forgot the explanation concerning capping of ye gillyflower
which my Ld Weymouth dos me the honour to desire of me. When I Said
that there was a round thin board put over the top of the flower, I did not
mean at So Smal a distance as to keep it from the air, but about a foot

above it, and the board to be no more than 5 Inches diameter So the air is
not much intercepted.¶

Sʳ John is brisk & there is hope that his health will be the better for this
journy. We have been to wait upon the Dean Since our arrival here, who is
very civil to us. I am full of respects to your family and very much

Sir   Your most faithfull Servᵗ
WByrd.

Sʳ John Send his Salutes.

Copy received by addressee.
Collection of Mr. Paul Mellon, Upperville, Virginia.
Photocopy, Virginia Historical Society.

Sir John Perceval to Digby Cotes

Penrith
18. Sept. 1701

To Mʳ Digby Cotes

giving Some Acct.
of my expedition to
Scotland

Dʳ Sʳ

Since my last, to which I have reciev'd no answer, I have been in the
ancient Kingdom of Scotland, where my first days accomodations were So
bad, that they deterr'd me from advancing farther to Edinborrough as I at
first intended.¶

The Town I din'd at goes by the name of Lanharf, to wᶜʰ place I was forc'd
over two Rivers up to my middle, for the[y] know not what a bridge is.
When I came there, I found the famous Town consisted of 5 mud houses
reckoning in the barns. The Kirk indeed was built of Stone, but cover'd like
the rest with turf. The best house was a Tavern where I met with very good
wine for an English Shilling a quart, which in Some measure made amends
for the want of bread, butter, cheese & meat. As Soon as we came to the
door, there issued a dirty Female without Shoose or Stockings, who it
Seems was our Landlady, & being told it was the custom to kiss our hosts to
make them give us the best, we desired her to wipe her mouth, & then fell
to our duty. Our horses all this while Stood in the open Air, for the Stable
door was So low they could not get in, and it being half uncover'd, & up to
the middle in dirt (for their Sheep & calves make use of the Same Tene-
ment) I thought 'twas better to let them eat without doors, which they did
not very heartily of Some oat Straw, which was all we cou'd procure for
'em.¶

After Saluting our Landlady, we desired to know what victualls She could
entertain us with. She told us She had geud breed & geud Wine: So She
brought us into another room where there was a table, 2 Stools, & a glass
window half a foot Square, a thing rarely Seen in this part of Scotland,
Neither was there a house within 16 miles as we were told that had a
partition like ours, which yet was no other than a curtain which hung down

& parted us from the Kitchen, where there was Such a Smoke diffus'd itself
that we were forc'd to feel where the glass Stood, whereby we unfortunatly
broak it, and were afterwards obliged to drink our wine out of the Pot.¶
The bread which was made of Oats was but half baked, and Standing
accidentally at the door, I took notice that the butter was of 20 colours, &
Stuck with hair, like Mortar, So I desired we might have the butter & hair
by themselves, that I might mix them as I pleas'd my Self. I enquir'd if they
had any cheese & they had none, but She Said we might get Some at the
geud Mans house, whereupon we Sent a Messenger to the Preacher, who
readily return'd him with a piece of mutton, kill'd I'me confident a fortnight before. This when drest I cou'd not eat, but Stuck to my oat bread &
Wine, which was all my dinner. I eat all the while in my gloves for fear of
the itch, wch boldly Shew'd itself on my Landladys fingers & legs, and put
me in mind of what an ⟨Coll! Daniel Dering⟩[2] Unkle Dering of mine was
wont to Say, that he had been but a fortnight in Scotland, and yet had got
their present State at his fingers ends. I was not So afraid of being lousie,
Since tis well known, that Set a louse upon a table, & he Shall dutyfully
direct his course Northward towards his Mother Country, So I was Sure if I
caught any, to leave 'em behind me.¶
I Shall Say nothing of the Stink which both the Woman & the House
favour'd us with, because the Smoke got the upperhand, & to our comfort
overpowr'd it, but at first entrance I thought I Shou'd have been Struck
down.¶
After all this, we were forc'd to thank our Lady for our good reception with
another Kiss, which had certainly brought up my dinner, had not the bread
been as heavy as lead in my Stomach. The bad Success of this forenoon
made me take a resolution to fly the Country, and I never look'd behind me
Till I got again within the borders of England.¶
I Shall be to morrow at Appleby, afterwards at Kendal, Lancaster, Wiggan
& Chester, where no body will be better pleas'd to hear from you than

      Dear S^r

                Y^r affect hum^{bl} Servt

                      J. Percival

Letterbook copy.
British Library, Add. Mss. 47025, ff. 54v-55v.

2. Marginal note, incorporated.

Bibliography

Manuscript Sources

Egmont papers, British Library.
    Additional Manuscript 47025, Letterbook of Sir John Perceval, 1697–1709.
    Additional Manuscript 47057, Tour diary of Sir John Perceval, 1701.
    Additional Manuscript 47058, Unfinished copy, with slight variations of Add. Mss. 47057.
    Additional Manuscript 47072, Autobiographical sketches of Sir John Perceval, c. 1715–1717.
Sloane manuscripts, British Library. 4061.
    Undated letter of Sir Robert Southwell to Sir Hans Sloane.
Byrd/Southwell correspondence, private collection, photostatic copies, Virginia Historical Society.

Printed Sources

An Account of the Gifts and Legacies that have been Given and Bequeathed to Charitable Uses in the Town of Ipswich. Ipswich, Suffolk, 1747.

Anderson, James. *A Genealogical History of the House of Yvery.* 2 vols. London, 1742.

Baines, Edward. *History of the County Palatine and Duchy of Lancaster.* 4 vols. London, 1836.

Bassett, John Spencer, ed. *The Writings of Colonel William Byrd of Westover in Virginia Esqr.* New York, 1901.

Bayne-Powell, Rosamond. *Travellers in Eighteenth-Century England.* London, 1951.

Binney, Marcus. "Holme Pierrepont Hall, Nottingham." *Country Life* 166 (1979): 842–45.

Blomefield, Francis. *An Essay towards a Topographical History of the County of Norfolk.* 5 vols. Fersfield and Lynn, Norfolk, 1739–1775.

Bowder, Diana. *Who Was Who in the Roman World.* Ithaca, New York, 1980.

Brome, Richard. *Travels over England, Scotland and Wales.* London, 1701.

The Builder's Dictionary. 2 vols. 1734; rpt. Washington, 1981.

Burke, John. *A Genealogical and Heraldic History of the Extinct and Dormant Baronetcies of England, Ireland and Scotland.* 2nd ed., 1841; rpt. Baltimore, 1977.

———. *A Genealogical and Heraldic History of the Landed Gentry . . .* London, 1837.

———. *Burke's Genealogical and Heraldic History of the Peerage Baronetage and Knightage.* Ed. Peter Townsend. 105th ed. London, 1970.

Butler, Lionel, and Chris Given-Wilson. *Medieval Monasteries of Great Britain.* London, 1983.

Campen, Jacob van. *Afbeeldin van 't Stadt Huis van Amsterdam.* Amsterdam, 1668.

Cassell's Gazetteer of Great Britain and Ireland . . . 6 vols. London, 1898.

Christy, Miller. "The Reverend John Ouseley (1645–1708), An Early Historian of Essex." *Essex Review* 21 (1912): 132–41.

Clifton-Taylor, Alec. *The Pattern of English Building.* London, 1977.

Cobb, Gerald. *English Cathedrals, the Forgotten Centuries—Restoration and Change from 1530 to the Present Day.* London, 1980.

Cokayne, George Edward. *The Complete Baronetage.* 5 vols. Exeter, 1900.

————. *The Complete Peerage.* 13 vols. London, 1910–1940.

Colvin, Howard. *A Biographical Dictionary of British Architects 1600–1840.* New York, 1978.

Colvin, Howard, J. Mordaunt Crook, Kerry Downes, and John Newman. *The History of the King's Works. Volume 5, 1660–1782.* London, 1976.

A Concise History of the Cathedral Church of Peterborough . . . Peterborough, 1782.

Cornforth, John. "Hutton-in-the-Forest, Cumberland." *Country Life* 137 (1965): 232–35, 286–89, 352–56.

————. "Newby Hall, North Yorkshire." *Country Life* 165 (1979): 1802–6, 1918–21, 2006–2009.

Cotton, Charles. *The Genuine Works of Charles Cotton, Esq.; containing I. Scarronnides, or Virgil Travestie. II. Lucian Burlesqued, or the Scoffer Scoft. III. The Wonders of the Peake. IV. The Planters Manual.* London, 1715.

Cox, Thomas. *Magnae Britannia et Hibernia, Antiqua & Nova. Or a New Survey of Great Britain* . . . 6 vols. [n.p.], 1720–1731.

Croft-Murray. Edward. *Decorative Painting in England 1537–1837. Volume 5, Early Tudor to Sir James Thornhill.* London, 1962.

Cromwell, Thomas. *History and Description of the Ancient Town and Borough of Colchester, in Essex* . . . 2 vols. Colchester, 1825.

Cross, R. L. *The Living Past—A Victorian Heritage.* Ipswich, Suffolk, 1975.

Dale, Samuel. *The History and Antiquities of Harwich and Dovercourt.* London, 1730.

Dalton, Charles. *English Army Lists and Commission Registers, 1661–1714.* 6 vols. 1892–1904; rpt. London, 1960.

Davies, Robert. "The Horn of Ulphus." *The Archaeological Journal* 26 (1869): 1–11.

Davis, Richard Beale. "William Byrd, Taste and Tolerance." In *Major Writers of Early American Literature,* ed. Everett Emerson. Madison, 1972.

De Blainville, P. *A Relation of the Journey of the Gentlemen Blathwayt into the North Part of England in the Year Seventeen Hundred and Three.* Ed. Nora Hardwick. Dursley, Gloucestershire, 1977.

Defoe, Daniel. *A Tour Through the Whole Island of Great Britain.* Ed. Pat Rogers. 1724–1726; rpt. Harmondsworth, Middlesex, 1971.

Dictionary of National Biography. Ed. Leslie Stephen and [Sidney Lee]. 66 vols. London, 1885–1901.

Dugdale, Sir William. *The Antiquities of Warwickshire Illustrated* . . . 2 vols. London, 1730.

————. *Monasticon Anglicanum: A History of the Abbies and Other Monasteries, Hospitals, Frieries, and Cathedral and Collegiate Churches* . . . *in England and Wales* . . . Ed. John Caley et al. 1817–1830; rpt. Farnborough, Hampshire, 1970.

Elliott, R. W. *The Story of King Edward VI School, Bury St. Edmunds.* Bury St. Edmunds, [1963].

Evelyn, John. *The Diary of John Evelyn.* Ed. John Bowle. Oxford, 1983.

Executive Journals of the Council of Virginia. Volume 2, August 3, 1699—April 27, 1705. Richmond, 1927.

Farmer, David Hugh. *The Oxford Dictionary of Saints.* Oxford, 1982.

Fetherstonhaugh, Mrs., and F. Haswell. "The College of Kirkoswald and the Family of Fetherstonhaugh." *Transactions of the Cumberland and Westmoreland Antiquarian Society,* n.s., 14 (1914): 196–237.

Fiennes, Celia. *The Illustrated Journeys of Celia Fiennes.* Ed. Christopher Morris. London, 1982.

Foster, Joseph. *Alumni Oxonienses; The Members of the University of Oxford, 1500–1714* . . . 4 vols. Oxford, 1891–1892.

————. *Pedigrees of the County Families of England* . . . *Volume 1, Lancashire.* London, 1873.

————. *The Register of Admissions to Gray's Inn, 1521–1889* . . . London, 1889.

Frantz, R. W. *The English Traveller and the Movement of Ideas 1660–1732.* 1934; rpt. New York, 1968.

Friedman, Terry. *James Gibbs.* New Haven, 1984.

Frost, Charles. *Notices Relative to the Town and Port of Hull.* London, 1827.

Fuller, Thomas. *The Worthies of England.* Ed. John Freeman. 1662; rpt. London, 1952.

Gibson, Edmund, ed. *Camden's Britannia, 1695.* 1695; rpt. Newton Abbot, Devon, 1971.

Gillow, Joseph. *A Literary and Biographical History . . . of English Catholics from the Time of the Breach with Rome, in 1534, to the Present Time.* 5 vols. [1885–1902]; rpt. New York, [1968].

Gimson, W. A. *Great Braxted.* [n.p.], 1958.

Habakkuk, H. J. "Daniel Finch, 2nd Earl of Nottingham: His House and Estate." In *Studies in Social History,* ed. J. H. Plumb. Freeport, New York, 1955.

Hainsworth, D. R., ed. *The Correspondence of Sir John Lowther of Whitehaven 1693–1698.* London, 1983.

Harris, John. *The Artist and the Country House.* London, 1979.

Harvey, Sir Paul, comp. and ed. *The Oxford Companion to Classical Literature.* Oxford, 1966.

Haverkamp-Begemann, E., and Anne-Marie S. Logan, comps. *European Drawings and Watercolors in the Yale University Art Gallery.* New Haven, 1970.

Hearnshaw, F. J. C. *Newcastle-upon-Tyne.* 1924; rpt. Wakefield, Yorkshire, 1972.

Hening, William. *The Statutes at Large* . . . 13 vols. Richmond, 1819–1823; rpt. Charlottesville, 1969.

Hepworth, R. "The Old Town Library, Ipswich." *East Anglian Magazine* 14 (1955): 455–60.

Hill, Oliver, and John Cornforth. *English Country Houses— Caroline, 1625–1685.* London, 1966.

Historical Manuscripts Commission. *Report on the Manuscripts of the Earl of Egmont.* 2 vols. Dublin, 1909.

————. *Thirteenth Report, Appendix, Part II, Report on the Manuscripts of His Grace the Duke of Portland, Preserved at Welbeck Abbey.* 2 vols. London, 1893.

Holinshed, Raphael, comp. *Holinshed's Chronical of England, Scotland and Ireland.* 6 vols. London, 1808.

Holmes, Geoffrey. *Politics, Religion, and Society in England, 1679–1742.* London, 1986.

Hudleston, C. Roy, and R. S. Boumphrey. *Cumberland Families and Heraldry* . . . Kendal, Cumbria, 1978.

Hunt, John Dixon, and Peter Willis, eds. *The Genius of the Place: The English Landscape Garden, 1620–1820.* London, 1975.

Hussey, Christopher. "Burghley House, Northamptonshire." *Country Life* 114 (1953): 1828–32, 1962–65, 2104–7, 2038–41, 2164–67.

————. "Ickworth, Suffolk." *Country Life* 117 (1955): 678–81.

Hutchinson, William. *The History of the County of Cumberland.* 2 vols. Carlisle, Cumberland, 1794.

Jackson, Gordon. *Hull in the Eighteenth Century: A Study in Economic and Social History.* London, 1972.

Jackson-Stops, Gervase. "Cockermouth Castle, Cumberland." *Country Life* 156 (1974): 146–49, 210–13.

Kent, Ernest A. "The Houses of the Duke of Norfolk in Norwich." *Norfolk Archaeology* 24 (1932): 73–87.

Kenworthy-Brown, John, Peter Reid, Michael Sayer, and David Watkin. *Burke's and Savills Guide to Country Houses. Volume 3, East Anglia.* London, 1981.

King, D. J. Cathcart. *Castellarium Anglicanum.* 2 vols. London, 1983.

Lansdowne, Marquis of, ed. *The Petty-Southwell Correspondence 1676–1687.* London, 1928.

Lees-Milne, James. *English Country Houses: Baroque, 1685–1715.* London, 1970.

Lees-Milne, James, and John Cornforth. "Chatsworth, Derbyshire." *Country Life* 143 (1968): 890–93, 958–62, 1040–44, 1110–13; and 144 (1968): 146–49, 220–23, 280–84, 496–500, 552–55.

Leigh, Charles. *The Natural History of Lancashire, Cheshire, and the Peak, in Derbyshire* . . . Oxford, 1700.

LeNeve, John. *Fasti Ecclesiae Anglicanae* . . . 3 vols. Oxford, 1854.

Leslie, John Henry. *The History of Languard Fort in Suffolk.* London, 1898.

Lincoln's Inn. *The Records of The Honourable Society of Lincoln's Inn.* 2 vols. London, 1896.

Lloyd, David. "The Benefactions of a Coal Magnate." *Country Life* 144 (1968): 92–94.

Locke, John. *Some Thoughts Concerning Education.* London, 1693.

London County Council. *Survey of London, Volume III. The Parish of St. Giles-in-the-Fields. Part I, Lincoln's Inn Fields.* London, 1912.

Lupson, Edward J. *St. Nicholas' Church, Great Yarmouth: Its History* . . . Yarmouth, Norfolk, [1889].

MacKenzie, Sir James D. *The Castles of England. Their Story and Structure.* 2 vols. New York, 1896.

McPherson, Robert G., ed. *The Journal of the Earl of Egmont: Abstract of the Trustees Proceedings for Establishing the Colony of Georgia 1732–1738.* Athens, 1962.

Marambaud, Pierre. *William Byrd of Westover 1674–1744.* Charlottesville, 1971.

Margary, Ivan D. *Roman Roads in Britain.* 2 vols. London, 1955.

Marrat, William. *The History of Lincolnshire, Topographical, Historical, and Descriptive.* 3 vols. Boston, Lincolnshire, 1814–1816.

Martin, Peter. *Pursuing Innocent Pleasures: The Gardening World of Alexander Pope.* Hamden, Connecticut, 1984.

Meschutt, David. "William Byrd and His Portrait Collection." *Journal of Early Southern Decorative Art* 14 (1988): 19–46.

Moir, Esther. *The Discovery of Britain.* London, 1964.

Morant, Phillip. *The History and Antiquities of the County of Essex.* 2 vols. 1763–1768; rpt. Wakefield, Yorkshire, 1978.

Muir, Ramsay. *A History of Liverpool.* 1907; rpt. Wakefield, Yorkshire, 1970.

Napper, J. H. et al. *Whitehaven: A New Structure for a Restoration Town.* Newcastle-upon-Tyne, 1971.

Nicolson, Joseph, and Richard Burn. *The History and Antiquities of the Counties of Westmoreland and Cumberland.* 2 vols. London, 1777.

North, Sir Roger. *Of Building: Sir Roger North's Writings on Architecture.* Ed. Howard Colvin and John Newman. Oxford, 1981.

"Notes and Queries." *Essex Review* 2 (1893): 54–63.

Oates, J. C. T. "The Deposit of Books at Cambridge under the Licensing Acts, 1662–79, 1685–95." *Transactions of the Cambridge Bibliographical Society* 2 (1957): 290–304.

Ogilby, John. *Britannia; or, The Kingdom of England and Dominion of Wales, Actually Survey'd* . . . . London, 1698.

———. *The Traveller's Guide: or a Most Exact Description of the Roads of England* . . . . London, 1699.

Oliver, George. *The History and Antiquities of the Town and Minster of Beverley* . . . Beverley, 1829.

Ormerod, George. *The History of the County Palatine and City of Chester.* 3 vols. London, 1882.

Oswald, Arthur. "Euston Hall, Suffolk." *Country Life* 121 (1957): 58–61, 102–5, 148–51.

Oxley, Geoffrey W. *Poor Relief in England and Wales, 1604–1834.* London, 1974.

Partridge, R. C. Barrington. *The History of the Legal Deposit of Books throughout the British Empire.* London, 1938.

Peacham, Henry. *The Complete Gentleman* . . . 1634; rpt. Ithaca, N.Y., 1962.

Pevsner, Nikolaus. *The Buildings of England.* 46 vols. Harmondsworth, Middlesex, 1951–1974.

Powicke, Sir F. Maurice, and E. B. Fryde. *Handbook of English Chronology.* London, 1961.

Redstone, Lilian J. *Ipswich through the Ages.* Ipswich, Suffolk, 1948.

Reps, John W. *Tidewater Towns.* Williamsburg, 1972.

Roque, Oswaldo Rodriguez. *American Furniture at Chipstone.* Madison, Wisconsin, 1984.

Royal Commission on Historic Monuments in England. *An Inventory of the Historical Monuments in Westmoreland.* London, 1936.

Shaw, William A. *The Knights of England.* 2 vols. London, 1906.

Singer, Charles, and E. J. Holmyard, A. R. Hall, and Trevor I. Williams. *A History of Technology. Volume 3, From the Renaissance to the Industrial Revolution.* 5 vols. Oxford, 1957.

Smith, Sir Thomas. *De Republica Anglorum.* Ed. Mary Dewar. Cambridge, 1982.

The Spectator. Ed. Donald F. Bond. 5 vols. Oxford, 1965.

Stewart, J. Douglas. *Sir Godfrey Kneller and the English Baroque Portrait.* Oxford, 1983.

Stone, Lawrence. *Sculpture in Britain: The Middle Ages.* Harmondsworth, Middlesex, 1972.

Suckling, Alfred. *The History and Antiquities of the County of Suffolk.* 2 vols. London, 1846–1848.

Summerson, John. *Architecture in Britain 1530–1830.* Harmondsworth, Middlesex, 1977.

Thompson, Francis. *Chatsworth, A Short History . . .* London, 1949.

Tickell, John. *The History of the Town and County of Kingston- upon-Hull . . .* [n.p.], 1798.

Tinling, Marion, ed. *The Correspondence of Three William Byrds of Westover, Virginia, 1684–1776.* 2 vols. Charlottesville, 1977.

Tipping, H. Avary. *English Homes, Period IV. Volume 1, Late Stuart 1649–1714.* London, 1920.

Venn, John, and J. A. Venn. *Alumni Cantabrigiensis—A Biographical List of All Known Students, Graduates and Holders of Office at the University of Cambridge, from the Earliest Times to 1900. Part I— From the Earliest Times to 1751.* 4 vols. Cambridge, 1922.

Victoria History of the Counties of England. 177 vols. London and latterly Oxford, 1901—.

Walpole Society. *The Twentieth Volume of the Walpole Society, 1931–1932: Vertue Note Books. Volume 2.* Oxford, 1932.

Wenger, Mark R. "Westover: William Byrd's Mansion Reconsidered." M.A. thesis, University of Virginia, 1981.

Wilson, David M., and D. Gillian Hurst. "Medieval Britain in 1962 and 1963." *Medieval Archaeology* 8 (1964): 231–99.

Wood, G. Bernard. "700 Years of an Archbishop's Palace." *Country Life* 130 (1961): 566–68.

Woodfin, Maude H. "William Byrd and the Royal Society." *Virginia Magazine of History and Biography* 40 (1932): 23–34, 111–23.

Woodfin, Maude, and Marion Tinling, eds. *Another Secret Diary of William Byrd of Westover, 1739–1741, with Letters and Literary Exercises, 1696–1726.* Richmond, 1942.

Wright, Joseph, ed. *The English Dialect Dictionary.* 6 vols. New York, 1898.

Wright, Louis B., and Marion Tinling, eds. *William Byrd of Virginia: The London Diary 1717–1721 and Other Writings.* New York, 1958.

Zimmerman, J. E. *Dictionary of Classical Mythology.* New York, 1964.

Index

Note: Numbers in italics refer to illustrations.